ENCYCLOPAEDIA OF INDIAN GOVERNMENT: PROGRAMMES AND POLICIES

ENCYCLOPAEDIA
OF
INDIAN GOVERNMENT:
PROGRAMMES AND POLICIES

Vol. 27

Health and Family Welfare

Edited by

Satish Tiwari

ANMOL PUBLICATIONS PVT. LTD.
NEW DELHI - 110 002 (INDIA)

ANMOL PUBLICATIONS PVT. LTD.
4374/4B, Ansari Road, Daryaganj
New Delhi - 110 002

Encyclopaedia of Indian Government: Programmes and Policies

First Edition, 2000
ISBN 81-261-0515-1 (Set)

PRINTED IN INDIA

Published by J.L. Kumar for Anmol Publications Pvt. Ltd., New Delhi - 110 002 and Printed at Mehra Offset Press, Delhi.

Contents

Preface

Encyclopaedia of Indian Government: Programmes and Policies contains authoritative information on about fifty departmental policies and their future developmental programmes.

Organised to be completed in 40 volumes, this gigantic work covers Agriculture; Atomic Energy; Chemicals and Fertilizers; Coal; Commerce; Communication; Culture; Defence; Education; Environment and Forests; External Affairs; Finance; Food & Consumer Affairs; Food Processing Industries; Health and Family Welfare; Home Affairs and Internal Security; Human Resources; Industry; Information and Broadcasting; Labour; Law, Justice and Company Affairs; Non-conventional Energy Sources; Ocean Development; Parliamentary Affairs; Personnel, Public Grievances and Pensions; Petroleum and Natural Gas; Planning and Programme Implementation; Planning and Statistics; Posts and Telegraphs; Power; Rural Development; Science and Technology; Social Justice and Empowerment; Space; States Affairs; Steel; Steel and Mines; Sugar and Edible Oils; Surface Transport; Textiles; Tourism; Urban Development; Water Resources; Women and Child development etc.

Based on the information derived from authoritative sources, this work contains authentic facts and figures. I am deeply beholden to all the scholars whose writings are cited or substantially made use of in the present work. I am also thankful to Anmol Publications Pvt. Ltd. for undertaking publication of this encyclopaedia. I am solely responsible for shortcomings in presentation of matter.

Encyclopaedic in nature, this will prove a dependable reference work for scholars and academics besides those appearing for different competitive examinations.

—**Satish Tiwari**

1

Introduction

Looking at the population situation in the country through the current century, one notices that during the earlier decades of the century the population of India was characterised by high birth rate, high death rate, high infant mortality rate, maternal mortality rate and low expectancy of life. After independence, effective programmes: for controlling killer diseases like malaria,: cholera and plague, as well as steady improvement in public hygiene and nutritional status of the population led to substantial control of diseases causing large scale deaths. As a result, death rate and infant mortality rate have reduced two-fold or more and life: expectancy at birth has similarly practically: doubled after independence. Birth rate has also declined form 40.8 in 1951 to 272 in: 1997 About 15.5 million people added to the: population of the country, annually.

Population of the country has multiplied: by more than four times during the century. It became 84.6 crore in the 1991 census and is presently expected to be around 974 crore. According to United Nations Fund Population Activities (UNFPA) estimates, world population is currently increasing at the rate of about 80 million per year. India alone is contributing to a fifth of the total increase in world population, every year. This is excessive as can also be seen from the fact that India has only 2.4% of the world land area, while its population constitutes 16% of the present world population. The already unusually large pressure of population on land in India, coupled with still continuing large annual increase indicates that the population situation in India is already critical.

Such large and still increasing population has big implications for availability and incidence of unemployment in the society. The pressure of population is also very relevant for the state of environment. The high levels of population on land, in air and in water in large parts of the country indicate that the carrying capacity of land and environment is being exceeded.

While, there are creditable achievements and hopeful signs in many states, the overall situation warrants concern. States/UTs of Kerala, Tamil Nadu, Mizoram, Nagaland, Sikkim, Pondicherry, Chandigarh and Goa, have already controlled birth rates and they are now below the replacement level of fertility. The situation in many other states like Karnataka, Andhra Pradesh, Maharashtra, Gujarat, Punjab and West Bengal holds out hope that they could also control birth rates sufficiently to reach below the replacement level of fertility.

The situation in regard to other large states is not yet so good as to warrant optimism. The Technical Group on Population Projections appointed by the Planning Commission, reported in August 1996 that if the current trends continued, the country as a whole can be expected to achieve replacement levels of fertility by the year 2026. Some of the most populous states will, however, achieve replacement level of fertility well after that It needs to be noted that even after replacement level of fertility is reached, the momentum of young generation keeps the population growing for one more generation aid only after that the population stabilises.

The UNFPA Population projections estimates that according to current trends, India would have a population of 152 crore by the year 2050 and it will surpass China as the most populous country in the world. These projections are, of course, based on the trends based on data during 1980-90, which will undoubtedly change for the better in coming years. Up to 1985, emphasis was not laid in a significant manner on population control measures. Substantially, nationwide programmes for Universal Immunisation, Oral Rehydration Therapy and Safe Motherhood were initiated only during the Seventh Plan and they acquired meaningful momentum only by the end of the Seventh Plan. Therefore, for most of the '80s, the overall problem of population and material/ child health has been addressed only in the last few years of the decade. The trends during this decade, therefore, indicate weak progress in this sector. This weakness fortunately has already been substantially removed and the Integrated Child Survival and Safe Motherhood Programme which started at the beginning of the Eighth Plan has covered the country by the end of the Eighth Plan. Increase in the pace of improvement as a result of these initiatives has been brought out by the Sample Registration System (SRS) findings for the year 1997 These findings indicate that the birth rate has been brought down to 272 and infant mortality rate has been brought down to 71 in 1997 If this pace of improvement is further strengthened in coming years, the goal of population stabilisation can be brought closer.

There is growing awareness in the country that the population situation is among the most critical issues before the country and unless this is controlled, there will be less scope for optimism in other sec tors. In the meeting of the National Development Council held in the early months of 1997 to consider the Approach Paper for the Ninth Plan, strong opinion was voiced by many states that the population situation should receive high importance during the Ninth Plan. During the special sitting of the Parliament coinciding with the celebrations for the 50th Anniversary of National, Independence, the population situation was one of the five themes highlighted in document placed before the Parliament for special debate. The resolution adopted by the Parliament stated: "that a vigorous national campaign be launched by all political parties to combat economically unsustainable growth of population, recognising that such growth lies at the root of most of our human, social and economic problems...".

Very good achievement on the population front in the states of Kerala, Tamil Nadu and Goa, hopeful signs in many states and strong policy support now becoming available for the programme, provides the opportunity for achieving faster progress than before in stabilising population early and in improving the RCH status of the citizens.

Background

The main objective of the Family Welfare Programme for the country has been to stabilise population at a level consistent with the needs of national development The Family Planning Programme was started in 1951 as a purely demographic programme. Subsequently, the element of public education and extension was included to facilitate outcomes under the family planning programme. During the seventies, the family planning programme was focused mainly on terminal methods and the programme received a setback due to the rigid implementation of a target-based approach. The programme has, however, remained full~ voluntary and the main effort of the government has been to provide services on the one hand and to encourage the citizens by information, education and communication on the other hand to use such services. The experiences gained within the country and outside had amply established that health of women in the reproductive age group and of small children (up to 5 years of age), is of crucial importance for effectively tackling the problem of the growth of population. This perception has led to change in the approach from Family Planning to Family Welfare. Since the Seventh Plan implemented during 1984-89, the FW programmes have evolved with the focus on the health needs of the women in the reproductive age group and of children below the age of 5 years on one hand and on the other hand, to provide contraceptives and spacing services to the desirous people. Thus, the family welfare programme has objectives of stabilising population of the country early and to ensure good reproductive and child health status of the existing population. These objectives are pursued by addressing contraception issues, maternal health issues, child survival issues and by encouraging citizens through IEC to use these services.

The Approach Paper to the Ninth Plan brought out by the Planning Commission has shown the inadequacy of the investment made for family welfare. This is a severe handicap, particularly when it is noted that in almost all respects, the health care system needs upgradation and it needs to reach out to many more people for the national goals to be achieved. While there is a steady improvement due to economic development, spread of education/literacy and empowerment of citizens, substantial problems in regard to education/literacy, particularly among the weak performing states and in regard to empowerment particularly of women, remain.

A look at birth rate, death rate and infant mortality rates (SRS 1997) clearly indicates deficiencies and weaknesses of the family welfare programme in individual states. While the birth rate is lowest at 79 in Nagaland and 14.2 in Goa, it is the highest at 33.5 in Uttar Pradesh, 32.1. in Rajasthan and 31.9 in Madhya Pradesh. The states with birth rate of 30 or more are Uttar Pradesh, Rajasthan, Madhya Pradesh, Bihar and Meghalaya. These are closely followed by Haryana (28.3) and Assam (28.2). In these states literacy levels are lower, support of the community for the programme is weak and efficiency of the state health system in delivering contraception and the RCH services is weak. An indication of the level of population control measures in these weakly performed states can be had by looking at sterilisations performed in some of the states during 1997-98. In 1997-98, six lakhs sterilisations were performed in Andhra Pradesh, and 5.7 lakhs in Maharashtra but with comparable population only 3 lakh sterilisations were performed in Uttar

Table 1.1

Achievements of the National Family Welfare Programme

Indicator	Past level	Current level
Crude Birth Rate	41.7(1951-61)	27.2(1997)
Crude Death Rate	22.8 (1951-61)	8.9(1997)
Infant Mortality Rate	146 (1951-61)	71(1997)
Maternal Mortality Rate	NA	4.37 (1991-92)
Life Expectancy at Birth (Years) Est. Male	37.1(1961)	62.4(1996-2001)
Female	36.1(1951)	63.4 (1996-2001)
Total Fertility Rate	6.0(1951)	3.5(1995)
Effective Couple Protection Rate	10.4 (1970-71)	45.4 (31.3.98)

Indicator	Past level	Current level
Immunisation Status(% Coverage)		
For Pregnant Women TT	40 (1985-86)	80 (1997-98)
For Infants		
BCG	29 (1985-86)	96 (1997-98)
Measles	44 (1987-88)	83 (1997-98)
DPT	41 (1985-86)	90 (1997-98)
Polio	36 (1985-86)	91 (1997-98)

NA: Not available (Relevant year in parentheses)

Pradesh, 2.24 lakhs in Rajasthan and 3.66 lakhs in Madhya Pradesh. Wide gap in the use of sterilisation facility in some of the weekly performing States compared to some of the better performing states like Tamil Nadu, Karnataka and Andhra Pradesh can be had from the table below:

Name of the State	No. of Sterilisations per 10,000 unsterilised couples with parity two and above
Uttar Pradesh	188
Madhya Pradesh	523
Rajasthan	447
Bihar	110
Tamil Nadu	934
Karnataka	1,297
Andra Pradesh	1,230

While to some extent the low figures of Uttar Pradesh, Madhya Pradesh, Bihar and Rajasthan are due to similarly fewer sterilisations having been performed, there in past years, but even the present levels are much lower than the size of the problem in these states indicate. These states are relying almost wholly on camps for sterilisation, because every district and sub division, either does not have doctors trained in sterilisation techniques, or trained doctors are not performing operations in hospitals even after training. The camp approach is unsatisfactory not only in terms of hygiene and after-care of patients, but because of unpredictability of schedule. Even some of the willing persons do not ultimately get sterilised. Summer months and monsoon season disrupts camps and therefore, it is not surprising that reliance on camps leads these states ultimately achieving a considerable lower figure at state level in sterilisations.

Infant Mortality Rate (IMR) among the major states is the highest at 96 in Orissa and 94 in Madhya Pradesh, while it is the lowest at 12 in Kerala. Even the next State after Kerala in infant mortality rate is Maharashtra with IMR of 47, which is much higher than it has been achieved in Kerala. Considering that developed countries have IMR in the range of 10- 15, higher level about that is avoidable. If one looks at the causes of infant mortality, it becomes clear that about two-thirds of infant mortality takes in the neonatal period (first 28 days). Within that period, also a large portion takes place in the first few days of life. It is thus obvious that if deliveries are conducted in hospital, survival of newborns can be assured with a greater degree of confidence. However, in Uttar Pradesh, Rajasthan, Madhya Pradesh and Bihar the institutional deliveries are only about 20%. Therefore, in these states, large decline of IMR can become possible only by canvassing institutional deliveries with the people. Apart from this, diarrhoea and the respiratory infections are the next most important causes of infant deaths. Treatment for both is available all over the country through ANMs and Primary Health Centres, but in the states with high IMR the efficiency of the state health system is unfortunately low because of which many children with diarrhoea or respiratory inspection do not get prompt treatment and many of such cases result in infant deaths.

The overall strategy of the Government of India (Department of Family Welfare) is to simultaneously strive for obtaining Reproductive and Child Health arrangements for the whole of the country's population and to promote and make available contraceptive/ terminal methods for desirous couples. It also needs to be observed that the measures through the health system alone do not and cannot assure success in either ensuring Reproductive and Child Health or in controlling population. These objectives are determined concurrently by the following:

— Policy support expressed publicly by opinion leaders in different sectors of the national system and by community at large. Without this kind of support, receptivity of people to make use of even available services cannot be ensured;

— Adequate resources for making available Reproductive and Child Health services to all rural and urban communities in the country;

— Accountability for performance among the health workers and efficiency of the health system. Without such efficiency, the quality of services to citizens or even effective access to health services cannot be ensured;

— Increased literacy among women and improved educational status of families. Similarly, improvement in economic status of families. The educated and economically well-off families can more rationally assess the options before them and acquire capability/willingness to assess consequences of their present actions for future. Therefore, the effort of the Department of Family Welfare is to collaborate with the related departments and non-governmental organisations for seeking support of their programmes for the Family Welfare Programmes. This in turn, will similarly improve the outcome of related programmes of those departments as well.

Evolution of Reproductive and Child Health Programme

The Universal Immunisation Programme (UIP) aimed at reduction in mortality and morbidity among infants and younger children due to Vaccine Preventable Diseases, was started in 1985-86. The Oral Rehydration Therapy (ORT) was also started in view of the fact that diarrhoea was a-leading cause of deaths among children. Various other programmes under Maternal and Child Health (MCH) were also implemented during the Seventh Plan. The objectives of all these programmes were convergent and aimed at improving the health of the mothers and young children and to provide them facilities for prevention and treatment of major disease conditions. While these programmes did have a beneficial impact, but the separate identity for each programme was causing problems in its effective management and this was also reducing somewhat the outcomes. Therefore, in the Eighth Plan, these programmes were integrated under Child Survival and Safe Motherhood (CSSM) Programme which was implemented from 1992-93.

The process of integration of related programmes initiated with the implementation of the CSSM Programme was taken a step further in 1994, when the International Conference on Population and Development in Cairo recommended that the participant countries should implement unified programmes for Reproductive and Child Health (RCH). The RCH approach has been defined as "People have the ability to reproduce and regulate their fertility, women are able to go through pregnancy and child birth safely, the outcome of pregnancies is successful in terms of maternal and infant survival and well being and couples are able to have sexual relations free of fear of pregnancy and of contracting diseases." This concept is in keeping with the evolution of an integrated approach to the programmes aimed at improving the health status of young women and children, which has been going on in the country. It is obviously sensible that the integrated RCH Programme would help in reducing the cost of inputs to some extent because overlapping of expenditure would no longer be necessary and integrated implementation would optimise outcomes at the field level. During the Ninth Plan, the RCH Programme, accordingly, has integrated all the related programmes of the Eighth Plan. The concept of RCH is to provide to the beneficiaries need-based, client-centred, demand-driven, high quality and integrated RCH services. The RCH Programme is a composite programme incorporating the inputs of the Government of India as well as funding support from external donor agencies including the World Bank and the European Commission.

The RCH programme incorporates the components covered under the Child Survival and Safe Motherhood Programme and includes two additional components, one relating to sexually transmitted diseases (STD) and the other relating to reproductive tract infection (RTI). The main highlights of the RCH Programme are:

— The Programme integrates all interventions of fertility regulation, maternal and child health with reproductive health of both men and women.

— The services to be provided will be client-centred, demand-driven, high quality and based on the needs of the community arrived at, through decentralised participatory planning and a target free approach.

— The programme envisages upgradation of the level of facilities for providing various interventions and quality of care. The First Referral Units (FRUs) being set up at sub-district level will provide comprehensive emergency obstetric and new-born care. Similarly RCH facilities in PHCs will be substantially upgraded.

— The Programme will improve access of the community to various services which are commonly required. It is proposed to provide facilities for MTP at the PHCs, counselling and IUD insertion at SCs in a phased manner.

— The Programme aims at improving the outreach of services, particularly for the vulnerable groups of population who have till now substantially been left out of the planning process:

— Special programmes will be taken up for urban slums, tribal population and adolescents.

— Non- Governmental Organisations will be involved in a much larger way to improve out-reach and make it people's programme.

— Skills of practitioners of ISM will be upgraded by training and research and development in ISM will be supported to improve the range of the RCH services.

— Panchayati Raj system will have a greater role in planning, implementation and assessment of client satisfaction.

Programme Interventions

The RCH programme is being implemented, based on a differential approach. Inputs in all districts have not been kept uniform because efficient delivery will depend on the capability of the health system in the district. Therefore, basic facilities are proposed to be strengthened and streamlined, specially in the weaker districts as the better-off districts already have such facilities and the more sophisticated facilities are proposed for the relatively advanced districts which have acquired the capability to make use of them effectively. All the districts have been categorised into categories A (58), B (184) and C (265), on the basis of Crude Birth Rate and Female Literacy Rate, which reasonably reflect the RCH status of the district. The districts will be covered in a phased manner over three years. The nationally uniform and differentiated RCH interventions would be as given in table 1.2.

Funding of the RCH programme

The estimated cost of the RCH Programme will be Rs. 5,112.53 crore during Ninth Plan starting 1997-98. The RCH initiatives in the form of nation-wide programmes will cost Rs.4,565.03 crore during the Ninth Plan. This would be supplemented by 24 District City Projects in 17 States costing Rs. 283.88 crore, which will be strengthened by inputs for infrastructure and facilities to bring them up to the State level. Some more District Projects (Rs. 263.62 crore) will be taken up during the World Bank assisted RCH-II

Integration of programmes

The integration of programmes ultimately leading to Reproductive and Child Health programme, which is currently under implementation, was formally, launched on 15.10.97 In 1985 Universal Immunisation Programme for six vaccine preventable diseases, oral rehydration therapy for controlling deaths resulting from dehydration as a result of diarrhoea and safe motherhood programme were separately, but concurrently taken up for implementation all over the country. During 1992-97, these programmes were integrated in the form of Child Survival and Safe Motherhood Programme. At this stage the International Conference on Population and

Development in 1994 helped in evolving a consensus for implementing a broad-based programme for Reproductive Health. This lent further support to the ongoing effort in India for evolving a holistic approach to family welfare programmes and during 1995-97 the Child Survival and Safe Motherhood programme was reassessed and the Reproductive and Child Health programme was evolved.

Important recent initiatives

Constructive reassessment of ongoing programmes led to two important policy initiatives during 1995-97 First was accepting the challenge of eradicating polio. The strategy of annual Pulse Polio Immunisation (PPI) programme consisting of two Immunisation days separated by about 6 weeks during the lean transmission season of winter was adopted and first round of PPI was taken up in December, 1995. In the first year, children below the age of 3 years were covered, but from 1996 children below the age of 5 years, have been provided Immunisation. During 1998-99, the fourth phase of Pulse Polio Immunisation was observed on 6th December 1998 and 17th January 1999. The coverage has been of the order of 137 million and the reported coverage has been around 109%. Larger than 100% coverage is due to vaccination of children above 5. The coverage under PPI; 1998-99 is about 4% higher than in previous year which will help in achieving more rapid decline in polio incidence in 1999. This has been made possible by inducting a group of secondary students on every PPI booth for noting down the families which do not come to PPI and for approaching them at their residences for immunisation of their children.

Urban slums and remote rural areas have been given larger attention an~ the Immunisation every year is being subjected to -both process evaluation and independent evaluation, the latter arranged through the local UNICEF organisation. It has been a heartening feature that the coverage has been found to be substantially above 90% in evaluations.

Surveillance system

PPI has been supplemented by a polio surveillance system. Ideally the surveillance system should have been put in place in 1995 itself, but in 1996 agreement was reached with DANIDA for assisting for a national surveillance system through the implementing agency of the WHO. The assistance is of US $ 36 million for the period of 5 years. In 1997, this arrangement has been put in place. A national surveillance team has been positioned in Delhi and 59 surveillance officers have been posted in various parts of the country. Their number is being increased to 86.

Separate office for the National team has been commissioned in the office complex at Jawaharlal Nehru Stadium, New Delhi, and the team has started functioning from this premises. The surveillance officers have been located at the state headquarters and at regional places in the case of larger states. They work independently but in close co-ordination with the state and Welfare Directorate and District Immunisation Officers. A regular weekly reporting system has been established and as a result of more meticulous search/ reporting, the number of reported cases of Acute Flaccid Paralysis increased from 1005 in 1996 to 2882 in 1997 and 3000 in 1998. The surveillance reports are considered by a Technical Advisory Group headed by the Secretary, Family Welfare with representatives from the WHO, DANIDA, UNICEF and other related agencies, every quarter and these are also considered departmentally in specially convened monthly meetings organised for this purpose.

An important improvement in the Pulse Polio Immunisation as Universal Immunisation Programme (regarding polio) in 1998 has been the use of vaccine vial monitor on all vial vaccine bottles. This has greatly enhanced quality assurance about the vaccine at the time of its administration to the children. The department has been insisting on testing of vaccine for its effectiveness in independent laboratories before the vaccine is despatched to States for use. Cold storage equipment is supplied all over the country to keep vaccines at prescribed low temperature. However, due to occasional breakdowns in equipment and more frequent power break-downs, temperature is always not maintained.

To maintain the effectiveness of vaccine, samples are drawn randomly all over the country all through the year and these are sent to laboratories for testing. In previous years, about 90% of the samples have been found to be effective, but for the 10% samples not found effective it has not been possible to withdraw them from use because the time the testing reports are received (which takes normally 6 to 8 weeks), much of the vaccines get used. This deficiency has been corrected from 1998 by use of colour monitors. Colour monitors or labels are put on vaccine bottles. Each label has a circle of deep blue colour. Inside it is a white square which changes colour and gradually becomes blue if vaccine bottle is exposed to higher temperature. When the colour of the white square becomes deep blue like that of the surrounding circle, the vaccine should be considered to have become ineffective. Therefore, by seeing the colour of the label at the time of administering the vaccine to children, the health worker can easily ascertain that the vaccine being given is effective.

This mechanism has been made mandatory in all procurement in 1998 except some vaccine which the government had to purchase from one of the companies in pursuance of Court order. This larger quality assurance will ensure that children will have better protection against polio in 1999 and this is expected to lead to a sharp decline in polio cases in 1999.

Community Needs Assessment Approach (CNAA)

Right since the beginning of the Family Planning Programme, targets for the year for individual contraceptives are being developed for the country and then these are conveyed to the States and from there to the districts. It has been known that this system of determining targets from above has many shortcomings. Firstly, the system is against the concept of empowerment of citizens because in a target driven programme, it is not the choice or preference of, citizens which guides the health workers, but the targets given from above. Secondly, targets reflect the perception of the persons above, rather than the felt needs of the citizens and therefore they are somewhat arbitrary. Thirdly, once targets are given, attainment of those numbers becomes primary and the quality of service becomes secondary. Finally, once targets are given, the health workers become pre-occupied with somehow reporting full achievement of targets and therefore the element of over-reporting comes in. Therefore, after very sizeable trials, during 95-96 and after consulting all the state governments, the practice of fixing targets from above was given up from April, 96. Now, in place, of targets the health workers are required to consult communities and ascertain their needs and preference for individual contraceptives for these to be made available. Giving up of targets does not mean that the objective of stabilising population early has been given up, on the other hand this community-based approach is intended to help in achieving goal of stable -population even earlier.

After the targets were given up, expectedly there was a slump in reported figures for contraception use. In some states like Uttar Pradesh, Bihar and Madhya Pradesh there were reports of feeling generated among health functionaries that giving up targets meant that health workers are no longer responsible for delivering any given quantum of work. In some of these states the reported figures for use of contraceptives declined by 30-50% during 96-97 However, a massive training and orientation effort covering all health workers in the country was taken up with the assistance of the UNICEF in 96-97 and this training effort is being continued now under the RCH programme. This has helped to restore improvement path in the use of contraceptives in 97-98. In 97-98 sterilisation reported by the state governments increased by 6.6%, IUD insertions by 71%, condom Users by 2.8% and oral pill users by 19% over 96-97 Figures reported by the state governments for 98-99 for first 8 months indicate that similar improvement is continuing in spacing method acceptors in 98-99 are above 1997-98 level, in IUD insertion 2.8 % above, in condom users 15.3 % above and in oral pills 3.9% above. It is important to note in this regard that the decline-sin birth rate during 96-97 and 97-98 has been actually slightly more than the average of 45 years during which contraceptives have been canvassed with the people. During 45 years of the programme the decline in birth rate has averaged slightly less than 0.3 per year, whereas during 95-97 it has been 0.55 per year, although the two year period is too short to reliably assess the decline in birth rate, but figures are still indicative that slump in reported contraceptive coverage during 96-97 has not hurt the birth control effort.

The F.W. programme-was being implemented under the 'Target Free Approach (TFA)' since Ist April 1996 all over India and under the system of decentralised participatory planning. TFA has been renamed as Community Needs Assessment Approach (CNAA) from

1997 Under this approach planning of family welfare services will be formulated in consulation with the community at the grassroot level. This approach is expected to bring about improvement in quality of services and client satisfaction. Under this new approach, monitoring and evaluation of the performance requires a fresh look with a view to ensuring quality of care at different levels of the primary health care system. Decentralised participatory planning implicates close association of the community and its leading lights and opinion leaders such as Village Pradhans, Mahila Swasthya Sanghs, Primary School Teachers, etc. in formulation of the PHC based family welfare and health care plan. The manual on CNAA on Family Welfare Programme has already been made available to all the States and UTs to provide guidance in formulation of decentralised planning,

The CNA manual envisages two key items, firstly working out need assessment for the year in the beginning of the year by each ANM and then its complication at PHC, district and state level to arrive at need assessment at these levels. Secondly, it involves monthly report from district level of not only contraceptive use, but also of other RCH services including availability of drugs and vaccines, so that monthly monitoring of work becomes possible and supplies can be rushed wherever there is shortage. The process of setting up these arrangements for annual need assessment and for monthly reporting has been initiated in 98-99 with the development and dissemination of the CNA manual. During 98-99, some districts and some states have managed to work out the need assessment and started sending monthly reports. However, this will need to be followed up and it is expected that during 1999-2000 annual need assessment and monthly reports will get made all over the country with desired regularity.

Strengthening working arrangements under the Target Free regime would require change in long-held attitudes and long-established working practices. Deriving optimum results under the target free working system will require continuing training and retraining programme and unceasing follow-up, which is in the process of being put in place under the RCH Programme.

Improvements during 1998-99

A number of improvements have been possible in the out-reach and effectiveness of Family Welfare programmes during 98-99. Some of these are as below:

Reorientation in strategy: Critical appraisal of the delivery system for Family Welfare programme shows that somehow the hospitals have persuaded themselves over the decades that responsibility for delivering Family Welfare Services to the people is exclusive responsibility of AN Ms. As a result of this, the hospital system created at huge cost is contributing very little to Family Welfare programme. While contraceptives are being supplied to States without any restraint, most hospitals do not offer contraceptives to citizens in a ready manner. An average citizen cannot go to a hospital and easily get contraceptives. Similarly, very few hospitals offer Immunisation facility and Vitamin A and ORS packets to citizens. While almost all hospitals at district and sub-divisional places and most Community Health Centres have operation theaters, these do not regularly offer IUD insertion facility or sterilisation facility in most States. Because of this the contribution of about 30000 district hospitals, sub divisional hospitals CHCs and PHCs remains low in Family Welfare programmes. If they start contributing to the Family Welfare programme, the total outcome with the already available investment will increase very substantially. This non-involvement of hospitals is particularly unfortunate because even in urban areas the participation rate of poor segments of the population and of population living in slums is quite low. To rectify this deficiency, State Governments are being pressed to make pointed efforts for involvement of hospitals in Family Welfare programmes. The States are being urged to ensure that at least in one operation theater IUD facility is offered every day and sterilisation facility is offered at least on a fixed day of the week so that no person coming for sterilisation on that day is turned back without sterilisation. The State Governments have also been requested to have a counter made near the entrance of the hospital where Immunisation should be offered to all those who seek it offered to all those who seek it. The ORS packets and contraceptives should also be put on the counter for being taken by the citizens freely. Many State Governments have already issued instructions to district officers for doing so.

Similarly a critical appraisal of the work of ANMs shows that despite drugs, vaccines and contraceptives being freely available, their use by citizens is only partial. Registration of pregnancies and ante-natal check-ups for pregnant women is also not total. On: being questioned, people invariably come up with the answer that ANM's visit to villages is not very regular and if they go to the Sub Centres, it is closed. This situation arises because ANM has been having instructions over the years to be touring villages all the time. Because of this construction or maintaining a Sub Centre on rent and investment made in furnishing, it remains largely irrelevant. To rectify this problem, the State Governments have been urged to formally order all ANMs to remain in the Sub Centre and keep it open at least on one or two fixed days of the week so that on those days citizens from the neighbouring area who desire to have Family Welfare services can come to the Sub Centres and obtain these services. Most State Governments have already issued instructions in this regard.

It was thought earlier that the urban population is quite well served by the network of Government, local body and non-Government hospitals in urban areas. Therefore, the focus of the Family Welfare programmes and services has been on the rural areas. However, experience has shown that a sizeable portion of poor Mohallas in urban areas do not effectively have access to Family Welfare services through urban hospitals. This is even more so in regard to urban slums which now account for about 10 crore population. Actually the RCH status and fertility rate in urban slums is even poorer than in the rural area as a whole. Therefore, the earlier decision to confine supply of drug kits to only rural areas is clearly not right. In 1998 this deficiency has been corrected and urban areas have been covered by the programme for supply of drugs kits. Procurement of drugs has been initiated on this basis and beginning in 1999 all urban areas in the country will also get covered by the drugs supply programme in regard to maternal and child health conditions.

Increasing the outreach

Similarly for the anaemia control programme so far only married women in reproductive age group were being provided iron folic acid tablets course. However, anaemia in adolescent girls is equally significant because if it is allowed to persist, such girls enter married life with anaemia and it affects their well being as well as the well being of their child when they become pregnant. Therefore, State Governments have been advised to instruct health functionaries to look after anaemic conditions of adolescent girls and to provide them iron folic acid course if they need it.

The urban slum population numbering about 10 crores is not so far covered by primary health care facilities. While the primary health care network of

Community Health Centres, Primary Health Centres and Rural Sub Centres covers rural area in the whole of the country adequately for primary health care, in urban areas the network of Post Partum Centres, urban Family Welfare Centres and urban Health Posts is sketchy and it provides primary health care to only a small fraction of urban slums. The population of urban slums is large and their needs for Family Welfare services are also large because RCH status of urban slum population is very poor. Therefore, the Department has paid special attention to this problem area. Under the World Bank assisted on-going IPP-VIII project whole of slum population of 10 cities in West Bengal, 11 cities in Karnataka and 73 cities/towns in Andhra Pradesh is being covered by primary health care by creating need-based facilities in the form of Urban Health Centres including facility for maternity.

Project proposals for these cities have been formulated in consulation with the State Governments concerned and these have been discussed with the World Bank for their concurrence. The Expenditure Finance Committee of the Government is considering these proposals for approval in January, '99 and if these are approved by the Government, these facilities would be operationalised during 1999. In addition to these, slum population in 25 larger cities in other States is being sought to be similarly provided primary health care by setting up need-based Urban Health Centres under the on-going World Bank assisted Reproduction & Child Health programme. State-wise project in these 25 cities are being prepared in consulation with the State Governments and the effort of the Department is to seek approval of the Government and of the World Bank for these city projects with a view to operationalising them during '99-2000.

The NGO programme emphasising decentralisation and envisaging unuptrusive but meticulous verification and concurrent evaluation has been operationalised during'98-'99 and the effort of the Mother NGOs is being focused for counselling so that citizens have full information and correct advice in regard to facilities and options available under the RCH programme. Simultaneously, some well established NGOs with large capability are being associated in complementing work of governmental system for provision of RCH services so that the population can get full range of RCH services. With this objective, a project to KEM Society, Pune for Poona district and to SEWA, Ahmedabad for Kheda, Banaskanta and Ahmedabad districts' is being sanctioned. A project for Delhi Metropolitan area has been developed by Indian Medical Association for involving more than 50 non-governmental hospitals and nursing homes for provision of RCH services to citizens. These are sizeable initiatives which will involve non-government sector in the RCH effort and if they succeed, they will become model for being replicated else where in the country.

While condoms and oral pills are supplied free of cost all over the country through Government hospitals and ANMs, their reach has attained a plateau. In such supplies there is always some uncertainty in regard to availability because of the less than regular tours of health functionaries. As a result many citizens do not use contraceptives because of lack of assurance about supply. The Government has been supplementing free supply by social marketing of contraceptives under which contraceptives are sold at subsidised rates through NGOs and companies. However, this effort has also not been reaching below small towns because the NGOs and companies find maintenance of supply system prohibitively expensive due to low volume of sales in individual villages. The rural population has lower couple protection rate than the national average and therefore is a high priority area if total fertility rate has to be brought down.

This can become possible only if arrangement for assured and unobtrusive supply can be made upto village level. In this regard a notable initiative has been started in December, 98 for Gwalior, Bhind and Morena districts of Madhya Pradesh through a Trust created by Hindustan Latex Ltd. This project for social marketing is being funded by the Government of India. It will offer not only condoms and oral pills but also weekly pills, oral rehydration packets and low cost sanitary napkins. The weekly oral pill will increase the options available to individual women for using oral pill for contraception, oral rehydration powder will enable families to use ORS for controlling diarrhoea in more cases and thereby reduce still large number of diarrhoeal deaths and use of sanitary napkins will help in bringing down the incidence of Reproductive Tract Infections which currently is very high and affects about 50% of all women.

To ensure interface with district health set up, an Advisory Committee headed by Commissioner, Gwalior Division has been constituted. The Trust will maintain warehouses at district and sub-divisional places for these five items. At village level ANMs and traditional birth attendants will be approached for becoming vendors on percentage commission basis. At Block level a number of youths have been given mopeds and they will tour every village on a fixed day of the fortnight. Initially they will provide vendors a stock worth Rs. 1000/- and then replenish it every fortnight while recovering the sale proceeds. To ensure continued motivation, the commission of village level vendors has been kept sizeable and the Block level youth have also been engaged on retainership, basis rather than as salaried employees with large portion of their monthly income coming in the form of commission on sales achieved. This arrangement will for the first time make it possible to as sure regular supply of these items right upto village level and it has the potential of making a breakthrough in the use of these items in villages. If this model proves successful, it can become a model for the rest of the country for being replicated in subsequent years.

Quality improvement

In regard to polio vaccine the Government of India has been having oral polio vaccine tested for quality, in independent laboratories before it is allowed to be dispatched by manufacturers to States for use. Subsequently, samples are drawn randomly from throughout the country during the year and they are similarly tested. The test reports indicate that about 90% of the samples are found effective. However, the testing takes about 2 months and because of this even the ineffective vaccine relating to 10% of the samples get used in vaccination by the time the report is received. Such deterioration in vaccine occurs due to occasional cold chain equipment failure but more frequently due to power failure which is quite common in large parts of the country. So far there has been no protection against this deficiency. However, in 1998 the Department has availed of a technological improvement which has come about in recent years to remove this weakness in the programme.

Chemically active coloured labels called vial monitors have become available recently. In these labels there is an outer circle of deep blue colour inside which there is a circle which is of white colour when the vaccine is bottled. If the vaccine bottle is exposed to higher temperature the colour of the inner circle gradually becomes blue and when it become a deep blue as of the outer circle, the vaccine is indicated to have become ineffective. Therefore, just by looking at the vial monitor while administering vaccine any health worker can easily determine whether the vaccine is still effective. This innovation has been utilised and vaccine vial monitors have been made compulsory on all polio vaccine procured in 98 except about 10% vaccine which had to be procured without vial monitors under Orders of the Court. The use of vial monitors will increase quality assurance about the vaccine and it will ensure that no child is given vaccine which is ineffective. This is expected to sharply bring down the number of polio cases in 1999.

In the vaccination programme all vaccines except polio are administered by injections including vaccination for tetanus to pregnant women. So far reusable syringes and needles are being provided to AN Ms for vaccination. ANM have been given sterilisation equipment and they are supposed to carry a box of sterilized syringes and needles when they go on tour to villages for vaccination. However, sometimes due to carelessness this always does not happen and sometimes the number of children to be vaccinated in the village exceeds the number of syringes and needles being carried by the ANM. In this situation the ANMs use the same syringe and needle on different children. This causes infection in some cases. This danger is becoming more grave due to increasing chance of HIV Aids infection and Hepatitis B infection. Therefore, the Department has decided to supply disposable needles and syringes to all hospitals and ANMs for vaccination programme form 1999 onwards. This will avoid transfer of infection from one person to the other. This will be a large improvement over the existing practice. Although chances of recycling of used needles and syringes are less in rural areas, but the possibility cannot be totally ruled out. Therefore, ideal answer to the requirement would be to use auto-destruct syringes and needles. So far only imported ones are available which are quite costly and therefore cannot be used for nation wide programme. However, two companies in India are on the verge of entering into a technology collaboration arrangement for manufacture of auto-destruct syringes and needles. These ate likely to become available during next two years and if their cost is somewhere in the range of the cost of disposable syringes and needles, the Department intends to switch over to use of auto-destruct syringes and needles for vaccination programme after two years.

A large proportion of deliveries in many States takes place at home or through AN Ms. For making such deliveries safe, Safe Delivery Kits are being recommended by the Government of India for long years. However, supply of Safe Delivery Kit has been limited to giving of such kits to Dais or ANMs when they are called for training. As a result of this, use of Safe Delivery Kits is not universal even in home deliveries. While the Government is canvassing hospital deliveries with the citizens for ensuring safety of mother and of the new born, procurement and supply of Safe Delivery Kit for home deliveries has been started by the Department. The procurement agencies of the Department have been instructed to procure Safe Delivery Kits and supply these to States as per their need. The supplies would become available to States during 1999 and will continue thereafter. This measure is expected to ensure greater safety in deliveries.

In a large number of home deliveries the women catch infection. This happens substantially because many families in the villages use the bed and bed sheets which they commonly use in daily life. During delivery the infection in these bed sheets and wetting of the bed sheets causes infection to the delivering woman. Studies have indicated that if sterilised rubber sheet is used in such cases, much of the risk of infection could be avoided. Therefore, in the eight States where presently percentage of home deliveries is high, the Government has decided to supply sterilised rubber sheet to every delivering woman which will be subsequently kept by her for her use and of the new born child. The process of procurement of sterilised rubber sheets has been started and supply to States will begin in 1999.

Increasing efficiency in distribution

The Government of India procures and supplies drugs, equipment kits, contraceptives and vaccines to States for use in Family Welfare programme. While the drug kits are supplied at district level, vaccines and contraceptives are supplied at State or regional level. The States have so far not created any specialised or dedicated system for receiving such supplies, storing them in acceptable conditions and for their distribution. The result is that drugs, equipment and contraceptives are kept in any available space which leads to sizeable deterioration in these items. Distribution to next lower level is by conveying to them by normal channels and expecting them lower levels to come and carry supplies. By the time supplies reach the PHC or the Sub Centre, 3 or 4 levels have to fetch their supplies. This involves large delay. Because of these arrangements on one hand excess supplies get wasted in some places while in other places short supplies do not get corrected and citizens remain without such supplies for long months. Therefore, supply arrangements have been streamlined in 1998-99. Vaccines and contraceptives are continuing to be procured by the Department directly While procurement and supply of drugs and equipment has been entrusted to professional agencies on assignment basis.

Hospital Services & Consultancy Corporation (HSCC) and Procurement Division of Hindustan Latex Ltd. has been engaged for procurement and supply of drugs and equipment. To improve things the drugs have been divided into two parts, one which are easily available in all parts of the country and frequently which have low cost and large bulk. For these HSCC will determine rate contract for the year by tender process and will keep a buffer stock at five or six places in the country from where States will be able to indent and procure necessary quantifies three or four times in an year.

This will enable avoiding unnecessary locking up of Government money for the whole year's supply and this will also avoid collecting high bulk and low value items from manufacturing places to a central place in the country for making kits and then again carrying this bulk to all the districts for use. Other items will be procured Centrally by the HSCC and these will be supplied as kits to districts. Procurement in this manner has been initiated for 99-2000 and supplies are expected to begin by the middle of 1999.

In addition to the above mentioned improvement, the problem of appropriate storage and efficient distribution remains. This is specialised work which requires professional and competent staff and organisation and storage space which is suitable for storing medical supplies. Investment in creating such arrangement has not been made in the past because supplies under Government of India programme have been increasing incrementally during last two decades and at no stage it was felt that these are now too large to be handled in a casual manner.

Now the value of annual supplies is about Rs. 500 crores and due to deterioration and inefficiencies loss to the extent of 20 - 30% is estimated to be taking place. Therefore by working with donor agencies proposals have been formulated for each major State through consultants engaged for the purpose. Proposals so developed envisage a specialised agency at State level for this work. It will create and manage warehouses at regional level for each cluster of 5 - 8 districts. These places will receive indent from each hospital in the area and will ensure delivery within 15 days through contracted transporter. To ensure efficiency, the State Government agency will be paid only on the basis of a percentage of supplies it handles.

Thus continued dependence of the Stage agency on grant from the Government of India for maintenance will be avoided. The proposals in this regard have been firmed up in consulation with the donor agencies and the State Governments and are being presently considered by the Government of India for approval. Government decision is expected in about the next three months. If the proposal is approved, these arrangements will be operationalised during '99-2000.

Inservice training

Inservice training of health managers, doctors and paramedics has been weak in the past. While there have been ad hoc, time bound training efforts frequently in the past in regard to a specific objective, regular inservice training arrangements have not been developed earlier. Inadequacies in the present working in regard to sterilisations, IUD insertions, anaemia control etc. clearly indicate need for upgrading the skills of health staff. In addition to this, the range of requirement of skills has increased with the starting of RCH programme. Therefore, there is need for a systematic and regular inservice training system in the country. This has been provided for in the RCH programme with the assistance of donor agencies. The Department has given high priority to this need and a network of 15 regional institutions called collaborating institutions headed by National Institute of Health & Family Welfare (NIHFW) at national level has been set up to identify training courses and training institutions, to channelise financial assistance to them and subsequently to monitor and enforce quality norms on training institutions.

The training courses will relate to not only specialised RCH interventions but will also relate to RCH management issues for senior level officers and to awareness building at Panchayat/district level in which Anganwadi workers and Panchayati Raj functionaries will also be involved. This arrangement has started becoming operational in '98-'99 and NIHFW has been able to channelise assistance to more than half the districts in the country during the year for awareness courses. Skill based courses are expected to become operational by the beginning of 99-2000.

The Department has been trying to improve training programmes at senior level by promoting multi-country training courses. During 97-98 assistance was arranged to NIHFW from UNFPA and they organised a course for district level officers, half of which were Indians and the other half from Indonesia. The training course of 6 weeks was also half in India and half in Indonesia. Such training course expose Indian officials-to foreign experience which enriches them and on the other hand it allows Indian expertise to be projected in foreign countries. During '98-99 three such courses have been facilitated by the Department with financial assistance of WHO. One course in Indian Institute of Health and Family welfare, Hyderabad has started on 28th December, 98. Two other courses, one in Institute of Economic Growth, Delhi and other the International Institute of Population Sciences, Mumbai, will start shortly. In each of these courses there will be tie up between the Indian institution and an identified foreign institution and the trainees will also be from both the countries.

IEC- In information, education and communication a number of meaningful initiatives have been possible during 98-99 For improving the quality and range of spot messages on TV/radio, the Department has been trying to engage professional agencies for production of such clips. During the year it has been possible to select a professional agency for such work and messages produced in the manner are expected to become available for telecast by the end of the year. In regard to films, the Department decided to avoid producing a large number of nonappealing films and decided to invite a small number of creative producers in the country for making films on any theme relating to Family Welfare. It has been possible to firm up proposals in regard to two films, one on women empowerment by Shri Amol Palekar and the other on generational perception in a Muslim family by Shri Shyam Bengal which will be a five part serial. These are expected to become available by the end of 1999. The effort of the Department will be to concentrate on making 4 or 5 such good quality films in a year which probably would be more influential with the public.

The Department has been able to operationalise the initiative for co-ordination with the literacy movement for IEC within individual districts through zilla Saksharta Samitis. Such collaboration will help both Family Welfare and literacy programmes and inter-district IEC would meaningfully supplement the national level effort through electronic and print media. Zilla Saksharta Samitis would utilise folk media and institutions within the districts to design and conduct IEC programme within the district. Proposals from individual districts for a two-year period were sought and response of Zilla Saksharta Samitis has been very good. In consulation with National Literacy Mission Authority 69 district proposals have been sanctioned and money has been made available to districts. It is likely that by the end of the year assistance would have been provided to 150 districts. This will be continued during '99-2000 for remaining districts. The Department is trying to work out an institutional arrangement for concurrent monitoring of the district programme so that the programme remains vibrant.

Another notable initiative which has become possible during '98299 is in regard to interactive panel discussions on TV. The Department has been seeking to promote informed debate in the country about population and Family Welfare issues through such discussions and also to indirectly enlist support of opinion leaders for the programme by inviting them on the panels in such discussions. During the year it has been possible to assign the work to a professional agency and actual organisation and recording of interactive panel discussion is expected to begin shortly. Telecasting is intended to be started around March, 99

Use of Indian Systems of Medicines The Department of Family Welfare has been trying to use Indian Systems particularly Ayurveda and Unani for Reproductive and Child Health to improve acceptability among people and to improve outcomes.. The RCH programme approved by the Government of India envisages use of Indian Systems also. During '98299 it has been possible to assist 30 Ayurvedic and Unani training institutions to provide short course training to Vaidyas and Hakims for upgrading their knowledge in regard to Reproductive and Child Health conditions and treatment. The RCH programme envisages promoting Vanaspati Van over degraded forestland or wasteland in sizeable large areas so that availability of Ayurvedic and Unani drugs improves and the problem of substitution or adulteration in such drugs is effectively countered. Proposals from Himachal Pradesh, Madhya Pradesh, Andhra Pradesh, Karnataka and Kerala have been received. The proposal in regard to Himachal Pradesh has been sanctioned. It is expected after expert Committees have visited the proposed sites, proposals in some more States may be found acceptable and sanctioned during the financial year. The Department is also attempting to use Ayurvedic drugs in the drug kit supplied to ANMs. There are some known effective drugs for maternal health and child health conditions. Seven such drugs have been identified in consulation with Ayurveda Experts and the Department of ISM and H. Proposal to begin procuring these drugs has been developed and has been proposed for consideration of the Expenditure Finance Committee. If Government approval becomes available for these proposals, IM drugs will start getting procured and supplied to ANMs in 1999.

Management information system.

Although large volume of inputs are being made in the Family Welfare programme from the national and State level, the monitoring at district level and below has been a weak point. A reliable picture in regard to this in the form of birth rate, death rate, infant mortality rate, etc. becomes available through Census at 10 year interval. In between National Family Health Survey in 9293 provided a very good picture of what is happening as a result of Family Welfare programmes., On annual basis Sample Registration System conducted by Registrar General of Census ascertains birth rate, death rate and infant mortality rate every year. However, during the year or even annually there is no way presently of ascertaining about which RCH services are actually reaching the people and to what effect. In 98-99 it has been possible to start two surveys, one Rapid Household Survey and the other Facility Survey. For both these surveys a network of 15 regional institutions headed by IIPS, Mumbai, has been set up to ensure objectivity in survey and in analysis of data. The Rapid Household Survey is ascertaining which RCH services are being used by people and to what extent. It has to be done for half the districts every year so that every district is covered every alternate year. In half the districts of the country the survey for 1997 has been conducted and the district reports are expected by the end of January, '99. For the other half districts survey for '98 will begin soon thereafter so that the results are available by June, '99.

The Facility survey will focus on hospitals and will ascertain which facility created in the hospitals for RCH are operational and to what extent they are being used. In each major State all hospitals of one district, in medium size States hospitals in a Sub Division and in small in States/UTs hospitals in a Block will be surveyed every month. These surveys are beginning in January, '99 and first monthly reports are expected in March, '99. These two surveys will provide a reliable assessment of RCH work which is actually taking place in each district/ country and therefore these will help in increasing accountability of health staff. These will also allow the Central and State Governments to take corrective actions without much loss of time.

The reporting system developed in the Community Needs Assessment approach after targets for individual contraceptives have been given up envisages need assessment in consulation with community at the beginning every year for the whole of the year and a monthly report of the inputs available and work done during the month from every district to the State Governments and Central Government. However, a bottleneck in operationalising this arrangement has been availability of NIC terminal in the district. To get over this difficulty it has been decided to provide personal computers to every district with connection to NIC terminal so that the District Health Officers can transmit annual and monthly information to the State Government and Central Government without difficulty. Each district office will also be provided with e-mail connection to improve communication between districts and State Governments and Central Government.

Strengthening for Zero polio incidence

While polio Immunisation as part of Universal Immunisation Programme (started in 1985-86 and which covered the whole of the country in 89-90) was meant to effectively control polio infection and bring down the number of polio cases, specific effort to eliminate polio was started in 1995 in the form of two Pulse Polio Immunisation rounds, one in December and other in January each year. This year PPI has been conducted for the fourth year. In order to take stock of the situation and see whether the country is on course for achieving zero incidence of polio and to see whether this goal can be achieved faster, during last four months an intensive review has been made in consulation with State Governments, Indian Council of Medical Research and experts, both Indian and foreign. The review has indicated that while the effort for eradicating polio has been extremely successful so far, the present trends indicate that zero incidence of polio can be expected some time during 2005-10. The Polio Surveillance System set up in 1997 is already very effective and it has matured faster than in almost any other country in the world. The experts, including experts of WHO, UNICEF and DANIDA, have advised that zero incidence of polio can be achieved by the year 2001 or 2002 by taking some additional strengthening measures. Such measures will include some additional rounds of polio Immunisation to reduce the gap between PPI rounds and to thereby break the chain of transmission which presently enables a small number of still infected children left in January to infect a large number of other children by the time of new PPI round in following December. The Department is consulting experts to firm up the proposal for strengthening measures and seeking Government approval for the modified strategy. The intention is to operationalise these strengthening measures in 1999 so that zero incidence of polio can be achieved by the year 2002.

Decentralised and local specific initiatives

India is a very large and diverse country and needs are different in different parts of the country. However, programmes tend to be generally the same all over the country because of the necessity of going through approval system at national level, though States and districts have the -flexibility of using more or less of individual items of programme. However, the problem of having a nationally uniform programme substantially remains.

To get round this problem the Department has worked with UNICEF to identify a cluster of 4-6 districts in about a dozen places in the country where specialists would study local situation and requirements and formulate specific additional programmes to meet these requirements. The objective for each cluster would be to bring down infant mortality rate below 30 and maternal mortality below over a three-year period. Decentralised management will be facilitated by giving control of the programme to local Committees headed by Commissioners or Collectors. Moderation of the programme will be ensured by coordinating the approval of the programme developed by specialists at national level by the

Department of Family Welfare in consulation with UNICEF-India. Subsequently, these agencies will monitor the progress of the programme to ensure that it does not get rountinised. Such a programme would also help UNICEF to point out sizeable achievement as a result of its assistance. For the State Governments such strategy would be helpful in developing a model for the other districts of the State for achieving similar good results in a time bound manner. This strategy has been discussed with the State Governments concerned and they have welcomed it. The Department is trying to have the district level programmes prepared as a project proposal by April, '99 so that they can be taken up for implementation from June, '99. This would be an effective initiative for ensuring that programmes in an area are in consonance with its special needs.

According to Planning Commission estimates, population figures are expected to go up from 856 million in 1991-92 to 938 million in 1996-97, showing an annual average growth rate of 18 per cent . If the growth rate remains around two per cent, this figure will go up to 955 million, According to current indications, the actual figure will be in between these two figures since the death rate has fallen below even the 2000-2001 and in any case will be below the rate of around two per cent as estimated by the current UN projections, of around 1,042 million in that year. If India is able to achieve a population growth rate of around 1.6 percent in the decade 2000-2001 to2010-2011, its population will reach 1,171 million, if the Planning Commission projections are used as a base. Even if this target is exceeded, the figure will be less than 1,224 million as estimated by the UN. These projections have not incorporated the detail of the 1991 census. The Registrar—General's Working Group on Population Projections set up conventionally by the Planning Commission, will have to firm up these alternative conjectural projections, in terms of underlying fertility, mortality and expected life span-behaviour, by age—group and rural-urban categories.

The other major category needing examination on this kind of perspective is the land or resource base of the economy. The Planning Commission has correctly projected that the net area sown or arable land of the country will remain constant at 141 million hectares. Growth in net area sown at around one per cent annually in the early period of planing fell to around 0.6 per cent and then to 0.3 per cent in subsequent decades and is now not growing at all. It is reasonable to assume that the exploitation of the geographical area of the country or the extensive land frontier has reached its limits. This is an important issue, the implications of which are not being realized with the urgency they deserve, since at a basic level resource constraints of a more severe kind faced by certain East Asian economies are now being approached in India. Organizations, communities, households and individuals will have to grasp this fact and live with it.

The intensive frontier for land use, however remains. It has been known for example that cropping intensity depends on irrigatin. Thus gross cropped area or harvested area has been shown in the past to be strongly determined statistically, in an econometric sense, by net irrigated area and irrigation intensity. This fundamental relationship can be used to project the intensive resource base of the economy.

Recognizing these problems the Finance Minister has been persuaded to introduce an Accelerated Irrigation Benefit Programme in the Annual Plan for this year. An outlay of Rs. 800 crore has ben provided for large irrigation project where substantial achievement can be expected—say in completing a section of the canal systems in the next two or three years and Rs. 100 crore for delivering water to the field in the next two agricultural years. These programmes will be strictly monitored. More important, a blue ribbon com-mission has been set up with the following terms of reference:

— To prepare an Integrated Water Plan for development of water resources for drinking, irrigation, industrial, flood control and other uses;

— To suggest modalities for transfer of surplus water to water-deficit basins by interlinking of rivers for achieving the above objectives;

— To identify important ongoing projects as well as new projects which should be completed on a priority basis together with phasing;

— Identify a technological and interdisciplinary research plan for the water sector with a view to maximizing the benefits;

— To suggest physical and financial resource generation strategies for the water sector; and

— Any other related issue.

The projections assume a vastly improved performance on the land and water management frontiers. It needs to be remembered that the balance ground water reserves towards the later half of the nineties will be nore and more limited. A very dramatic effort will be needed to harvest and carefully use the available water. Otherwise, the projected increase in cropping intensity will simply not take place. Cropping intensity increased from around 1.3 in the early nineties. In the nixt two decades, this effort needs to be considerably strengthened, so that cropping intensity can increase from 1.3 to 1.5. Harvesting of rainwater, recycling water from agricultural drainage systems, more judicious use of water for cropping, will all be required, Non-agricultural use of water will have to be far more econmical.

Another way of looking at the severe land constraint is to see that a net area sown per person will go down from around 0.17 ha to around 0.10 ha. The gross area sown per person currently around 0.2 ha will, even if cropping intensity increases very rapidly, go down to around 0.15-0.18 ha.

It has been shown elsewhere that limited co-operation in waer use has been successful in many watershed projects in resolving the land constraint. The same is true of lower level surface irrigation systems. Community involvement is also important for judicous management of aquifer systems and ground water use. In many cases, land management questions are equally important and are inextricably linked with water management, eg land shaping in hill slopes and on farm investment in irrigation commands.

The technology interface is important, both for land and water management and for cropping and non-crop farm systems that are optimal, in this class of issues. While a lot of research has been done and is available, the real issues are policy rules for fast replicability of existing knowledge and success stories. Community institutions have to be at the heart of this process. ICAR, its centres and sponsored institutions, have not easily participated in this process.

Work force: This kind of development is simply not possible if the functional literacy skills of the farm population arenot improved and if the peasant who works on the land, does not have rights to make improvements on it. There are a number of significant examples where based on local initiative, educational and training institutions led to knowledge-based growth in rural areas. These include the Charotar Vidya Mandal at Vallabh Vidyanagar (later Sardar Patel University), Dharamasthala Educational Trust (efforts of Veerendra Heggade) and many co-operative sponsored institutions in Maharashtra (for example the Pravara Ecucational Trust at Loni). Recognizing the importance of such efforts, the government of India has set up a National Council for Rural Institutes. The ICAR and its affiliates must be one of the major thrust institutions in this effort and its educational and extension wings must sponsor, acredit and support the effort.

The government's Basic Minimum Services (BMSDs) Programme also has the same objective. It consists of the following programmes which need integration with our agricultural strategy:

— 100 per cent coverage of provision of safe drinking water in rural and urban areas.

— 100 per cent coverage of primary health service facilities in rural and urban areas.

— Universalization of primary education.

— Provision of public housing assistance to all shelterless poor families.

— Extension of mid day meal programme in primary school to all rural blocks and urban slums and desadvantaged sections.

— Provision of connectivity to all unconnected villages and habitations.

—s Streamlining the public distribution system with the focus on the poor.

India's population, as on 1 March 1991 stood at 846.30 million (439.23 million males and 407.07 million females). This includes the projected population of 7.72 million of

Jammu and Kashmir. The second largest populous country, India is the home of 16 per cent of world's population. The country, however, accounts for 2.42 per cent of the total world area.

The population of India as recorded at each decenial census from 1901 has grown steadily except for a decrease during 1911-21. In absolute terms the country's population has increased by 162.97 million during the decade 1981-91. Decadal growth of population from 1901, is shown in table 1. An encouraging feature revealed by the provisional results is the decline in growth rate of the population in the last decade compared to 1971-81. It marginally decreased from 24.66 per cent recorded in 1971-81 to 23.85 per cent during 1981-91.

In most states the growth rate declined during the decade. However, Andhra Pradesh, Arunachal Pradesh, Madhya Pradesh, Maharashtra, Nagaland, Tripura, West Bengal, Daman and Diu, Lakshadweep and Pondicherry which account for one third of the country's population, recorded increase in growth rate. Nagaland registered the highest growth rate of 56.08 per cent while Keral the lowest 14.32 per cent.

India's population, as on 1 March 1991 stood at 846.30 million (439.23 million males and 407.07 million females). This includes the projected population of 7.72 million of Jammu and Kashmir. The second largest populous country, India is the home of 16 per cent of world's population. The country, however, accounts for 2.42 per cent of the total world area.

The population of India as recorded at each decenial census from 1901 has grown steadily except for a decrease during 1911-21. In absolute terms the country's population has increased by 162.97 million during the decade 1981-91. Decadal growth of population from 1901, is shown in table 1. An encouraging feature revealed by the provisional results is the decline in growth rate of the population in the last decade compared to 1971-81. It marginally decreased from 24.66 per cent recorded in 1971-81 to 23.85 per cent during 1981-91.

In most states the growth rate declined during the decade. However, Andhra Pradesh, Arunachal Pradesh, Madhya Pradesh, Maharashtra, Nagaland, Tripura, West Bengal, Daman and Diu, Lakshadweep and Pondicherry which account for one third of the country's population, recorded increase in growth rate. Nagaland registered the highest growth rate of 56.08 per cent while Keral the lowest 14.32 per cent.

The NSS estimates of per capita consumption of different sections of the urban population in 1967-68 suffer from similar underestimation. In column 2 of the Table we have reproduced the NSS estimates of per capita consumption of the urban population in 1960-61 only slightly revised to bring them in accord with the official estimate of per capita national consumption. In column 2 are given the NSS estimates of per capita consumption in 1967-68 at 1960-61 prices. It will be seen that the NSS estimate of per capita urban consumption in 1967-68 (Rs. 325.7) is 8.6 per cent below the NSS estimate of urban consumption in 1960-61. Therefore, the estimate in 1967-68 is clearly an underestimate. The nature of underestimation becomes evident from column 4 where the NSS estimates for 1967-68 are expressed as percentages of corresponding estimates for 1960-61. These percentages increase progressively from 77.2 per cent for the poorest 5 per cent to 99.6 for the population lying between 60-70. Thereafter the percentages decline rapidly, implying that the upper middle and the richer sections of the urban population did not do comparatively as well as the middle sections. This is incredible and the conclusion is inevitable that the underestimation of urban consumption has been more serious in the case of the upper middle and the richer sections than in the case of other sections.

Hence, the NSS estimates of urban consumption in 1967-68 need to be revised. As in the case of the NSS estimates for rural consumption, we shall do the necessary revision conservatively in two steps. In the first stage (columns 5 and 6), we suppose that the percentages in column (4) should not decline as they do after reaching the value 99.6 for the class 60-70; hence we hold them at 99.6 for all classes above 60-70. The results are given in colum (5). It will be seen that this revision causes the NSS estimate for 1967-68 to rise from Rs. 325.7 to Rs. 346.7. It is nevertheless still below the estimate of per capita consumption in 1967-68 namely Rs. 364.9. In fact, it needs to be raised by 5.25 per cent to bring it to that level. We do this by raising uniformly the revised estimates of consumption of all sections (column 6) by 5.25 per cent. The results of this second and final revision are given in columns 7 and 8.

In column 8, the per capita consumption of different sections in 1967-68 are expressed as percentages of corresponding consumption in 1960-61. The results are eye-opening. The lower middle and poorer sections constituting the bottom 40 per cent of the ruban population have not benefited at all by the economic development of the past decade. Indeed, the evidence is that their per capita consumption has declined and greatly so among the poorest 10 per cent. This is not impossible. It is this class which sufferes from rise in prices as was witnessed in the past decade. There are other important reasons for such serious deterioration in the living standards at the bottom of the urban population. We shall refer to them a little later.

Other sections of the urban population have benefited variously. The per capita consumption of the middle sections lying between 40-60 increased by between 1.0 and 3.0 per cent; of the upper middle and the richer sections constituting the top 40 per cent of the urban population, the per capita consumption increased by 4.8 per cent. All visible and audible evidence points to the possibility that the consumption of the richer sections, the top 10 per cent or the top 5 per cent certainly, has increased much more. But in the absence of positive evidence, we prefer to be conservative. We should be thankful that statistcis could catch even as much of the reality as we have been able to discover.

The statistical evidence on growth of inequality is thus clear. A superficial examination and comparison of the NSS estimates of consumer expenditure in 1960-61 and 1967-68, as is commonly done, gives an impression that the inequalities in the distribution of consumer expenditure have narrowed down during the past decade. Unfortunately this is not true. The NSS estimates of consumption in 1967-68 are gross underestimates and the underestimation is particularly serious in the case of consumption of the upper middle and richer classes. The statistical evidence on both these counts is conclusive. Hence the NSS estimates of per capita consumer expenditure in 1967-68 must be corrected for underestimation.

As we have seen, even a conservative revision makes clear that all sections of the population have not benefited equally from the economic development of the past decade. The gains of development have remained largely confined to the upper middle and the richer sections constituting the top 40 per cent of the population. While the overall per capita consumption increased by about 3.9 per cent in seven years, the consumption of the upper 40 per cent of the rural population increased by at least 4.4 per cent and that of the upper 40 per cent of the urban population increased by at least 4.8 per cent. These increases are not extraordinary and they certainly are not undesirable. Unfortunately they have remained largely confined to the upper middle and richer sections of the population. The middle, lower middle and poorer sections of the rural population showed much smaller increases in their per capita consumption and the per capita consumption of the poorest 5 per cent actually declined a little. The situation in urban areas appears even more serious. The per capita consumption of the lower middle and poorer sections constituting the bottom 40 per cent of the urban population declined and the consumption of the poorest 10 per cent declined by as much as 15 to 20 per cent. Such unequal distribution of the gains of development inevitably leads to growing inequality and a widening gulf between the rich and the poor.

Urban situation

We have earlier noted that, during the period from 1960-61 to 1967-68, the rural-urban disparity has narrowed down a little. Thus, while in 1960-61 the per capita urban consumer expenditure was 37.7 per cent higher than the per capita rural consumer expenditure, in 1967-68 the urban per capita expenditure was only 35.9 per cent higher than the rural per capita expenditure. We shall now examine how this slight reduction in the rural-urban differential came about. In particular, we shall ask whether the reduction in the rural-urban differential came about because of a reduction in the differential between the rural-urban rich or the rural-urban poor. We have put together the relevant data. In columns (4) and (7) of the Table we have expressed the per capita urban consumer expenditure as per cent of the per capita rural consumer expenditure for each of the 12 sections into which we have divided the population.

To begin with, we should not that even in 1960-61, the rural-urban differential was much greater between the rural-urban rich than between the rural-urban poor. For instance, the per capita consumer expenditure of the 30 per cent urban poor was then about 27 per cent higher than the per capita consumer expenditure of their rural counterparts. On the other hand, the per capita consumer expenditure of the 20 per cent urban rich was then about 47 per cent higher than the per capita consumer expenditure of their rural counterparts.

The corresponding data for 1967-68 are given in column (7) of the Table. It will be noticed that the differential between the rural and urban upper middle and richer classes was practically the same in 1967-68 as it was in 1960-61 It increased only slightly. The urban upper middle and richer classes seem to have done compartively a little better than their counterparts in rural areas. But the situation is quite the contrary in respect of the middle, the lower middle and the poorer sections. These classes in urban areas have done distinctly worse comparatively to their counterparts in rural areas so that the differential between them has narrowed down. This is more true of the lower middle than the middle classes and even more true of the poorer classes than the lower middle classes. The narrowing down of the rural-urban differential is on account of the lower middle and poorer classes in urban areas having thus moved closer to their rural counterparts.

What has happened to the 10 per cent poorest in rural and urban areas is the most striking. As we have noted, the 10 per cent rural poor have stayed practically where they were at the beginning of the decade. On the other hand, the 10 per cent urban poor have difinitely suffered. As a result, they have moved close to the rural poor. In 1960-61, the consumption of the urban 5 per cent poorest was 27.2 per cent higher than the consumption of their rural counterparts; in 1967-68, it was only 4.5 per cent higher. The same is true of the 5 per cent poor next above them. In 1960-61, their consumption was 29.2 per cent higher then their counterparts in the rural areas; in 1967-68, it was only 10.2 per cent higher. These small margins are certainly not adequate to compensate the higher cost of urban living at this level. It means that in 1967-68 the living standard of the 10 per cent urban poor was worse than that of their rural counterparts.

It is necessary to understand the meaning of this deterioration in the living standards of the urban poor. It does not necessarily mean that the same people were worse off in 1967-68 in comparison with their condition in 1960-61. This is not imposible. But more generaliy it means that new migrants have moved from the rural area into the growing urban centres and have been compelled to accept life at a level much below what used to be the case a decade ago and hardly distinguishable from the life they left behind and to escape which they moved into the cities. It is thus that the rural-urban disparities have somewhat narrowed down.

We should conclude. During the past decade, the per capita private consumer expenditure increased by less than half a per cent per annum. Moreover, the small gains have not been equitably distributed among all sections of the population. The condition of the bottom 20 per cent rural poor has remained more or less stagnant. The condition of the bottom 20 per cent urban poor has definitely deteriorated; and for another 20 per cent of the urban population, it has remained more or less stagnant. Thus, while the character of rural poverty has remained the same as before, the character of urban poverty has deepened further. This is the consequence of the continuous migration of the rural poor into the urban areas in search of a livelihood, their failure to find adequate means to support themselves there and the resulting growth of pavement and slum life in the cities. All the latent dissatisfaction about the slow progress of the economy and the silent frustration about its failure to give the poor a fair deal, let alone special attention, appear to be gathering in this form. Its shape today is probably no more than hideous; allowed to grow unheeded and unrelieved, it will inevitably turn ugly.

The Urban land (Ceiling and Regulation) Act, 1976 came into force on 17 February 1976. It applies to all the state governments and union territories except Jammu and Kashmir, Kerala, Nagaland and Sikkim hich have not adopted the Act so far. It also excludes Tamil Nadu which had enacted its own law in 1978. The Act was enacted in order to prevent concentration of urban land in the hands of a few persons and also to curb speculation and profiteering therein with a view to bring about an equitable distribution of urban land to sub-serve the common good. The Act is mainly implemented by the state governments through the competent authorities appointed by them for performing various functions under the provisions of the Act.

As per the information furnished by various state governments/union territories, 2,19,506 hectare of land has been estimated as excess vacant land. Out of this, 40,480 hectare of excess vacant land has been vested in the state governments/union territories. The state governments/union territories have acquired physically 14,816 hectare of excess vacant land. On the front of the social housing, 2,980 schemes were approved involving 5,320 hectare of vacant land for the purpose of construction of 4,02,449 dwelling units for the weaker sections of society. In order to make the Act more workable and to simplify the procedure various amendments to the Act have been fomulated and are under consideration of the Government.

Urban Water Supply and Sanitation is a State subject. Schemes are formulated, implemented, operated and maintained by the state governments/union territory administrations. Funds are provided for the purpose under the state plans. As per the information available, the coverage of urban water supply and sanitation till December 1991 was 85 per cent and 46 per cent respectively. The working group for the formulation of the Eighth Plan recommended to provide drinking water facilities to cent per cent population and with sewerage and sanitation facilities to 75 per cent of the urban population by the end of the Eighth Plan (1992-97). In order to achieve the objective, the Working Group envisaged amount of Rs. 23,634.56 crore for the Eighth Plan. However, only an outlay of * Rs. 1,114.54 crore has been provided for the Annual Plan 1993-94 under the state sector. During 1994-95, an amount of Rs. 16.99 crore was distributed amongst those staes which were considered earlier for the first instalment. Various training programmes have been initiated for human resource development in planning, design, operation and maintenance and management of urban water supply and sanitation schemes. The Government has introduced use of micro-computer for planning and designing of water supply distribution and sewerage systems besides imparting training to pubblic health engineers. Financial assistance was provided to several state agencies dealing in urban water supply and sanitation sector for procuring micro-computers. The agencies have procured the computers and accessories and installed them in their organisations.

The Ministry sponsors research and development projects to various institutions in the country in order to develop appropriate technologies in the field of water supply and sanitation which can be applied not only in implementation of the project but also in their operation and maintenance and to acheive an overall improvement in the sector. The Urban Development Ministry has developed a Managment Information System (Mis) which has been disseminated to state public health engineering departments and water supply and sewerage boards for implementation. The Ministry provides technical advice and accords technical approval for urban water supply and sanitation schemes in order to get loan assistance from LIC, World Bank and other bilateral agencies.

The Scheme of Urban basic Services for the Poor (UBSP) was launched in 1990-91. The scheme is based on the covergent provision of social and physical inputs in low income, urban neighbourhoods through the programmes of various specialist departments with the active participation of community groups. The cardinal objective of scheme is to improve the overall quality of life of slum dewllers. The Cabinet has approved the scheme for the Eighth Plan period. From the inception of the Eighth Five Year Plan, the programme is being implemented on a 60:40 sharing basis between the Central and state governments. Further, the per capita expenditure will be Rs. 75 in the first year and Rs. 50/- from the second year onwards after the basic infrastructure hs been established. A total outlay of Rs. 100 crore has been provided for the scheme for the Eighth Plan period. The scheme is to be implemented in collaboration with the state sector scheme of Environmental Improvement of Urban Slums and the Centrally-sponsored scheme of Nehru Rozgar Yojana. By the end of the Eighth Plan period, it is expected that the benefit of the scheme will extend to urban areas having a total slum population of about 70 lakh and, on a national basis, targets 500 cities and towns. The National Plan of Action (NPA) on Children which is a follow-up of the promises made by the global fraternity at the World Summit for Children in 1990, reiterates and re-affirms India's commitment to the cause of women and child development. NPA goals became opertional from early 1992. One of the major objectives of the UBSP scheme is to achieve the goals of the NPA on Children in the urban poor localities by planning and organising various programmes being implemented by different ministries/ departments.

Upto March 1995, over 3,622 neighbourhood development committees comprising primarily of urban poor women have been set up in around 283 towns taken up for provision of basic services all over the country. This represnets community based structures covering around 48.26 akh low income women and children. It is expected that approximately 70 lakh beneficiaries will be covered under UBSP programme by; the end of Eighth Five Year Plan. On a national basis, the Eighth Five Year Plan targets 500cities and towns. Around 2,997 mini plans have already been prepared and 460 community organisers are in the field working as catalysts for enriching community participation. In order to monitor the scheme a National Level Monitoring Committee has been set up under the Chairmanship of Secretary, Ministry of Urban Affairs and Employment.

The Scheme of Urban Micro-Enterprises (SUME) is being implemented from June 1990 under the Nehru Rozgar Yojana (NRY). The scheme covers unemployed urban poor whose family income is less than Rs. 11,850 per annum in metropolitan areas, cities and towns, not covered by Integrated Rural Development Programme (IRDP).

Under the scheme, subsidy at the rate of 25 per cent of the project cost is given to each beneficiary subject to the ceiling of Rs. 5,000 for SCs/STc and women beneficiaries and Rs. 4,000 for others. Repayment is made in three to five years with the suitable monthly/quarterly instalments depending upon the surplus cash generation. The applications are sponsored by the Urban Local Bodies (ULBs) viz., Nagar Panchayats and Municipalities which act as nodal agency. Applicants should * have lived in the locality at least for three years. The security for the loan will be the asset created out of the loan and no security or third party guarantee is necessary. While 30 per cent of the funds would be utilised for women beneficiaries, SCs/STs are to be given weightage in proportion to their population share in total urban poor of the ULB concerned. During 1993-94, an amount of Rs. 12,647.69 lakh was sanctioned against 1,78,956 applications.

Prime Minister's Rozgar Yojana (PMRY) for educated unemployed youth was launched on 2 October 1993. the objective of the scheme is to provide sustained employment to about 10 lakh educated unemployed urban youth in micro-enterprises during the Eight Five Year Plan. These enterprises cover manufacturing, service and business ventures. The scheme was implemented in urban areas during 1993-94 and from 1 April 1994, throughout the country. Self-Employment Scheme for Educated Unemployed Youth (SEPUY) has been subsumed with PMRY from 1 April 1994. The salient features of the scheme are: (i) Youth between the age of 18 and 35 belonging to families having incomes of less than RS. 24,000 per annum would be eligijble for assistance under the scheme; (ii) These educated unemployed entrepreneurs would be given a subsidy of 15 per cent subject to a ceiling of Rs. 7,500 each for starting the micro-enterprises; (iii) They would be required to bring in five per cent of the project cost as margin money; (vi) Each entrepreneur will be eligible for a loan upto a ceiling of Rs. one lakh and this loan would not require a collateral gurantee; (v) The entrepreneurs selected under the scheme would be provided training before the loan is granted; (vi) Not more than 30 per cent of the micro-enterprises would be from the business sector; (vii) Besides matric passed or failed students and ITI passed youth, all the persons who have undergone Government sponsored technical courses for a minimum duration of six months will be eligible for assistance under the scheme; (viii) Reputed NGOs would also be associated in the implementation of the scheme especially in the selection training of entrepreneurs and preparation of the project under the scheme; (ix) A reservation of 22.5 per cent for SCs/STs and 27 per cent for other backward castes (OBCs) has been provided; (x) Women shuld be given preference and the beneficiary should have been a permanent resident of the urban area for three years. Upto December 1994, 60,513 applicants have been sanctioned loans amounting to Rs. 32,226.65 lakh (by all Indian scheduled commercial banks).

With approximately 27 per cent of its population living in urban areas, India is one of the least urban countries, but with an urban population of 217 million (1991) it is also a country with one of the largest urban populations. India's towns and cities could, by themselves, make up the third largest nation of the world.

Urban India consists of close to 3500 towns varying in size from the smallest district towns with a population of 5,000 to the large urban agglomerations exceeding 10 million people. Nearly two-thirds of the urban population is concentrated in 317 'Class I' towns, or cities with a population of over 100,000 of which half lives in 23 metropolitan areas with populations exceeding 1 million. The four largest cities—Bombay, Calcutta, Delhi and Madras—between them account for one sixth of the urban total. the Class I towns are the fastest growing urban areas in India. Greater Bombay, with apopulation of 12.57 million, and Calcutta with 10.86 million, are among the largest metropolitan areas in the world.

While over the past four decades the popultion of India has more than doubled, during the same period the urban population has more than quadrupled. The growth has come as much from net migration as from natural increase (about 40 per cent each), with the balance due to reclassification and inclusion of new towns.

The National Commission on Urbanization (1988) states that "these urban centres have also generated tha most brutal and inhuman living conditions, with large sections of the citizens living in squatter settlements. The overcrowding in the slums and the desperate lack of water and sanitation leads not only to severe health problems but to abject degradation of human life." It further remarks that "in the decades to come, who knows how much political tension and physical viloence will be triggered off by the flrgrant display of wealth which coexists with the rising expectations of the poor and with the appalling conditions of congestion and pollution which form their environment?"

The estimate of proportion of urban people living in slums varies from about 20 per cent to 30 per cent. Looked at by class of town, the highest percentage of people living in slum areas is in the cities with a million plus population and the least in towns with less than 100,000 population. The growth rate of the slum population, largely through continuing in migration, is significantly faster than that of other segments of the urban population. While this phenomenon is in no way unique to India, it is the sheer size of the problem in India that is staggering.

About 27 per cent of the urban population lives below the poverty line, 30-40 per cent of the population of the larger metropolitan areas live in slums, 27 per cent does not have access to water-borne sanitation. Indian cities also have very high levels of air and water pollution. As a result, the environment that the rural migrant has to live in, is as harsh a choice between environment and development as one can pose.

And yet the choice is made. It is made by over 13,500 people each day who move from rural to urban environments and the several million who continue to live in the highly degraded areas of urban India. The urban slum is their 'gateway'. It is the 'solution' rather than the 'problem' of urban living. It is both a low cost housing solution and a low cost transportation solution, as the slum is usually close to the place of work. But it makes nevertheless for squalid surroundings. It is a price that is paid, and paid consciously—because the option, where it even exists, is worse. Urban poverty is preferred to rural poverty.

Air pollution is a problem in some urban areas. Heavy vehicles cause 47 per cent of the pollution while accounting for 8 per cent of the total number of vehicles on Indian roads. The production of automobiles in India has increase from 1,891 in 1955 to 116,564 in 1988. Two and three wheelers constituting 63 per cent of the number of vehicles cause 13 per cent of the total pollution. While this pollution does cause localized problems, the number of vehicles is so small that it has negligible impact at the global level. Efficient public transport options, which will cut down on both fossil fuel consumption and pollution need to be explored.

The noise levels in many of the Indian cities is much above the safe limit. This is due to diverse factors which include industrial manufacturing activities, excessive use of vehicle horns, and unregulated use of loudspeakers at social, political and religious events. Awareness must be created in this regard.

The question that is difficult to understand is not so much why the poor decide to stay in slums, but rather how much remains to be done about improving conditions in these areas. The Report of the National Commission on Urbanization feels that "For whatever reason, resource allocation in the urban field seems to follow a problem rather than anticipate it." Furthermore, "the inefficiency of our cities and towns is being perpetuated by obsolete, rigid and irrational laws, regulatory provisions and norms. The urban centres, with their concentration of diverse activities, should be generators of wealth; instead, they have degenerated into parasites looking elsewhere for support."

The family Welfare Programme has helped in containing the growth rate of population. Total Fertility Rate has declined from 4.5 in 1981 to 3.5 in 1993 as per the estimates of Sample Registration System (SRS). The Crude Birth Rate has decreased from 33.9 per provisional estimates of the SRS. The Crude Death Rate has also declined from 12.5 to 9 per thousand population over the same period. The Infant MOrtality Rate dropped from 110 per thousand live births in 1981 to 74 in 1995. The annual average exponential population growth rate has come down marginally from 2.22 per cent during 1971-81 to 2.14 per cent during 1981-91. The population, however, continues to grow as the decline in birth rate has not been as rapid as the decline in the death rate.

There are, however, inter-State differences in the achievements of the Family Welfare Programme. At one end of the spectrum are the States like Kerala, Tamil Nadu and Goa which have already achieved replacement level of fertility. At the other end, are the large States like Uttar Pradesh, Madhya Pradesh, Rajasthan and Bihar where fertility levels and bjirth rates continue to be higher than the national average. Therefore, decline in the rate of growth of population for the country as a whole depends upon how the large northern States perform in the family welfare programmes in the future. Unless effective steps are taken to bring about significant improvements in the programme, the performance in containing the growth of population at the All India level may not change significantly.

Recognising the close relationship between high birth rates and high rnfant mortality, high priority has been accorded to the Maternal and Child Health (MCH) programme since 1985. In order to achieves the main objective of MCH, (i.e. to improve the health status of women and children and to reduce maternal, infant and child morbidity and mortality rates), the Universal Immunisation Programme (UIP) was launched in 1985. From the year 1992-93 the UIP has been strengthened and expanded into the Child Survival and Safe Motherhood (CSSM) programme. Under this programme, apart from strengthening the existing MCH, initiative has been taken to expand the pilot projects on Acute Respiratory Infection Control and Traditional Birth Attendants training. For this, a provision of Rs.350 crore has been made in the 1996-97 budget as against Rs.220 crore in 1995-96 (BE).

From 1.4.1996, the Family Welfare Programme is being implemented on the basis of the "Target Free Approach" (TFA). This approach envisages replacement of the system of setting contraceptive targets from the top by a system of decentralised participatory planning at the Primary Health Centre level.

Pursuant to the World Health Organisation (WHO) goal to eradicate poliomyelitis (polio, a major crippling childhood disease) by the year 2000 A.D., the Pulse Polio Immunization (PPI) was launched in 1995-96. About 87 million children aged 0-3 years were administered as supplemented dose of oral polio vaccine on 9.12.1995 and 93 million on 20.1.1996, irrespective of their routine immunisation status. Since PPI received an overwhelming response from the public, the exercise was repeated on 7.12.1996 and 18,1.1997 covering about 120 million children in the age group of 0-5 years.

A Special School Health Check-up Scheme for Primary School Children was carried out in 27 States/ UTs in July 1996, and in the remaining 5 States between August and October 1996. The objectives of this Scheme were to detect common health related problems among primary school children; to conduct screening of children for appropriate referral and check up; to generate health awareness in the community; and to ensure arrangements for follow up and treatment at higher level medical facilities. Reports from 441 districts show 75.9 per cent coverage of schools and 84.9 per cent coverage of enrolled children.

In order to foster community involvement in the Family Welfare Programme, two new schemes have been started on a pilot basis. Under one of these, one revenue village in every district, among villages with a population of 500 or more, will be given an award of Rs. 2 lakh for achieving a reduction in the Crude Birth rate, Infant Mortality Rate and Child Mortality Rate. The second schemes aims to integrate family welfare and health care into the ongoing National Wastershed Development Project for Rainfed Areas (NWDPRA) of the Ministry of Agriculture. Under this scheme, the watershed level community based management structures, known as the

'Mitra Krishak Mandal' (MKM) will conduct surveys and prepare watershed level family welfare and health care plans. An amount of Rs. 5000 will be given to each village in the watershed areas, for specified activities like emergency obstetric care and purchase of essential medicines.

The Prenatal Diagnostic Techniques (Regulation and Preventation of Misuse) Act, 1994, has been brought into force from 1st January, 1996. This Act makes it illegal to use prenatal diagnostic techniques like amniocentesis for determining the sex of the foetus, a practice that often leads to abortion of female foetuses. Statutory machinery for implementation of the Act has been established.

Uttar Pradesh continued to be the largest state, population wise with 16.44 per cent people of the country living there (13,91,12,287) followed by Bihar with 10.21 per cent (8,63,74,465) and Maharashtra with 9.33 per cent (7,89,37,187). West Bengal occupied fourth place accounting for 8.04 per cent (6,80,77,965) of the country's population followed by Andhra Pradesh with 7.86 per cent (6,65,08,008). Ranking of the states and union territories according to population size is in table 2.

Bombay metropolis continued to be the most populated city of the country with urban population of 12.60 million, Calcutta taking the second place having 11.02 million. Delhi ranks third with a population (urban) of 8.42 million followed by Madras 5.42 million.

Population factors

One of the important indices of population concentration is the density of population. It is defined as the number of persons per square kilometre. The population density has gone up from 216 in 1981 to 267 persons in 1991 (excluding Assam and J&K). In 1901 it was 77 persons per sq km followed by Chandigarh (5,632). Lakshadweep which has the smallest population size is the fourth most densely populated area with a density of 1,616 persons per sq km. Arunachal Pradesh is the most sparsely populated area of the country with 10 persons per sq km.

The 10 heavily populated districts of the country are Calcutta, Madras, Greater Bombay, Hyderabad, Delhi, Chandigarh, Mahe, Howrah, Kanpur City and Bangalore. All of them have density of above 2,000 persons per square kilometre and 5.01 per cent of the country's population lives in these districts. The average density of these districts is 6,888.

In any study of the population, analysis of the sex composition plays a vital role. The sex composition of the population is affected by the differentials in the mortality conditions of males and females, sex selective migration and the sex ration at birth.

Sex ratio is defined as the number of females per 1000 males. In India, it has generally been adverse to women. The ratio has also declined over the years except in 1981 when it slightly improved to 934 from 927. In 1991, there has been a fall by seven points to 927 per thousand males. But Kerala represented a different spectrum. The state has a higher number of females than males, 1,036 females for thousand males

In the Indian context, a sex ratio of 950 and above can be considered as favourable to females. The states and union terrtories coming under this category besides Kerala are Himachal Pradesh (976), Andhra Pradesh (972), Goa (967), Karnataka (960), Manipur (958), Orissa, (971), Tamil Nadu (974),

Dadra and Nagar Haveli (952), Daman and Diu (969) and Pondicherry (979). Chandigarh accounted for the lowest number of females per thousand males with 790.

Socio-economic dynamics

Overall economic growth in terms of Gross Domestic Product (GDP) at constant factor cost improved from 0.8% in 1991-92 to 6.3% in 1994-95 and 7% in 1995-96 aided by a growth rate of 2.4% by agriculture and allied sectors, 11.7% by industry and construction sector and 7% by services. Overall economic growth during the first four year of the 8th Plan (1992-97) averaged 5.9% per annum compared with the planned target of 5.6%.

The domestic savings rate measured in terms of gross domestic savings as a proportion of GDP at current market prices increased from an average rate of 21.3% in 1992-93 and 1993-94 to 24.4% in 1994-95. The rate of domestic investment measured in terms of gross domestic capital formation as a proportion of GDP at current market prices increased from 21.6% in 1993-94 to 25.2% in 1994-95.

Industrial production which was virtually stagnant in 1991-92 increased by 9.4% and 12.1% in 1995-96 supported by a growth rate of 6.9% in mining, 13.6% in manufacturing and 8.1% in electricity generation. As per the latest information available, industrial growth deceleration to 8.5% in April-June 1996 due to deceleration of growth rates in all the sub-sectors (3.6% in mining, 10.4% manufacturing and 2.2% in electricity generation). As per growth rates by use-based classification, capital goods sector recorded a growth rate of 14.2%, intermediate goods 11.9%, consumer durables 11.1% and consumer non-durables 8.6% in April-June 1996. However, the growth rate of basic goods sub-sector having a weight of 39.4% in the overall industrial production was only 4% in April-June 1996.

Seven infrastructural sectors, namely, electricity, coal, steel, cement, crude oil and petroleum product &

fertilizer with a combined weight of 31% in the Index of Industrial Production (IIP) recorded a growth rate of 7.8% in 1995-96. But their growth rate decelerated to 3.2% in April-August 1996 due to poor performance of electricity generation (growth rate of only 2.4%) and crude oil production (decline of production by 10.4%).

The outlook of agricultural production in 1996-97 is excellent with foodgrains output likely to reach 197 million tonnes compared with 185 million tonnes in 1995-96. This is primarily due to this year's rainfall distribution being the best in the past five years. The late withdrawal of monsoon has further ensured bright prospects for rabi production this year.

The estimate of foodgrains production in 1995-96 has been scaled down to 185 million tonnes representing a sharp decline of nearly 6 million tonnes over the prec * eeding year. The shortfall was substantial (about 3 million tonnes) in wheat output, besides short-fall of production of rice and coarse cercals. Consequently wheat procurement dropped steeply to 8.2 million tonnes compared to 12.3 million tonnes in the preceding year. Public stock (Central Pool) of foodgrains was about 22.1 million tonnes as on September 1, 1996.

There are 23 districts in Assam of which Cachar, Karimganj and Hailakandi are the three plain districts and Karbi Anglong and North Cachar Hills are the two hill districts in its southern part. Karbi Anglong is known as the biggest district in southern Assam covering an area of 10,434 sq. kms in contrast to Hailakandi being the smallest district with the area of 378 sq. kms. The two hill districts cover 68% of the total area in South Assam. Out of 33 lakh population, 75% of it live in the three plain districts and the district Cachar alone gives shelter to 36.7% of its total population.

Over the years there has been consistent rise of both population and density in South Assam. The density of populaltion has increased from 75 per sq. km. in 1960–61 to 98 per sq. km. in 1970–71 and further to 149 per sq. km. in 1990–91 as against the corresponding figures of 286 persons in all Assam and 267 persons at the all India level. In contrast Karimganj has been observed to be the most thickly populated district in South Assam with the highest density of 457 persons per sq. km.

Out of 33 lakh population in South Assam, 15.89 lakh are living in the Cachar district alone as against 0.69 lakh in N.C. Hlls. The percentage of female population to total population is varying from district to district from the lowest of 46.16% to the highest of 48.61%. It is estimated that 76% of the total female population are living in the plain districts and percentage of female has been higher in rural areas than that of the urban areas in all the five districts in South Assam.

Urbanization is one of the important indcators of development in an economy. South Assam's economy being a part of the Indian economy is no exception to this. It is found that about 3.2 lakh population in South Assam are living in the urban areas. Among these urbanites 37.4% are living in the Cachar district and 22.1% in Karbi Anglong. It is estimated that 67% of the total urbanites are lliving in the plain districts only. The extent of urbanization is found to be too less in Kailakandi and N.C. Hills in comparison to other three districts in South Assam.

According to 1960-61 census reports, there were only one lakh of urban population in South Assam. However, there has been slow but a continuous rise in their number over different census periods. The number has increased from 1.51 lakh in 1970–71 to 3.19 lakh in 1990–91. In other words, the percentage of urban population to total population has increased from 6.04% to only 9.64% in 1990–91. The figure of 9.64% is comparatively too low to the al India average of 25.7% and all Assam average of 11.1%. The highest growth rate of urban population of 22.87% is observed in the N.C. Hills district. Growth of urban population has been observed to be relatively higher in the hill districts than that of the plain districts.

Literacy being another important indicator of socio–economic development reflects the relative position of the region in the country. It is estimated that 14.5 lakh of people in South Assam are literate of which 40.4% are living in the Cacher district alone. Only a measure 4.8% of the total literates live in N.C. Hills. It also reveals that 79% of the total literate in South Assam live in the three plain districts. There has been slow but a steady rise in the growth of literacy in the region. During 1960–61 the lliteracy rate was at the level of 26.7%. This was increased to 28.5% in 1970–71 and further to 43.9% in 1990–91. Comparing this literacy rate of 43.9% in South Assam with the corresponding rate of 42.5% in Assam and that of 52.2% in India it can be said that not only South Assam but also the whole of the Assam state is lagging behind in this respect. Moreover, within South Assam the lowest literacy rate of 35.9% is observed in the Karbi Anglong district as against 48.3% in Cachar.

Surprisingly female literacy is much better in this part of the state in Assam. It is estimated that 5.6 lakh females are literates. The percentage of female literacy is relatively at a higher level of 38.4% as against the corresponding rates of 35.2% in Assam and that of 24.8% at the all India level. However, it is in much worse a positon compared to Nagaland and Mizoram where the rates are 45.5% and 64.1% respectively. As far as different districts are concerned, there is no significant variation in the female literacy rates in South Assam.

The Central Statistical Organisation (CSO) conducted the first economic census in 1977 to bridge the data gaps in the unorganised sectors of non-agricultural economy. The economic census was aimed at providing basic information on distribution of non-agricultural enterprises and to provide a frame for follow-up surveys for collection of detailed information about the structure of enterprises, investments, input, output, emploument, etc. The first economic census was followed by two sample surveys-one in 1978-79 relating to unorganised manufacturing and the second in 979-80 devoted to trade, transport, hotels and restaurants, storage and warehousing and services.

The second Economic Census was conducted in 1980 during the houselisting operations of 1981 Population Census with increased scope and coverage. It covered all enterprises (establishments and own-account enterprises) in the non-agricultural sector excluding crop production and plantation. Based on the information thrown up by this Census, three follow-up surveys were carried out, one in 1983-84 on hotels and restaurants, transport, storage and warehousing and services; second in 1984-85 on unorganised manufacturing and third in 1985-86 on wholesale and retail trade. The frame of 1980 Census was updated during 1987-88 in 64 towns. On the basis of Economic Census 1980 and updated frame, four sample surveys were conducted.

The third Economic Census 1990 was conducted along with the houselisting operations of 1991 Population Census in all states/union territories except Jammu and Kashmir. The data processing of Economic Census 1990 was undertaken in a decentralised manner by state/ union territories. Some of the states/union territories utilised the services of Regional Computer Centres at Calcutta and Chandigarh. The all India results of

Economic Census 1990 brought out shortly by the CSO for which processing and tabulation has been done by the Computer Centre, Department of SAtatistics. On the basis of the frame thrown up by Economic Census 1990, a follow-up survey covering sectors of mining and quarrying and storage and warehousing was conducted during 1992-93 and another survey on hotels and restaurants and transport was conducted during January to September, 1994.

According to 1980 Economic Census, there were 18.4 million enterprises in the country (excluding Assam) employing 53.6 million persons. Among these, these were 16.9 million enterprises (58.4 per cent in rural areas) engaged in non-agricultural activitties employing 50.7 million persons (43.3 per cent in rural areas). As per of the results of Economic Census 1990, there were 25 million enterprises out of which 22.7 million were in the non-agricultural sector. The total number of persons usually working were of the order of 72.1 million out of which 40.2 million were hired workers. A total of 17.7 million enterprises operated without any hired labour on a regular basis and were mainly run by the households themselves.

Ministry of Finance is responsible for administration of finances of the Government. It is concerned with all economic and financial matters affecting the country as a whole including mobilisation of resources for development and other purposes. It regulates expenditure of Government including transfer of resources to the states. This Ministry comprises three departments, namely, (i) Economic Affairs, (ii) Expenditure and (iii) Revenue.

The Department of Economic Affairs consists of seven main divisions namely, (i) Economic, (ii) Banking, (iii) Insurance, (iv) Budget, (v) Investment, (vi) External

Finance and (vii) Currency and Coinage. This Department inter alia monitors current economic trends and advises Government on all matters of internal and external economic management including working of commercial banks, term-lending institutions, investments regulations, external assistance, etc. Preparation of the Budget of the Union of India as well as the state governments and union territory administrations with legislature when under President's rule and their presentation to Parliament is also the responsibility of this Department.

The Department of Expenditure comprises eight main divisions, namely, (i) Plan finance Division, (ii) Establishment Division, (iii) Cost Accounts Branch, (iv) Controller General of Accounts, (v) Finance Commission Division, (vi) Implementation Cell, (vii) Integrated Finance Division and (viii) Staff Inspection Unit.

Department of Revenue exercises control in respect of revenue matters relating to direct and indirect Union taxes through two statutory boards namely, Central Board of Direct Taxes and the Central Board of Excise and Customs. This Department is also entrusted with the administration and enforcement of controls and regulatory measures provided in the enactments concerning Central sales tax, stamp duties, gold control, foreign exchange and other relevant fiscal statutes. Control over production and disposal of opium and its products is also vested with this Department.

Industrial production grew by 9.7 per cent in the first seven months of 1996—97, 1.9 percentage points slower than the 11.7 per cent growth in the first seven months of the previous year, which was the highest in 25 years. The growth of 9.5 to 10.5 per cent would still be the second highest growth rate in 25 years. It says, "the good performance of industrial production in 1996—97 is due entirely to the manufacturing sector, which has maintained its high growth." During the first seven months of the year the rate of growth of the manufacturing sector was 12.1 per cent, virtually the same as 12.3 per cent in 1995—96.

The Survey attributes the slowing of industrial production to the dramatic fall in the rate of growth of electricity production and a slowing down of growth in the mining sector, mainly because of the 10 per cent decline in crude oil production. During the first seven months of the year, electricity production has grown only by 3.4 per cent compared to 10.1 per cent in the corresponding period of 1995—96. If despite slowdown of electricity generation, manufacturing has recorded good growth, one possible reason could be captive generation, which is increasingly being used as a backup to public supply, the Survey adds. This hypothesis is supported by the growth of about 22 per cent in the volume of diesel imports.

Another noteworthy aspect of industrial production in 1996—97 has been acceleration in the rate of growth of capital goods production to 16.5 per cent from 15 per cent in the first seven months of the previous year. In contrast capital goods inports have declined by six per cent in the first seven months of the year. This according to the Survey, shows the increased competitiveness of the domestic capital goods industry.

The Survey also refers to the deceleration in the growth rate in the production of consumer durables, such as cars, to 9.8 per cent in the first seven months of 1996 97, compared to 30.2 per cent in the first seven months of the previous year. The delisensing of investment in consumer durable and decontrol of imports of parts of these goods, contributed to boom in investment and production in the sector. The decline in growth during

1996—97 suggests that the pent—up demand in the domestic economy has been met. Further growth will depend on increased cost competitiveness, which requires fuller exploitation of the comparative advantage that India has in the production of labour—intensive parts. Some analysts, however, seen in the sudden saturation of the demand a falacy in the general belief of the size of the middle class with good purchasing power, estimated at 200 million.

The Survey rates as poor the overall performance of the core and infrastructure sectors during the first 8 months of 1996—97 (April—November). Six industries, namely electricity generation, coal, steel, crude oil, petroleum products and cement, with a combined weight of 28.8 per cent in the Index of Industrial Production (IIP), averaged a growth of 4.1 poer cent in April—November, 1995. It says the previous Surveys had emphasised the need to accelerate, widen and deepen reforms of th non—tradable infrastructure and energy sectors, to avert an impending mismatch between economic growth and provision of these services. The new government, it says has repeatedly stressed its firm determination to reform the infrastructure and energy sectors and has take a number of policy decisions and new initiatives.

The Survey says continuing restraint on money supply growth is among the factors that have kept the prices in check. Despite the recent rising trend inthe growth of WPI, the average inflation for 1996—97 is expected to be at least one percentage point less than the average inflation in the previous year. There was complete change in the sectoral pattern of price changes du;ring 1996—97. The annúal rate of inflation accelerated sharply in the "fuel, power, light and lubricants" and primary articles, while decelerating in the "manufactures" group. The annual rate of price increase in the fuel—power group went up to 17.4 per cent in January 1997 from 1.1 per cent a year ago because of administered price increase, while that of primary articles to 11.7 per cent from 2.6 per cent. The rate of growth in prices of manufactured goods declined to 3.6 poer cent from 6.9 per cent in the previous year. The rise in prices of primary goods has largely been due to rise in prices of cereals and fruits and vegetables.

Money supply growth has been higher in 1996—97 than in 1995—96, the Survey says, adding "Upto the fornight ended January 17, 1997, broad money (M3) grew by 10.6 per cent as against 8.2 per cent growth in the corresponding period of 1995—96. The average call money rate declined from a high of 13.75 per cent at the beginning of the currently financial year to a range of 5 to 11 per cent in September 1996 and ruled between 10 and 11 per cent in December 1996, before falling to low single digits in January 1997. The reversal of the 1997—96 excess demand for funds for investment in 1996–97 has led to a general softening of interest rates during the year. The cut—off yields on 91—day treasury bills has come down from 12.4 per cent in the first week of July to around 7.5 per cent at the end of January 1997.

Control over fiscal deficit was identified by the Update to the Economic Survey, presented by the United Front Government last year as one of the three challenges for economicpolicy. The Budget for 1996—97 envisaged a reduction of the fiscal dificit by 0.8 per cent of GDP to 5 per cent from 5.8 per cent in 1995—96 (RE). The primary deficit is also budgeted to fall from 1.1 poer cent of GDP to 0.2 per cent, while the revenue deficit to 2.5 per cent of GDP from 3 per cent in 1995—96.

The reduction in fiscal deficit has been attempted through an increase in revenues coupled with a reduction in expenditure. Revenue receipts (net) are budgeted to increase by 18.3 per cent during 1996—97 (BE). Despite a larger outgo on account of interest payments, subsidies and provision for revision of salaries and pension, total revenue expenditure is budgeted to grow at a lower rate of 12.7 per cent compared to 17.5 per cent in the previously year (RE). This deceleration in the growth of revenue expenditure has led to a decline in revenue expenditure to GDP ratio from 13.1 per cent in 1995—96 to 12.9 per cent in 1996—97 (BE). This favourable outcome, the Survey claims, is largely on account of containment of non—interest, non—plan expenditure growth at 9.3 per cent during 1996—97, about half the growth of 18.6 per cent in 1995—96 (RE). Consequently, non–interest revenue expenditure as a proportion of GDP is budgeted to fall to 8.1 per cent from 8.3 per cent in 1996—97 (RE). The revenue deficit is budgeted to fall by 0.5 per cent point of GDP. One may, however, note that the comparison of Budget estimates (BE) with Revenue Estimates (RE) is not very realistic.

Attainment of industrialisation over the last 48 years has been striking feature of Indian economic development process which was launched as a conscious and deliberate policy in the early fifties. In pursuance of this policy, large investment has been made in building up capacity over a wide spectrum of industries. Industrial production has made rapid strides in terms of variety, quality and quantity. There has been a substantial diversification of industrial base during this period with the consequent ability to produce a very broad range of industrial goods. Self-reliance has been achieved in basic and capital good. Indigenous capabilities have now been established to the point of virtual self-sufficiency so that further expansion in various sectors such as mining, irrigation, power chemicals, transport and communication can be based primarily on indigenous equipment. Process of industrialisation has also fostered entrepreneurship and development of a wide variety of technical, managerial and operative skills. Today, the country is in a position to provide consultancy services as well as managers, technicians and skilled workers for setting up industrial projects aborad.

The Industrial Policy Resolution of 1948 marked the beginning of the evolution of Indian Industrial Policy. The resolution not only defined the broad contours of the policy, it delineated the role of the State in the industrial development both as an entrepreneur and as an authority.

Successive policy resolutions also reiterated this basic tilt in favour of the public sector. The Industrial Policy Resolution of 1956 gave the public sector a strategic role in the economy. It categorised industries which would be the exclusive responsibility of state or would progressively come under state control and others. Earmarking the pre-eminent position to the public sector, it envisaged private sector co-existing with the State and thus attempted to give the policy framework flexibility.

The Industrial Policy initiatives undertaken by Government since July 1991 have been designed to build on the past industrial achievements and to accelerate the process of making Indian industry internatinally competitive. It recognises the strength and maturity of the industry and attempts to provide the competitive stimulus for higher growth. The thrust of these initiatives has been to increase domestic and external competition through extensive application of market mechanism and facilitating forging of dynamic relationships with foreign investors and suppliers of technology. The process of reform has been continuous.

As on 31 March 1993 there were 245 central public sector undertakings, comprising of eight in the construction sector, 72 in services and remaining 165 in the manufacturing. The number of CPSUs as indicated above exclude nine companies, six insurance companies and three financial institutions with Central Government investment but without direct responsibility of management.

The total capital employed in the 245 CPSUs increased from Rs. 1,179.91 billion in 1991-92 to Rs. 1,399.33 billion in 1992-93. The overall rate of return on capital employed in the PSUs also increased from 2.0 per cent in 1991-92 to 2.43 per cent in 1992-93.

The number of small scale units as at the end of 31 March 1994 were 2.38 million comprising of 1.77 million registered units and 0.61 un-registered. The overall production in the small scale sector during 1993-94 has been estimated to have reached Rs. 2,416.5 billion. The total value of exports of these units has been Rs. 177.85 billion in 1992-93.

Agriculture

The rate of agricultural growth of the order of around 3.2 per cent per annum during the fifties was derived from acreage increases to the extent of 70 per cent. In the sixties, the rate of growth which was only 2.1 per cent in this sector and did not neutralize even the rate of increase of population in that decade, could be derived from acreage increase to the extent of 30 per cent only. The scope for any further increase in acreage for increasing agricultural peoduction has exhausted in the seventies and the entire increase in farm production had to come from improvement in per acre productivity. This has required high level of capital–intensive effort in the development of the agricultural sector.

According to a competent study, the capital output ratio in Indian agriculture has already touched the figure of four and is close to the same scale as is required in industry. For the same reason, the fact has to be reckoned with that absorption of labour in agriculture through a significant rise in yields on land has tended to be a comparatively limited and expensive process and this process alone cannot be relied upon to solve the growing unemployment problem. The running controversy on priorities as between agriculture and industry, in particular heavy industry, is thus futile and misleading in the context of the realities of Indian economic situation and its growth prospects. The idea that India enjoys a comparative advantage in agricultural output inIndia is now crucially dependent on growth of inputs from industry. The need is thus not to fforeclose available resources in the economy for the so called development needs of the agricultural sector but to mop up a substained part of the surpluses and incremental incomes generating in the agricultural sector to meet the investment requirements of infrastructural development, including heavy and intermediate goods industries,to inputs for agriculture at a rapid and accelerating pace.

If much credit is taken for achieving self—sufficiency in food grains relative to effective domestic demand, there is now much brave talk of making India one of the few "grain powers" in the world even while large number of Indian people still do not have access to adequate food. Agriculture in India will have to go a long way yet before it can feed the Indian people. It is too early to talk of India becoming a "grain power." But the official policy has already veered to the postion that the government would not come in the way of the farmers exporting their produce and these exports would not be banned "merely" for bringing supplies and prices down for the domestic consumers. The upshot has been that while good grains have been exported, two million tonnes of wheat are being imported in the current year, 1996—97 to meet even the effective demand in the domestic market. The danger inherent in this position is not imaginary.

The widening disparities in incomes and levels of living combined with growing concentration of land and the swelling ranks of landless rural labourers are manifest. It is not amiss either to consider the pricing of agricultural produce, more especially food grains—the primary wage goods—and examine its influence on the general price trend and structure of relative prices in the Indian economy. The Agricultural Prices Commission, to start with, recommended a particular set of prices based on its studies of the cost of production, fair return to the farmer and fair prices for the consumer. It has been a practice, by and large, to improve upon the prices recommended by the APC in order to provide additional incentives to the surplus farmers to increase production for the market. After the launching of the so—called economic reforms in 1991, however, the baalance between the claims of the surplus farmer and the consumer has been tilting sharply in favour of the former and the inflationary impact of "incentive prices" for good grains and other agricultural produce has been ignored. Subsidised farming by way of what are called "incentive prices" for farm produce and subsidised inputs for agriculture like chemical fertilizers, private irrigation facilities like tubewells and pumpsets, power andcomparative soft—term credit, was conceived in the wake of the disastrous drought years of 1964-65 as the means of stimulating agricultural production for the market and securing control over a substantial part of the marketable surpluses so produced.

There were probably compelling reasons under the given ownership pattern in cultivable land for adopting this strategy when shortages of agricultural commodities, especially of food grains, ad emerged as an endemic problem of the economy—its stability and further growth. But the concomitant of this development has been the growing commercialization of agriculture and emergence within it to prominence of that segment of farmers with their commercial interests which produce and control agricultural surpluses. In the course of time, however, as shortage in cereals or other crops are overcome relative, of course, to effective market demand at the present low-level of purchasing power in the economy, the system of subsidised production and marketing in agriculture has become in essence a mechanism to ensure to the surplus producer a monopoly to all the gains arising from incrreases in production and productivity.

Among the vast numbers of Indian farmers, only a small fraction, and móre than 10 per cent of the total, commanding the best cultivable land produces for the market on any scale. They also monopolise the subsidised supply of inputs and credit and benefits of infrastructural facilities such as irrigation and power created by public investment.

Agricultural crop production in 1996—97 is expected to show good recovery from the slower growth in 1995—96. Growth is projected at 3 per cent after a fall of 0.4 per cent in 1995—96. The sharp decline in foodgrains production by 3.4 per cent, which was responsible for the slow growth in 1995—96, is expected to be reversed by an increased of 3.3 per cent in 1996—97. Foodgrains production is expected to recovery is primarily due to coarse cereals, as well as an anticipated rise in wheat production which suffered a sharp setback in 1995—96.

As the agricultureal year runs from July to June, the estimates for 1995—96 were only firmed up after the end of the financial year. A large downward revision (of 3 million tonnes) was made in the estimate of wheat production for 1995—96. The revision was unexpected and unexplained, because average rainfall in 1995—96 was quite normal. The revision, late in calendar year 1996, also created severe problems for the management of the food economy.

Commercial crop production has done extremely well in 1996—97 with oilseeds and cotton expected to reach record levels of 24.1 million tonnes and 14.3 million tonnes, respectively. Jute and mesta have also shown a growth of 3.4 per cent this year. Sugarcane output is, however, unlikely to maintain the record level of 283 million tonnes attained in 1995—96.

Industrial production (as measured by the index of industrial production–IIP), grew by 9.8 per cent in the first seven months of 1996—97, 1.9 percentage points slower than the 11.7 per cent growth in the in the corresponding period of 1995—96. The good performance of industrial production in 1996—97 is due entirely to the manufacturing sector, which has maintained its high growth.

The slowing of industrial production is clearly attributable to the dramatic fall in the rate of growth of electricity production and a slowing of growth in the mining sector mainly because of the 10 per cent decline in crude oil production. During the first seven months of 1996—97, electricity production (as measured by the index) has grown by only 3.4 per cent compared to the 10.1 per cent growth in the corresponding period of 1995—96. It is somewhat surprising that manufacturing sector growth has been barely affected by the slow growth in electricity production. One possibility is that captive electricity generation, which is increasingly used as a back—up to public supply, has substituted for the lack of generation by electricity boards. The high growth of diesel imports, about 22 per cent by volume in the first seven months of 1996—97 (with total refinery throughput growing in the normal range of around 4 per cent), is consistent with this hypothesis. At present, electricity statistics incorporate little or no data on captive power generation.

Another noteworthy aspect of industrial growth this year is the acceleration in the rate of growth of capital goods production to 16.6 per cent in the first seven months of this year from 15 per cent in the first seven months of last year. This has off—set the decline in the rate of growth of consumer goods and basic goos. In contrast, capital goods imports have declined by 6 per cent in the first seven months of 1996—97. This shows the increased competitiveness of the domestic capital goods industry.

The overall performance of the core and infrastructure sectors during the first 8 months of 1996—97 (April—November) has been poor. Six industries namely, electricity generation, coal, steel, crude oil, petroleum products and cement, with a combined weight of 28.8 per cent in the Index of Industrial Production (IIP), averaged a growth of 4.1 per cent in April—November, 1996, less than half the 8.9 per cent, in April—November, 1995. The deceleration in the growth rate of these infrastructure industries is mainly due to a decline in crude oil production and power generation. Hydro power generation declined by 7.7 per cent, and thermal power generation grew by only 6.4 per cent in the April—November, 1996 as compared to 14.6 per cent in the April—March, 1995—96. Coal, cement and refineries' throughput have grown faster in April—November,

1996—97 compared to the corresponding period of 1995—96. Growth of sectors such as railways, ports and telecommunications, which do not appear in the IIP, also slowed. The rate of growth of railways' revenue earning goods traffic decelerated marginally from 7 per cent during 1995—96 to 6.3 per cent for April–November 1996. Growth of cargo handled at major ports and new telephone connections provided decelerated more sharply to 4.7 per cent in April—November, 1996 (from 9.1 per cent in 1995—96) and 8.3 per cent in April—November, 1996 (from 23.3 per cent in 1995–96), respectively. The slower growth in cargo handled by ports in probably the result of a deceleration in the growth of external trade. The telecomunications slowdown, however, suggests that the pace of implementation of telecommunications reform needs to be accelerated and its scope widened to include Department of Telecommunications as a service provider. Given the parlous financial state of many public utilities, particularly the State Electricity Boards, the possibility of crises worsens with each passing year. The new government has repeatedly stressed its firm determination to reform the infrastructure and energy sectors. In line with this commitment, a number of policy decisions have been taken and new initiatives launched.

High Yielding Variety Programme was started in 1966-67 as a major plan of agriculture strategy for increasing production of foodgrains in the country. Cropwise details are shown in table 3. The programme is supported through a number of Centrally-sponsored schemes and thrust has been shifted from single crop to cropping system approach since 1994-95. Identifying potential areas, the country has been grouped in three major cereal based cropping systems viz., (i) Integrated Cereal Development Programme in Rice Based Cropping System Areas (ICDP-Rice); (ii) Integrated Cereal

Development Programme in Wheat Based Cropping System Areas (ICDP-Wheat); and (iii) Integrated Cereal Development Programme in Coarse Cereal Based Cropping System Areas (ICDP-Coarse Cereal).

These thrust programmes are designed to increase the productivity and production of foodgrains through adoption of latest scientific production technology. Minikit demonstration programme aims at popularising newly released varietity and getting the newly released evolved varieties tested under field conditions. For this a large number of seed minikits containing 0.25 kg to 10 kg seed are distributed at a nominal cost to farmers. State level training programmes are being organised at agricultural universities and ICAR research institutes in collaboration with concerned state agriculture departments to disseminate the latest crop production technology to the district/block level extension officers.

About 990 lakh hecare area in the country is rainfed accounting for 70 per cent of the net sown area of 1,410.6 lakh hectare. Crops grown and cropping practices followed in these areas entirely depend on the rainfall which is often erratic and unpredictable. Bulk of the crops like rice, jawar, bajara, other millets, pulses, oilseeds and cotton are grown in this area under rainfed conditions. Farmers in these areas, particularly, small and marginal, are still practising subsistence farming and are in the vertex of vicious circle. Wide fluctuations in production occur in these areas year after year. Increasing and stabilising agricultural production in these areas is, therefore, of crucial importance.

Government has given high priority for the development of dryland areas and, therefore, several programmes and projects have been launched for utilisation of potential of these areas for: (i) realising the projected requirement of about 240 mt of annual food production by 2000 AD and to smoothen out fluctuation in annual production; (ii) reducing regional disparities between irrigated and vast rainfed areas; (iii) restoring ecological balance by greening rainfed areas through appropriate mixture of trees, shrubs and grasses; and (iv) generating employment for rural masses and reducing large-scale migration from rural areas to already congested cities and towns. Holistic approach for integrated farming system development on watershed basis in rainfed areas would be main pursuit of the development activities under the National Watershed Development Project for Rainfed Areas (NWDPRA) in the Eighth Plan.

Allied sectors

The gross value of output from livestock sector (at current prices) is estimated to account for 26 per cent of the total value of output from Agriculture sector. This excludes the contribution of animal draught power. Animal husbandary is an important source of self employment and subsidiary occupation in rural and semi-urban areas and more so for people living in the drought prone, hilly, tribal and other poorly developed areas, where crop production on its own may not sustain them fully. As revealed by NSS, 1987-88 was 4.15 per cent as against 1.1 per cent for the agriculture sectore as a whole. The recent Land and Livestock Holding Survey (NSS, forth-eitghth round) further reveals that during eighties there was a substantial growth of dairy farming in the country.

The ratio of in-milk bovine stock to 100 households rose from 37 in 1981-82 to 46 in 1991-92. It also highlighted that the rise in ratio during eighties was most pronounced in the states with relvatively high average in milk stock, like Punjab, Haryana and Fajasthan. On the other hand, there was little improvement in the ratio in

Kerala, Orissa and Tamil Nadu. The marginal and small holdings constitute the core of the milk production sector accounting for about 66 per cent of the in-milk bovine stock (1991-92 estimate).

In 1995-96, the country produced 66 million tonnes of milk. This represents an average annual growth of 4.5 per cent since 1990-91.

Poultry Farming has become an important activity providing additional income to the weaker sections of the population in rural and semi-urban areas. Poultry farming has made good progess due to research and developmental efforts of the Government and the organised private sector. Egg production is expected to have increased to about 27 billion during 1995-96. Land and Livestock Holding Survey (NSS, forty eighth round, October, 1996) point out that there has been a rapid growth in poultry farming during 1970s and 1980s. The poultry stock per hundred households rose steadily from 107 in 1971-72 to 195 in 1991-92. In 1991-92, the marginal category of farm households (constituting 48 per cent of the households) alone accounted for 55 per cent of poultry stock.

Under the cattle insurance policy, cover is provided for the sum insured or the market value of the animal at the time of death, whichever is less. Animals are normally insured upto 100 per cent of their market value. General Insurance Corporation (GIC) implements various cattle insurance programmes through its four companies under their "Market Agreement on Cattle Insurance". Buffaloes, calves/heifers, stud bulls, bullocks etc. of specified age groups are insured against death due to accidents inclusive of natural causes like fire, lighting, floods, storm, earthquakes, famine diseases, surgical operation, riot, strike and civil commotion and risk of breeding an calving. Insurance policy can also be extended to cover permanent total disability on payment of extra premium. Cattle purchase under poverty allevation programmes are insured under Master Policy. The animals are insured at concessional rate and part of the premium is subsidised by the Government. Under the Cattle Insurance Scheme, at present, about 10 per cent of the total cattle population is covered. The projected target for insuring cattle during 1996-97 was 88 lakhs out of which 48 lakhs was for 'scheme' animals and 40 likhs for 'non-scheme' animals. The position regarding number of cattel covered, premium collected and claims paid during the past 5 years. After taking into account management expenses and incentives, the scheme is presently operating on no-profit-no-loss basis. The scheme is thus operated by the Insurance Companies on their own risk.

India is the seventh largest producer of fish in the world and, perhaps, second in Inland fish production. Fishery sector plays a vital role in sustaining a fairly large proportion of population along the long 8129 kms. coast line. The contribution of fisheries to the net domestic product has increased from Rs. 1479 crore in 1984-85 to Rs. 9826 crore in 1994-95 at current in 1994-95 at current prices showing about six and a half times increase in ten years. The trend of fish production and exports. The target for fish production in 1996-97 is 51.40 lakh tonnes comprising 28.57 lakh tonnes from marine and 22.83 lakh tonnes from Inland waters. An area of 3.86 lakh hactares has been brought under scientific fish culture and 5.04 lakh farmers have been trained in improved practices upto 1995-96 through active support provided under Fish Farmers Development Agencies. Development of brackish water aquaculture through Brakish Water Fish Farmers Development Agencies have been established in the coastal states for providing a package of technical, financial and extension support for shrimp farming.

2

Policy and Legislation

National population policy

In pursuance of one of the recommendation of the Committee on Population of the National Development Council, a Group of Experts was constituted on 19th July, 1993, under the chairmanship of Dr. M.S. Swaminathan, for preparation of a preliminary draft of the National Population Policy. The Group submitted the draft National Population Policy on 24.05.1994. The Report has been tabled in both Houses of Parliament on 14th June,1994.

On the basis of comments received from other Ministries and States on the preliminary draft, a Statement on National Population Policy was drafted. This draft was laid on the Table of both Houses of Parliament during December, 1996 in reply to Starred Question. This draft Statement on National Population, Policy, along with a draft Statement on National Population Policy, along with a draft Note for the Cabinet was circulated among Ministries/Department concerned for final comments before seeking the approval of the Cabinet.

The Note for Cabinet, seeking approval of the National Population Policy, was prepared taking into account the comments of the Central Ministries/ Departments, States/ Union territories and discussions in the two Houses of Parliament during the Special Session of Parliament on the occasion of the 50th Anniversary of India's Independence.

The Cabinet approved the National Population Policy on the 20th November 1997, with directions to table the Policy in both the Houses of Parliament. On account of the two Houses of Parliament being adjourned sine-die on the dates on which tabling of this Policy document was scheduled in the business of the two Houses, followed by the dissolution of the Eleventh Lok Sabha, the Policy could not be tabled in the Parliament.

After the new Government assumed office, further consultations with the Experts have been held. In the light of the discussions held, necessary modifications have been carried out in the draft of the National Population Policy.

Approval of the government is being sought for the draft of the National Population Policy with the objective of tabling it in the Parliament during Budget Session of 1999.

The constitution (Seventy-Ninth Amendment) Bill, 1992

The Constitution (Seventy-Ninth Amendment) Bill, 1992 was introduced in the Rajya Sabha in December, 1992. This Bill was in pursuarce of one of the recommendations of the Committee on Population of the National Development Council. Under the provisions of the proposed Bill, a person shall be disqualified for being chosen as, and for being a Member of either House of Parliament, or either House of the Legislature of a State, if he has more than two children. However, it will not apply to those who already have more than two children or those who beget an additional child within one year of the commencement of the Act. Thus, the Bill is not applicable to persons who already have more than two children. Once passed, these provisions will also apply to

Panchayats and Nagarpalikas, by virtue of Articles 243F (1) (a) and 243V (1) (a).

The Bill has been recommended by the Standing Committee of Parliament on HRD for consideration and passage, with the recommendation that before moving the Bill for consideration, a meeting of the leaders of political parties may be convened to arrive at a consensus. A meeting of the leaders of political parties was held in August, 1997 and it was decided in that meeting that further consultations are necessary to arrive at a consensus. The process of seeking political consensus continued during the year.

Implementation of prenatal diagnostic techniques

Under the Prenatal Diagnostic Techniques (Regulation and Prevention of Misuse) Act, 1994, prenatal diagnostic techniques can be conducted, and genetic counselling can be offered only in genetic clinics, genetic laboratories and genetic counselling centres registered under the Act. Use of prenatal diagnostic techniques is allowed only for detecting any of the abnormalities and subject to the fulfillment of the conditions specified in the Act. Disclosure of the sex of the foetus is prohibited. Punishments are prescribed for violation of the law. Although the Act and Rules thereunder have come into force on 01.01.1996, no case of violation of the law has been reported from any part of the country so far.

Appropriate Authorities and Advisory Committees under the Act have been appointed/constituted in 21 States and 6 Union Territories UTs. In respect of 3 other States and one UT, appropriate authorities have been appointed, but Advisory Committees have not been constituted. These are Bihar, Mizoram, West Bengal and Lakshadweep. The 'Central Supervisory Board' under the Act has been constituted by notification in the Gazette of India dated 05.02.1997, and it has met on 24th April, 1997, 9th September, 1997 and 31st August, 1998.

The Government of India expects State governments to effectively implement the provision of this Act, so as to eliminate the practice of female feticide. Effective -implementation will also require the active involvement of socially committed non-governmental bodies and individuals.

Medical Termination of Pregnancy (MTP) Act, 1971

After the introduction of the MTP Act, 1971 the number of approved MTP facilities increased from 1,877 in 1976 to 8,722 in 1997-98. Similarly, the number of reported MTP cases increased from 3,81,111 in 1972-76 to 5,17,179 in 1996-97 However, these figures are only the tip of the iceberg, as unauthorised abortions are still widespread and not reported.

The MTP Act has been reviewed in consultation with experts in connection with the larger exercise being coordinated by Cabinet Secretariat for review of all laws to update them.

There are three amendments proposed in the MTP Act, 1971. The first amendment is in the definition of "lunatic" to bring it in conformity with Mental Health Act, 1987. The second amendment proposed is in the definition of "minor", where it is proposed that decision to seek abortion should be available to a minor if she is married. The third proposal is to make unregistered clinics and untrained persons performing abortions punishable and punishment made stiffer.

The proposal already has the administrative approval of the Minister. It will be presented in the Parliament through the Cabinet after consulting the Law Ministry.

Medical Termination of Pregnancy (MTP) is a reproductive health measure that enables a woman to opt out of an unwanted/ unintended pregnancy in certain specific circumstances without endangering her life and well being.

India legalised medical termination of pregnancy on broad socio-medical grounds through MTP Act, 1971. The aim of the Act was to reduce maternal mortality and morbidity due to illegal/unsafe abortion. To make safe abortion services available to all women in the country, the Government of India, under the RCH programme is expanding and improving the MTP facilities and their utilisation.

Assistance from the Government of India will be in the form of training, supply of MTP equipment and provision for engaging doctors trained in MT to visit PHCs to perform MTP on fixed days, once in a week or once in a fortnight. Assistance in the form of equipment and training will be provided to well run and competent medical clinics in the non-government sectors, if they have functional Operation Theatres and trained doctors/ nurses.

3

Infrastructure for Implementation

Introduction

Department of Family Welfare is one of the three departments under the Ministry of Health and Family Welfare. The ministry has a common minister but each Department is separately headed by an independent Secretary. The Secretary is assisted by three Joint Secretaries and a Chief Director (Statistics) in the same grade. Out of the three joint Secretaries, one is Financial Adviser to the Ministry and looks after the work of other two departments of the Ministry-also. The other two joint Secretaries are Programme Officers, looking after various programmes relating to family welfare.

The senior officers in the Department are taken from broadly three groups, firstly administrative services officers from All India Services and Central Secretariat Services, secondly medical officers from Central Health Services and thirdly statistical Officers. The joint Secretary, Reproductive and Child Health is assisted by Programme Divisions for NGOs, IEC, Donor Coordination Division relating to International assistance, Infrastructure Division, Maternal Heath Division and Child Health Divisions. The other joint Secretary is assisted by programme divisions for Area Projects, Policy Division, Training Division, Research & Studies Division and Supplies Division. The Chief Director (Statistics) is incharge of the large Division relating to data and Statistics.

In the States there are Departments of Family Welfare supported by Directorates of Family Welfare. Generally, Principal Secretary (Health and Family Welfare) is incharge in the States of the whole of Health and Family Welfare and is assisted by one Secretary for Health matters and the other for Family Welfare matters.

All Family Welfare Programmes are implemented through the State Government set ups. For service delivery the set up for urban areas has 1562 Post Partum Centres which are either located in the medical colleges or in District Hospitals. These are supported by 1,291 Urban Family Welfare Centres and 871 Urban Health Posts.

The latter two only have paramedics as its staff. For rural areas in addition to the Director/Sub-divisional Hospitals, there are 2,622 Community Health Centres. In addition there are 1,36,339 Rural Sub Centres. The Rural Sub Centres have one Male Multipurpose Health Worker and Auxiliary Nurse Midwife and are provided for about 5,000 population. A Primary Health Centre is provided for about 30,000 population and a Community Health Centre is provided for 1.2 lakh population in a block. The Primary Health is headed by a Doctor and is assisted by 15 other persons.

Community Health Centre has four Specialists in Gynaecology, Paediatrics, Medicines and Surgery and other staff. Rural Sub Centres are supported by the Government of India but only about 4,000 Primary Health Centres created in the beginning are supported by the Government of India. Rest of PHCs and CHCs have been set up by the State Governments. At District level, there is District Family Welfare Officer who along with his team is supported by the Government of India. At State level by the Directorate of Family Welfare is supported by the Government of India.

Infrastructure division of the Department looks after programmes in respect of Urban and Rural Health Services in India.

Urban Health Services

The Post Partum Programme was started during the year 1969 in 59 District Level Hospitals.

The Post Partum Programme is defined as a maternity centred hospital based approach to Family Welfare Programme to motivate women within the reproductive age group (15 - 44 years) or their husbands to adopt small family norms through education and motivation particularly during pre natal, natal and post natal period.

Over the years, the concept of Post Partum has changed considerably and accordingly the functions of Post Partum Centres have also undergone a change. The Post Partum Centres also function as referral centres for providing MCH and Family Welfare Service 550 Post Partum Centres are functioning at the District Level.

The success of the Programme at District Level encouraged the Government of India to extend the Post Partum Programme to Subdivisional / Taluka Level Hospitals also. At present, 1012 Sub-district Level Post Partum Centres are functioning under the programme.

Under the Post Partum Programme, a set pattern of inputs in the form of staff, equipment, construction of a ward and operation theatre etc., is provided. The programme is 100% centrally assisted and is implemented through State Governments.

The performance under Post Partum Programme at Sub-district Level during 199697 and 1997-98 is at Table 1.

Table 1

Percentage distribution of various acceptors of Family Welfare methods at Sub-District Level during 1996-97 and 1997-98 is as follows:

Family Welfare Method	Sub-District Level 1996-97 Number of Acceptors	Percentage Acceptors	1997-98 Number of Acceptors	per-cent
Tubectomy	341694	53.0	353075	52.3
Vasectomy	6889	1.1	6007	0.9
IUD	229932	35.6	242213	35.9
Eq. OP Users	66749	10.3	73234	10.9
Total	645264	100.0	674529	100.0

PAP smear test facility programme

PAP Smear Test Facility Programme for early' detection of cervical cancer among women has been approved by Government of India in 105 Medical Colleges which are equipped with full fledged Department of Pathology and Services of a Senior Pathologist i.e. Professor of Pathology.

Under the Programme a post of Cyto Technician for preparation/examination of slides and contingent expenditure for purchase of glassware and chemicals etc., have been provided by Government of India.

Contribution of post partum programme

The contribution in terms of performance of Post Partum Programme both at District and Sub-district Level is quite encouraging.

The performance under the programme for 1997-98 is as Table 2.

Table 2

Performance of PAP smear Test Facility Programme

Item	Number
Number of Centres approved by Government of India	105
No.of slides prepared and examined	53684
No.of slides found normal	30625
Percentage found Normal	57.05
No.of slides found positive for carcinoma	1446
Percentage found positive for carcinoma	2.69

Sterilisation bed scheme

It was introduced during the year 1964 by reservation of Sterilisation beds in Government/Voluntary Organisation and Local Body Institutions. The purpose of introduction of this scheme was to provide facility for tubectomy operations as the beds for such cases were not readily available in the hospitals. Under the Scheme, a total of 3170 bed are functioning at present (as on 1st April 1998).

A recurring amount of Rs. 4500 per bed per annum is admissible for maintenance of the Sterilisation beds to Local Body/Voluntary Organisation on achievement of 60 tubecto-mies per bed per annum.

Urban revamping scheme urban health posts

The Urban Revamping Scheme has been introduced with a view to provide improved service / delivery out reach services of primary health care, family welfare and maternity services in urban areas particularly slum areas. The State Governments have established 871 Health Posts and 10 City Family Welfare Bureaux. The City Family Welfare Bureaux are entrusted with the responsibility of coordination, monitoring, supervision etc., of the Family Welfare Services provided by various institutions in the city.

Urban family welfare centres

Urban Family Welfare Centres are on ground since 1950 to provide Family Welfare Services in urban areas. There are three types of Urban Family Welfare Centres based on the population covered by them. In all there are 1083 Urban Family Welfare Centres functioning in the States/ Union Territories as on 1st April 1997 These Urban Family Welfare Centres; will be reorganised into Health Posts gradually as and when these cities will be considered for expansion under Urban Revamping Scheme.

Primary health care institutions in rural areas

The Primary Health Care infrastructure has been developed as a three tier system and is based on the following population norms:

Centre	Population Norms	
	Plain Area	Hilly/Tribal Area
Sub Centre	5000	3000
PHC	30000	20000
CHC	120000	80000

Sub Centres (SCs)

It is the most peripheral contact point between the Primary Health Care System and the Community. It is manned by one Multi-Purpose Worker (Male) and one Multi Purpose Worker (Female) /ANM. Only 97 757 Sub-Centres established after 1st April 1981 are funded by Ministry of Health and Family Welfare, out of a total number of 136818 Sub centres functioning in the country at the end of June, 98. The rest are being funded under the State Minimum Needs/ Basic Minimum Services (BMS) Programme.

Primary Health Centres (PHCs)

PHC is the first contact point between village community and the Medical Officer. These are established and maintained by the State Governments under the Minimum Needs Programme (MNP)/BMS. A PHC is manned by a Medical Officer supported by 14 paramedical and other staff. It acts as a referral unit for 6 Sub Centres. It has 4 - 6 beds for patients. The activities of PHC involve curative, preventive, promotive and Family Welfare Services. Number of PHCs functioning in the country was 18,965 by 1st April 1990 which rose to 22991 by the end of-June, 1998.

Community Health Centres (CHCs)

CHCs are being established and maintained by the State Government under MNP/BMS. It is manned by four medical specialists i.e. Surgeon, Medicine, Gynaecologist and Paediatrician supported by 21 paramedical and other staff. It has 30 indoor beds with one O.T., X-Ray, Labour Room and Laboratory facilities. It serves as a referral centre for 4 PHCs. On 1st April 1990, the number of CHCs functioning was 1,910 which rose to 2712 by the end of June, 1998.

Rural family welfare centres

These are 5435 Rural Family Welfare Centres functioning in the country. These centres were established at all the block level PHCs sanctioned upto 1st April, 1980. The states have integrated the Rural Family Welfare Centres into their Primary Health Care System. There is therefore no separate identity for these RFWCs today. They are functioning as Primary Health Centres. The Government of India however, continues to provide financial support for maintaining these centres sanctioned before April, 1980. A provision of Rs. 265.00 crores has been made in B.E. 1998-99 for providing financial support to the states.

The details of staff sanctioned at each Centre is as under:

Assistant Surgeon	-	1
Block Ext. Educator	-	1
LHV	-	4
F.P. Health Assistant	-	1
Computer	-	1
ANM	-	1
Accountant	-	1
Driver	-	1
Vill. Worker		
(@ Rs. 50/- p.m.)		

Budget Allotted for Rural & Urban Health Schemes

(Rs. in Lakhs)

Name of the Scheme	Outlay for 1998-99
Sub-Centres	34, 000
Health & Family Welfare Centres	700
Training of ANMs (M)	2,500
Training of MPWs (M)	600
Village Health Guide Schemes	1, 000
Rural Family Welfare Centres	26, 500
Post Partum Centres	4, 000
Sub Distt. Post Partum Centres	6, 000
Sterilization Beds	170
Urban Revamping Scheme	3, 400
Urban Family Welfare	3, 000

Gaps in infrastructure

As per the existing population norms, the existing infrastructure is not adequate in some states even if we take 1991 census population in to account. The number of sub centres, PHCs and CHCs required as per 1991 rural population, number in position and the resulting short-fall is given in Annexure-I. However, if we take into account the projected rural population for 2002 (closing year of 9th Plan), then the state-wise requirement and short-fall are as given in Annexure-II.

It may be seen from Annexure-I and Annexure-II that the present short-fall (as on 31st Dec. 1997) at the all India level is as in Table 3.5.

Table 3

Centre	Shortfall as per 1991 Population	Shortfall as per Projected population for 2002
Sub Centre	7686	22930
PHCs	1521	4182
CHCs	2903	3757

Funding for bridging the gaps

The Department of Family Welfare is not directly providing financial assistance for setting up new Sub-centres and only maintenance grant is being given since 1st April 1981 for 97757 sub-centres out of a total number of 136815 sub centres. PHCs and CHCs are opened and maintained by the State Governments under the Minimum Needs Programme (MNP) which has since been reorganised into Basic Minimum Services (BMS) Programme. In view of the limited resources available, targets during the Ninth Plan period for establishing the subcentres, PHCs during and the CHCs have been kept at the level of shortfall as per 1991 population. While the progress of establishing SCs and PHCs may be viewed satisfactory, the gap in case of CHCs, the crucial First

Referral Units (FRUs), is still wide. During the Ninth Plan the highest priority is to be given to bridge this gap through restructuring and strengthening of existing it frastructure and redeployment of existing staff.

Each Sub-Centre is manned by one Male Health Worker and one Female Health Worker (Auxiliary Nurse Midwife). In order to train the required number of ANM in the rural areas, there are 480 ANMs Training Schools functioning in the country with an annual admission capacity of 16455 candidates (for 357 reporting schools). The duration of the training is 18 months. 10th pass girls preferably from the local villages where their services will be utilised later at the Sub-Centres and Primary Health Centres are admitted for the basic course.

Female health assistant training programme

One Female Health Assistant supervises the work of six Sub-Centres in the rural areas. She provides technical guidance and supervision to the ANMs who are working in rural areas. The senior ANMs with a minimum of 5 years working experience are trained for 6 months to take up the post of LHV, which is a promotional post. 42 LHV training schools with an admission capacity of 2596 (for 38 reporting schools) are functioning in the country.

Village health guide scheme

The Village Health Guide Scheme was initially started as Community Health Workers' Scheme on 2nd October, 1977 in all the States except Arunachal Pradesh, J &K, Kerala and Tamil Nadu. The Scheme was renamed as Village Health Guide Scheme in 1981 when it was made 100% centrally, sponsored scheme under Family Welfare Programme. According to the scheme the village community selects a volunteer as Village Health Guide who after training acts as a link between the community and the governmental health system. He/She mainly provides health education and creates awareness on MCH and Family Welfare Services. He/She has to keep track of communicable diseases, treat minor ailments and provide first aid to the patients.

At present about 3.23 lakh VHGs are reported to be working. Each VHG is paid an honorarium of Rs. 50/- per month. ~he Scheme has recently been reviewed by a committee of expert which has looked into various aspects of the scheme such as the usefulness of the scheme, the work done by VHGs, capability of VHGs in the context of institutional arrangements available in the country, enhancement of honorarium and other facilities available to VHGs etc. The committee obtained feedback from the states and visited some of the states to get first hand information and it has submitted its final report / recommendations and the same is being examined in the Ministry.

Multi-Purpose worker (Male)

As per the norms, each sub-centre is required to be manned by a trained Female Health Worker (ANM) and a trained Male Health Worker known as Multi-purpose Worker (Male). The Government of India had initiated a scheme of training and thereby converting the uni-purpose workers under various programmes to multipurpose workers. The scheme of basic training for MPW (Male) was initiated during the 7th Plan period because of the shortage of MPWs (Male) at Sub-Centre level. Under this scheme, 10th pass candidates are selected and trained for one year before they are inducted into service.

The basic training of MPW(M) was initiated in 47 Health and Family Welfare Training Centres throughout the country as 100% Centrally sponsored Scheme. During 7th Plan (1985-90). It was observed that the training capacity was not enough to meet the requirement of

MPW(M) in all the Sub-Centres, and hence the financial sanction to establish 50 new MPW(M) basic schools were given by the Government of India. At present, there are 28 HFWTCs and 23 New Basic MPW(M) Schools which are providing basic training to MPW(M).

Health and Family Welfare Training Centres (HFWTCs)

Health and Family Welfare Training Centres are established in the country with the objective of giving in-service training of health personnel in the rural health sector.

These training centres are up with 100% financial assistance from the Central Government. There are 47 HFWTCs in the country at present.

The category of health personnel given in-service training at HFWTC and the period of training is as below:-

Medical Officer	2 weeks
Health Assistants (Male and Female)	2 weeks
Health Workers	2 weeks
Block Extension Educators	2 weeks
Key Trainers of ANM School and M.P.W. (M) basic schools	2 weeks

In addition to the above training, the HFWTCs take up in-service training under various vertical National Programme as well. From 1982, HFWTCs are giving basic training to MPWs(M) also the HFWTCs are funded under 100% Central Assistance from the Family Welfare Budget.

Regional health office

There are 17 Regional Offices of Health and Family Welfare functioning under Ministry of Health and Family Welfare located in the Capitals namely Hyderabad, Shillong, Lucknow, Ahmedabad, Imphal, Bhubaneswar, Patna, Chandigarh, Pune, Shimla, Jammu/Srinagar, Bangalore, Tiruvananthapuram, Bhopal, Jaipur, Calcutta and Chennai covering all the States/Union Territories. These offices have been established with the aim of liason and coordination of various National Health and Family Welfare Programmes with the States, monitoring of centrally sponsored Health and Family Welfare schemes, on the spot Technical guidance, test checking of records in the State, maintenance of Malaria clinic, review and analysis of monthly technical re ports, supervision of Health information and field units and association in various implementation and grant sanction committees.

On the Family Welfare side there are 13 posts in every Regional Health Office headed by a Regional Director. Out of 17 Regional Directors, 11 are drawing salary from Family Welfare side and remaining 6 are from the Health side. However, the administrative control of all the 17 offices lies with Directorate General of Health Services of this Ministry. This department receives feedback in respect of all the National Health and Family Welfare Programmes by Monthly Progress and Tour Reports.

Family welfare training and research centre, Mumbai

Family Welfare Training and Research Centre, (FWTR & RC) Mumbai, is a Central Training Institute, responsible for the in-service training in Health and Family Welfare for the states in Western zone of the country, which includes the states of Gujarat, Madhya Pradesh, Andhra Pradesh, Goa, and the Union Territories of Daman, Diu and Dadra and Nagar Haveli.

Training related to Primary Health Care, Family Welfare and other integrated National Health Programmes is imparted to various categories of health professionals of State and District levels, i.e. District Health Officers, District Extension and Media Officers, Key trainers from the Health and Family Welfare Training Centres of the above 1 states. This Centre is also conducting a one year Post-graduate academic course of Diploma in Health Education (D.H.E.) for candidates deputed from all over the country and also for candidates sponsored by the World Health Organisation (WHO)/UNICEF/ UNDP/DANIDA etc. The first course of D.H.E. was started in the year 1987-88 and the XIIth course is in progress at present.

Apart from training and teaching, F.WT. and R.C., Mumbai is also involved in

Regional Health Officers

Regional Director	States under their	Sources of Funds Jurisdiction
Hyderbad	Andhra Pradesh	Health
Shillong	Assam, Meghalaya and Arunachel Pradesh	Health
Lucknow	Uttar Pradesh	Health
Ahmedabad	Gujarat, Dadra and Nagar Haveli	Health
Imphal	Manipur, Nagaland and Mizoram	Health
Bhubaneswar	Orissa	Health
Patna	Bihar	F.W.
Chandigarh	Haryana, Punjab and Chandigarh	F.W.
Pune	Maharastra, Goa Daman and Diu	F.W.

Regional Director	States under their	Sources of Funds Jurisdiction
Shimla	Himachal Pradesh	F.W.
Jammu/Srinagar	Jammu and Kashmir	F.W.
Bangalore	Karnataka	F.W
Tiruvananthapuram	Kerala, Lakshwadeep	F.W.
Bhopal	Madhya Pradesh	F.W
Jaipur	Rajasthan	F.W.
Calcutta	West Bengal, Sikkim, Tripura and A and N Islands	F.W
Chennai	Tamil Nadu, Pondicherry	F.W

Health Services Research and Community-based Research in Health and F.W. and also delivering the comprehensive health services through Health Camps, organised at rural and urban areas.

Training programmes on Health and Family Welfare are also conducted for the W.H.O. Fellows, deputed through the Ministry of Health and F.W.

During the year 1998-99, training, education, research and clinic services of the Centre, were conducted as below:

Training activities

A training Programme on "Population and Sex Education" for the girl students of Regional Vocational Training Institute (R.V.T.I), Mumbai has been arranged by F.W.T. and R.C., Mumbai from 26th June 1998 to 27th June 1998. A total of 80 students were present for the above programme.

A workshop for launching the training programme for para-medical personnel working in F.W. programme has been arranged on 14th Oct. 1998, at F.WT and R.C., Mumbai.

Research activities

F.W.T and R.C., Mumbai, has been identified as a Regional Co-ordinating Centre to supervise the Annual Sentinel Surveillance activities, which has been already conducted for the states of Rajasthan and Himachal Pradesh.

F.W.T and R.C., Mumbai, has undertaken the "Evaluation of Family Welfare Radio sponsored programmes" - "Haseen Lamhe" and "Yeh Bhi Khoob Rahi" during the year.

The research study "To develop a programme of preventive education on AIDS for the underprivileged adolescent boys and girls in urban slums" has been completed. The dissemination workshop will be conducted during the month of December. The report has been finalised and dissemination workshop is to be conducted to disseminate the research findings to the researches and administrators working in the same field.

A research proposal on "Study of sexual practices in relation to HIV/AIDS and STDs in selected tribal community of Maharashtra and Madhya Pradesh" has been submitted to NACO, New Delhi, for approval and funding.

Fellowships

Dr. (Mrs.) S.O. Verma, C.M.O. (NFSC) has been awarded a British Council Fellowship to attend a training course of Participatory and Rapid Appraisal for Evaluation in Health at Keel University, U.K., from 1st Sep. 1998 to 6th Sep. 1998 (A Collaborative Project of Nuffield Institute, Leeds, U.K. and NIHFW, New Delhi).

I.E.C. programme

F.W.T. and R.C., Mumbai has organised a health exhibition at Chhatrapati Shivaji Terminus (CST), Mumbai, on creating the awareness among the people regarding F.W, and AIDS from 12-13 Nov. 1998 (on the occasion of Nehru Jayanthi).

Clinical services

Service delivery to the mothers and children continued at the centre during the year 1998-99 through its Clinic and Laboratory. Medical and Health Care Services were delivered to the patients attending the clinic during the year. Along with M.C.H. services, counselling in Family Welfare is also imparted by the Centre.

International institute for population sciences, Mumbai

International Institute for Population Sciences, Mumbai is a "Deemed University" functioning under the administrative control of the Ministry of Health and Family Welfare, to confer training, conducting research and providing consultancy services in the field of Population Studies. The Institute has six specialised department viz. Department of Mathematical Demography and Statistics Department of Fertility Studies, Department of Public Health and Mortality Studies, Department of Migration and Urban Studies, Department of Population Policies and Programmes and Department of Development Studies. In addition, there is a Department of Development Studies. In addition, there is a Department of Extra Mural Studies functioning since 1993 on project basis.

Training: The Institute offers four regular courses viz. (a) The Diploma in Population Studies (DPS), (b) Master of Population Studies (MPS), (c) Master of Population Studies through correspondence and (d) Diploma in Health Education (DHE). In addition to the above courses, the Institute offers Ph.D. Programme. During the year 1997-98, 09 students (China - 05, Bhutan -02 and India -02) have attended DPS course. 23 students have attended MPS Course, 68 students were admitted to

MPS Course. 16 students were admitted to DHE course. 72 students have been registered for Ph.D. Degree. The Institute had also organised a Short-Term Training Programme on "Population Planning and Evaluation" for 10 officials from Sri Lanka during September 22-26, 1997 and on "Planning Management and Evaluation of Population Programme" during December 01, 1997 to January 01, 1998.

Research: The Institute has completed 15 Research Projects during 1997-98. There are 8 on-going research projects which were initiated during 1997-98 and are in different stages of completion. Also, 15 new research projects are being taken up during the year 1998-99, including two funded by other agencies. The new Research Projects are as under:

- Levels, Differentials and Determinants of Fertility: A District-wise Analysis of 1991 Census Data.
- Fertility, Mortality and Gender Inequality in India: A District Level Analysis of 1991 Census.
- Evaluation and Adjustment of 1991 Census Age Data and Estimation of Demographic Indicators for the Districts of Selected Indian States.
- Multi-region Demographic Analysis of India.
- Measuring Morbidity Diversity in India: A Spatio-Temporal Analysis.
- Reproductive Preferences and Achievement: An Investigation from Two Points Household Surveys.
- A Study of the knowledge, Attitude and Behaviour of the Elected Members of Gram Panchayats on Population Issues and Health and Family Welfare Programme in Uttar Pradesh.
- A Study of Highway Communities Exposed to the Risk of HIV/AIDS.

- Causal Linkages Between Migration, Regional Disparities and Urbanization in
- India (Analysis of 1991 Data for Migration, Regional Development and Urban Economic Structure of Class I Cities).
- Survival Study of Tobacco and Food Related Cancers in Mumbai.
- Impact of Changes in vital Rates on Ageing Process in some Selected Stated of India over the Periods 1971-81 and 198191: An Analysis Based on Census Data.
- Proposal for Action Research Programme.
- Nirodh Use and Its Wastage in India: an Investigation from Field Study in Three States (Haryana, Maharashtra and U.P.)

Funded by other agencies

Social Assessment Survey (Beneficiaries) in Thane and Latur (Funded by Dept. of Health (Medical), Directorate of Health Services and Govt. of Maharashtra).

- Reproductive Behaviour of Women in Greater Mumbai: An Investigation from the Field Study (Funded by Public Health Deptt. Municipal Corporation of Greater Mumbai).
- In addition there are three research project viz. (i) Capacity Building in the area of Re productive Health, (ii) National Family Health Survey- II and (iii) Rapid Household Survey under RCH Programme are under taken. These are funded by foreign agencies.

NFHS-II - Keeping in view the large utility of the valuable data for population management collected in the NFHS-I, the decision was taken to conduct the NFHS-II with the financial assistance of the USAID for total US $ 3.5 million for the local costs. The main purpose of NFHS-II is to measure changes over time and to gain a better grasp of the factors related to improvements in the population and health area. Under this survey, 25 States and I U.T. (Delhi) and about 94,000 ever married women in the age group of 15-49 years will be covered~ The three new and important feature of NFHS-II are (a) anaemia test for all respondent women and their children below 3 years of age, (b) Test of Iodine content in cooking salt and (c) Lead testing in the blood of children below 3 years in Delhi and Mumbai. UPS, Mumbai will function as Nodal Agency to make overall coordination and to disburse the funds to consulting Agencies, to finalise the questionnaires and sampling design and tabulation plan, under overall technical support of M/s. Micro International, Washington to prepare preliminary and final report at national level and to arrange dissemination of survey results through various forums and media.

Seminars/Conferences/ Workshops organised by the Institute

The following workshop/seminars were organised by the Institute during 1998-99:-

- State Institute of Health and Family Welfare (SIHFW) and IIPS jointly organised a seminar on Population and Development in Orissa from March 04-06, 19 98 SIHFW, Bhuvaneshwar.
- Questionnaire workshop on NFHS-II during March 19-20, 1998 at IIPS, Mumbai.
- Workshop on sampling design for NFHS-II during March 24-25, 1998.
- Workshop on Reproductive Health under the auspices of Ford Foundation Project on capacity

building for PRC personnel 'and NGOs during April 6-8, 1998.

- Workshop on the use of Qualitative Research Methods on Health Research for the Research Staff of the Indian Institute of Health Management Research (IIHMR), Jaipur, September 29 to October 02, 1998.
- Consultancy Services: During the year 1997-98 the Institute provided consultancy services to various Institutions in India in the field of Population.
- Publications: The Institute brings out a quarterly Newsletter which furnishes details about various on-going activities of the Institute. During 1997-98 the Institute published four issues of IIPS Newsletter.
- Library: There are a total of 63100 books, 9945 bound periodicals and 13706 reprints in the Library. The Library receives 250 journals regularly, out of which 150 journals are by way of subscription and others are received as gifts or on exchange basis.
- *Data Centre*: Data Centre has been identified as "POPIN focal point" of the South Asian countries by Asia Pacific POPIN for three years period. Further it acts as "Supporting Centre" for "POPLINE" and getting the support from centre for population programmes, JHU, Baltimore, USA.
- *Notable Achievement of the Institute:* Institute is designated as a nodal agency to supervise and conduct the Rapid household survey (RCH Programme) with the help of 15 regional agencies in 50% of Districts of India.
- Institute is also entrusted with responsibility of being nodal agency for conducting NFHS-II covering above 1,00,000 household scattered all over the districts. Institute is also conducting projects funded by Ford

Foundation to build capability of researchers in research on Reproductive Health. The Institute has been recognised on Popin Supporting Centre by UN ESCAP Bangkok for coming 3 years.

- The details of Rapid Household Survey and Facility Survey conducted by 15 Regional Institutions led by IIPS, Mumbai are given in Chapter-I under Management Information System.

National Institute of Health and Family Welfare, New Delhi

The National Institute of Health and Family Welfare, New Delhi is an autonomous body under the administrative control of the Department of Family Welfare. It is registered as a Society under the Societies Registration Act XXI of 1860 as extended to the 'Union Territory of Delhi. It was set up in 1977 as an apex technical Institute with the objective of promoting Health and Family Welfare Programme in the Country through education, training, advisory, consultancy and specialised services, research and evaluation. The focus of these activities are the two major goals of Health for all by 2000 A.D. and Net Reproductive Rate- 1 by 2011-16 A.D. The Institute has a faculty strength of 48 including its Director.

Education: In the area of basic education, the Institute continued to conduct (i) a three-year Post-Graduate Degree Course M.D. in Community Health Administration, (ii) a two year Post Graduate Diploma Course in Health Administration, (iii) a one-year Post-Graduate Certificate Course in Health & Family Welfare Management through Distance Learning; and (iv) a one-year Post- Graduate Certificate Course in Hospital Management through Distance Learning. During the year 18 students pursued the M.D. Course in Community Health Administration but discontinued later; 126 students were enrolled in the Certificate Course in Health and Family Welfare, and 133 students were enrolled in the Certificate Course in Health Management.

In-service Training: The in-service training programme of the Institute during this year included Integrated Skill Based Course in Health and Family Welfare, particularly in the area of Management, Communication, Training Methodology and Clinical Skills. The training highlight of the year included the Maternal and Child Health training course, which was previous conducted in collaboration with the Lverpool School of Tropical Medicine, UK, and which was conducted during the year exclusively in India by the NIHFW. The Training Courses and workshops, numbering 33, covered a wide range of Health and Family Welfare personnel. The participants from all over the country are trained in the areas of Health and Family Welfare Communication, Management, Health Systems Research and ,Training methodology, clinical skills research methodology in biomedical research by participatory methods with hands on training in the field, hospital and laboratory.

Research: The research studies/ projects conducted by the Institute during the year were based upon crucial issues of the Health and Family Welfare Programmes and included monitoring and evaluation. The Institute has developed methodology for identifying research needs and conducting studies. NIHFW undertook different studies as a part of its regular activities. 14 studies were completed and 26 studies were in various stages of progress during the year. These are as under:-

Completed studies

- Policy Research on Private Practice by Government Doctors.
- Concurrent Evaluation of Pulse Polio Immunisation (PPI) Programme December 7, 1997 and January 18, 1998

- Development of Low Cost Pregnancy Test Kit.
- Third Evaluation of the Strategies for health for All by the Year 2000 A.D.
- Evaluation and Standardisation of Health Management Training Courses in India (Under Health Management Consortium).
- Social Marketing of Contraceptives.
- Implementation Completion Report of India Population Project-VI.

Completed Studies under M.D. (CHA) Programme

- A Study of Health Care Services Provided to the Inmates of a Jail in Relation to their Health Problems.
- Assessment of IEC Activities in a District.
- A Study of the Existing Monitoring System for Select National Health Programmes and to Suggest Monitoring Indicators for these Programmes in a District.
- Evaluation of Quality of Maternal and Child Health Services at Maternal and Child Welfare Centre under the Municipal Corporation of Delhi.
- A Study on problem of Malaria and implementation of its Control Measures in Urban Slums of Delhi.
- Evaluation of National Child Survival and Safe Motherhood Programme in a District.
- A Study of Hospital Waste Management in a Tertiary Care Hospital.

On-Going Studies

- Assessment of Sperm Steriod Binding Proteins for the Regulation of Fertility in the Human.

- A Study on Willingness and Economic Capacity to pay for the Health Care Services.
- Integration of Health and Family Welfare Services in the States.
- Follow up Evaluation Study of Orientation Training Courses for District Extension and Media Officers in Communication Skills.
- Study on Selective Versus Comprehensive Features of Primary Health Care implementation in selected States in India.
- Development of Health Care Delivery Model for the Tribal Areas.
- An Evaluation Study of Bharat Gyan Vigyan Samiti's Literacy to Health project.
- An Epidemiological Study on Reproductive Health Problems among Males and Females in a District.
- A Study on Pre-marital Sexuality and Unmet Needs of Contraception among Sexually Active unmarried Youths in the Cities of India - Delhi and Lucknow.
- Development of Evaluation Tool Bank for Training.
- An evaluation study of Community Health Centres and Primary Health Centres in selected States.

  A Study on Involvement of Health, Care Providers in Delivery of Comprehensive Primary Health Care.
- A Study of Effectiveness of Integrated In-service Training on, performance of Health Personnel in the Delivery of Health and Family Welfare Services in IPP-VII, States - a Three Phased Study.
- Partnership between Government and NGOs as an Alternative approach of Maximising Quality of PHC Services in North-East Hills.

Study of organisation and Management of selected NGOs in four States of India (Under Health Management Consortium).

- Assessment of Training Needs of Primary Health Care Functionaries in Context of Reproductive and Child Health in a State.
- A Study on the Evaluation of National Malaria Eradication Programme in the States of Haryana and Rajasthan.
- Follow-up Evaluation Study of Hospital Administrations Courses conducted at NIHFW
- An Evaluation Study of Child Survival and Safe Motherhood Programme.
- HSP Gwalior Project - "Integrated Intervention Strategies".
- Evaluation of Obligatory Free Medical Care Services provided by Charitable Hospitals in Delhi.

On-going Studies under M.D. (CHA) Programme

- Study on Training Needs Assessment of Panchayat Raj Members in the Context of Local Decentralised Development Planning including Health.
- A Study of selected Health Problems of Elderly in a District.
- Assessment of Block Extension Educative Activities for Promoting Health and Family Welfare programmes at Block level experience for trainers of all categories of health personnel, providing primary health care. In addition, management Institutes were also identified to conduct management training for health managers at district and State levels.

Specialised services: Specialised services of the Institute included services for MCH/infertility/endocrinological disorders provided at its clinic, the documentation and Library services provided through its National Documentation Centre and its research publications and course modules. The Institute also provided advisory and consultancy services to various national, international and voluntary organisations in various capacities during the year.

Regarding Training Administrative Unit in NIHFW, the information has been detailed in the Chapter for Training.

Hindustan Latex Limited (HLL), Thiruvananthapuram

HLL, a public sector undertaking under the administrative control of the Department of Family Welfare, commenced its manufacturing operations on April 5, 1969 and is today one of the largest manufacturers of condoms in the country. It also manufactures Copper-Ts, Oral pills including 'Saheli'- the once-a-week non-steroidal contraceptive pill, Blood Bags, Hydrocephalus Shunts and is also marketing Surgical Sutures, an important Component for the hospital industry. HLL has three manufacturing plants two at Peroorkada and Akkulam in Thiruvananthapuram, Kerala and one at Belgaum, Karnataka.

Capital Structure: The issued and paid up share capital of the Company is Rs. 1553.50 lakhs. The total capital employed is Rs. 49744.23 lakhs as on 31st March 1998.

Memorandum of Understanding: Hindustan Latex has signed the Memorandum of Understanding with the Department of Family Welfare, Government of India, for the financial years from 1991-92 onwards. HLL's performance has been rated 'Excellent' for its consistently achieving targets, on the basis of the performance criteria set by the Government of India during the year 1996-97

Performance: The sales turnover of the company was

Rs. 66.06 crores for 197798 against Rs. 81.88 crores for 1996-97 The total sales achieved for its various products for 1997-98 were:-

a)Condoms	568.74	Min.Pcs
b)Latex Gloves	5.56	Min. Pcs
c)Saheli Once a week Contraceptive Pill	9.41	Min. Tablets
d) Mala D/N	11.62	Min.cycles
e) Copper-T	0.87	Min.Pcs
f)Hydrocephalus Shunt 2514	pcs	
g) Blood Bags	0.94	Min.Pcs
h) Sutures (Trading)	0.053	Min.Dozen

Technological Expertise: Over the past twenty-nine years, HLL has acquired technological expertise and are today leaders in the area of Latex Dipped Goods.

R&D Department: The Company's R&D Department has made significant contribution for the improvement of the quality of the Company's range of condoms together with the indigenisation of raw materials and other equipments that were imported.

Quality Assurance: The Company lays great emphasis on effective quality control at every manufacturing stage.

Hindustan Latex have been granted ISO 9002:1994 Certification, for the topmost quality management systems for its two Plants.

- At Peroorkada - Manufacturing Condoms
- At Akkulam - Manufacturing
  - (i) Copper-T's
  - (ii) Blood Bags and
  - (iii) Hydrocephalus Shunt.

The ISO 9002:1994 certification signifies that the quality systems in force at its manufacturing units is a Model one, for quality assurance in - production, installation and servicing. This international acknowledgement for the Quality systems at HLL was awarded by the NQA Quality Systems Registrar Ltd., accredited by the Dutch Council for Certification; one of the topmost certification agencies of Europe. Earlier, in 1995 HLL was awarded the N F Mark - the official Quality Certification by the Premier French LNE after a detailed Quality Laboratory Audit.

Again HLL is the only manufacturer from India to be awarded the prestigious CE Mark certification is a prerequisite for entry into the vast and competitive European Market. HLL condoms today conform to the rigorous specifications prescribed by WHO, AFNOR (French Standards), ASTM (American Standards). Recently, HLL also received the SABS Mark from the South African Bureau Standards and the GMP Certificate from the Zimbabwe Regional Drug Control Laboratory.

Marketing and Exports: The Company has regional marketing offices at Delhi, Madras, Bombay, Calcutta and Lucknow besides the headquarters at Thiruvanthapuram. Direct marketing operations of its own domestic brands includes:-

- Moods, a premium brand, is the first of such brands introduced in the market on a national scale, other brands introduced later were Share, Ustad, Rakshak Nymph and Moods Supreme.
- HLL introduced the world's first non-steriodal Once-a-week Oral Contraceptive Pill Saheli in 1992.
- Marketing of Mala-D Oral contraceptive Pill in the states of Rajasthan, Madhya Pradesh, Kerala, Tamil Nadu and Karnataka started in July, 1993.

- Other additions have been the high-tech medical aid for Neuro Surgeons-the Ceredrain Hydrocephalus Shunt; Surgical Suturees both - absorbable and nonabsorbable; and Blood Transfusion Bags, at its most modern facility at Thiruvananthapuram.

- During 1997-98 HLL achieved a sale of 169.83 Mln. Pcs. of condoms under the social marketing programme, 40 lakhs cycles of Mala-D and 94.03 lakhs tablets of Saheli oral pills.

- HLL has been retained by the Ministry of health and Family Welfare as a Procurement Consultant for their Reproductive and Child Health (RCH) programme. An agreement was signed between HLL and the Ministry to this effect on 30.4.98. As per the agreement, HLL has to procure 13 drug items and hospital rubber sheets. These items are to be assembled into Drug kit W and Drug kit 'B'. These kits are then to be delivered to 250 consignees located in various States/UTs. The Hospital rubber sheets are to be distributed in the States of Assam, Bihar, Rajasthan and Madhya Pradesh. The total value of procurement is estimated to Rs. 40.00 crores. HLL invited bids through advertisements and after evaluation of bids submitted the documentation to this Department of Family Welfare. After the approval of the competent authority in the Ministry, HLL placed orders on the firms. The total value of order of drug kits 'N and 'B' is Rs. 32.00 crores approximately. The total quantity to be procured is 1,33,600 no. each of Drug kit W and Drug kit 'B'.

- HILL has recently awarded a three year project by the State Innovation in Family Planning Service Agency (SIFPSA), Lucknow for marketing contraceptives in the rural areas of Uttar Pradesh. SIPFSA is a voluntary organisation set up with the

Financial Assistance from U SAID. Under this project, HLL will set up a marketing network to market 89 million condoms, 70 million Oral contraceptive pills and 5.75 lakhs Copper-

- This project is to set up marketing infrastructure at an estimated cost of Rs. 4.22 crores over a period of 3 years. The Company has also been awarded a contract by AIDS Prevention and Control (APAC), Chennai, and envisage a market spending of Rs. 17 lakhs financed by the agency for a period of one year.
- Hindustan Latex Family Planning Trust (HLFPPT) promoted by HLL has been awarded a project for Social Marketing of Condoms, Contraceptive Pills, ORS and Sanitary Napkins, in around 2500 villages of Gwalior, Bhind, and Morana districts of Madhya Pradesh. The development objectives of the project include distribution of Social Marketing brands of contraceptives through unemployed, educated and mobile rural youth, supported by a comprehensive local media based IEC programme, thereby contribution to the reduction of total Fertility Rate (TFR) in the rural areas and also advancement of Family health through the promotion of sanitary napkins and Oral Rehydration Salts (ORS).

HLL's Branded Condoms and Examination Gloves received the 510 K certification from FDA (Food and Drugs Administration) USA, which is essentially a clearance for marketing these products in the US.

The International division of the company was set up in 1993. HLL's exports during 1996-97 touched Rs. 11.92 crores. HLL exported its products during 1997-98 to 37 countries all over the world.

Population research centres

The Union Ministry of Health Welfare has established a network of 18 Population Research Centres (PCS) in various Universities (11), other Institutions (6) of national repute and one in Madhya Pradesh, scattered over 17 major States of India on the basis of facilities and other infrastructure available. These Centres are responsible for carrying out research on various topics of Population Stabilisation, Demographic and Socio-Demographic Surveys and Communication aspects of Population and Family Welfare Programme.

These Population Research Centres are autonomous in their functioning with 100% financial assistance, in the form of grants-in-aid on year to year basis towards salaries of staff, books and journals, stationery, vehicle for field for field surveys and the infrastructural equipments etc, from Government of India. At present there are two types of PRCs, one designated as 'Fully Developed' and others 'Not Fully Developed'. Staffing pattern varies according to the type of PRC. These grants-in-aid are released to the PRCs in three instalments in a year on receipt of essential prescribed documents/ bonds and undertakings. The staff of these PRCs is also imparted training, both Nationally and Internationally, with a view to enhance the research capabilities and improve the quality of research.

These centres are monitored centrally to ensure that the research effort is not merely academic but also action oriented.

Strengthening of PRCs

The changes envisaged on the basis of the recommendations of the three committees

- *Permanent Status:* It is proposed to as sign permanent status of an Institute to the PRCs;

- *Pensionery Benefits:* Introduction of an element of flexibility is proposed. Staff can opt for Pension/ CPF Scheme.
- *Ceiling on Non-salary Items:* The ceiling on non-salary items is proposed to be enhanced considerably to increase capability of PRCs.
- *Staff Strength:* A Fully Developed PRC will have a full time Director in the pay scale of a Professor assisted by two Readers and two Lecturers. A Non-fully Developed PRC will have full time director in the scale of Professor assisted by one Reader and two Lecturers. Approval of budget for these measures is being obtained for IX Plan.

Studies conducted by the PRCs Most of the studies conducted by these PRCs are on varying topics such as:-

- Population Growth;
- Socio-economic characteristics of rural/ urban population;
- Evaluation of Family Welfare Programme for non-acceptance of Family planning methods;
- Evaluation of Special School Health Check up Scheme; and
- Fertility and Socio-economic Indicators.

Some of the important topics of research covered by these Centres, in addition to the studies assigned by the Government of India are as under:-

- Integrated Nutrition and Health Programme: A Base-line survey Report of Andhra Pradesh;
- Multi-Indicator Cluster Survey in Urban Slums and Rural Areas;

- Status of Women and Reproductive Behaviour Among Urban Indian Women Understanding the linkages;
- Study to evaluate the Impact of TV Advertisement for Deluxe Nirodh and Mala-D in Madurai City;
- Population Growth and Quality of Life.

The ongoing process of regular monitoring and ensuring that the research effort is not merely academic but also action oriented has been further strengthened. A set of 15 studies on varying topics, has been assigned to the PRCs for completion during 1998-99 and 1999-2000. List of studies selected and assigned to t he Population Research Centres is as follows:-

- Verification of Authenticity of reported cases of Sterilisations (by each technique separately and IUD insertions by obtaining list of persons shown to have been sterilised or women shown to have been provided IUD insertions by the District Family Welfare set up and to verify from such persons whether actual sterilisation/ IUD insertion was made. In regard to IUD insertions also to verify the duration after which it has to be taken out and reason for taking out the IUD. To be taken up completely.
- Installation and utilisation of equipment supplied under CSSM. List of equipment should be obtained from the department of Family Welfare (Govt. of India) and from the Director, Family Welfare of the State Government. It should be verified through visits, when equipment was delivered at district level and when these have been shifted to the user hospitals and whether they are presently in use. To be taken up for a block of half the districts.

- Survey for functioning of RTI/STI Clinics. It should be ascertained from Chief Medical Officer of the District/ Director, Family Welfare of the State Government in which RTI/STI clinics are sanctioned and verification should be made by visits whether these clinics have distinct and visible identity, whether (and how many) doctors are posted exclusively for the clinic and how many men and women (separately) have availed these clinics in last three or six months. This study should be taken up for a block of roughly half the districts in the state chosen for study.
- Verification of last doses of vaccines for various vaccination programmes and verification of third pre-natal check up of pregnant women and third post natal checkup of women after delivery. This study should be taken up district as a unit but wherever it is taken up 100% verification should be ensured.
- Ascertaining and assessing the factors responsible for unwanted pregnancies-Study or selected areas. The study can be also for different religious groups of women.
- To ascertain availability of condoms and oral pills at village level. This study may take block sub-division or district as a unit and may ascertain for individual villages whether there is any out- let from where people of the village can obtain condom and oral pill when they require it.
- Assessment-of prevalence of Reproductive Tract Infections and Sexually Transmitted Infections in representative samples of population in selected areas.
- Assessment of Implementation status of Pre-natal Diagnostic Techniques Act, 1994. To ascertain in

identified Districts situation in regard to registration of clinics and situation in regard to prosecution under the Act.

- Assessing prevalence/incidence of Neo-Natal Tetanus in selected districts.
- Verification of utilisation of buildings constructed under IPP-V, IV & VII Projects. Whole state should be taken for such assessment. List of buildings constructed may be obtained from Director, Family Welfare of the state Government and utilisation should be ascertained by field visits.
- Study of the functioning of State Training Institutes of Health and Family Welfare. Position in regard to adequacy of building, training equipment, adequacy of faculty members and regularity/extent of training programmes may, be ascertained. If there are shortcomings, the reasons for that may be ascertained.
- Assessment of effectiveness of Mahila Swasthya Sanghs in selected districts and to assess what impact their functioning has had on population control/RCH objectives.
- Assessment of effectiveness of Nehru Yuvak Kendras in selected districts: assess what impact their functioning has had on population control/RCH objectives.
- Assessment of effectiveness of Village Health Guides in selected districts and to assess what impact their functioning has had on population control/RCH objectives.
- Abortions Needs Assessment
- An amount of Rs. 8.00 crore has been earmarked for the above PRCs during 1998-99.

The ongoing process of regular monitoring and ensuring that the research effort is not merely academic but also action oriented has been further strengthened.

(Rs. In lakh)

S.No.	Name of State	Assistance Fund	Total Amount
1st Phase			
1.	Kerala	248.80	
2.	Madhya Pradesh	248.80	
3.	Rajasthan	248.80	
4.	Tamil Nadu	224.00	970.40
IInd Phase			
	Money released with IEFC sanctions dated 28.12.1998		
1.	Andhra Pradesh	256.00	
2.	Karnataka	256.00	
3.	Orissa	208.00	
4.	Punjab, D & N Haveli Daman & Diu, Pondicherry, and Manipur	227.20	947.20
IIIrd Phase			
	EFC sanction accorded on 05.01.1999		
1.	Andhra Pradesh	540.00	
2.	Gujarat	90.00	
3.	Haryana	72.00	
4.	Uttar Pradesh	360.00	
5.	West Bengal	234.00	1296.00
			3213.60

Transport

Mobility is a vital input for effective implementation of Family Welfare Programme.

The Government of India has provided 8089 vehicles to the States/UTs. The latest position regarding availability and entitlement of vehicles is as per Annexure-III

Monitoring and evaluation of the existing fleet was done from 5th July 1998 to 15th Jan., 1999 during the year 1998-99 in the States of Kerala, Tamil Nadu, Andhra Pradesh, Himachal Pradesh, Punjab, Haryana, Rajasthan, Uttar Pradesh, Bihar, Madhya Pradesh and Maharashtra.

POL and maintenance charges for the family welfare vehicles was made available to the States at the rate of Rs.15,000/- per vehicle per annum for diesel driven vehicles and Rs.20,000/- per vehicle per annum for petrol driven vehicles.

Mopeds to ANMs

Since 1996-97 with the assistance of UNFPA a project is being implemented under which ANMs are given interest free loans from a corpus fund for purchase of mopeds to enhance their mobility. The following States have received assistance under the project so far.

4

Funding for Family Welfare Programme

Introduction

India is the first country to have officially started Family Welfare Programme in 1951. The resources made available for the programme have always been short of the requirement and therefore only partial achievement of the objective of stabilisation of the population could be achieved. Outlay in successive plan periods are shown in table 1.

A unique feature of the programme is that it continues to be cent percent centrally sponsored plan scheme with very insignificant non-plan support. The plan size therefore looks very impressive but this is because no part of the maintenance expenditure created over the plan periods since inception has ever been transferred to the non-plan as is the normal practice for other schemes. The department of the Family Welfare took up the issue of funding with Ministry of the Finance, Planning commission and also with the two previous Finance Commissions. But unfortunately the commissions did not include any recommendation for transfer of any part of Family Welfare maintenance expenditure to state sectors.

However, the case has again been placed before the Eleventh Finance Commission. The N D C committee on population had recommended in 1993 that states should meet 10% of the expenditure of Family Welfare

Programme. This issue was taken up with the States in the Central Council of Health & Family Welfare where Ministers of State Government are members) but the states strongly resisted sharing any burden in this regard.

The performance under Post Partum Programme at Sub-district Level during 199697 and 1997-98 is at Table 1.

Table 4.1. Outlays under the Family Welfare Programme from the 1st Five Year Plan.

Period		outlays (Rs. in crores)
First Plan	(1951-56)	0.65
Second Plan	(1956-61)	5.00
Third Plan	(1961-66)	27.00
Annual Plans	(1966-69)	82.90
Fourth Plan	(1969-74)	285.80
Fifth Plan	(1974-78)	285.60
Annual Plan	(1978-79)	111.80
Annual Plan	(1979-80)	116.20
Sixth Plan	(1980-85)	1309.00
Seventh Plan	(1985-90)	2868.00
Annual Plan	(1990-91)	675.00
Annual Plan	(1991-92)	749.00
Eighth Plan	(1992-97)	6195.00
Annual Plan	(1997-98)*	1750.35
Annual Plan	(1998-99)*	2239.35

The expenditure on maintenance of infrastructure created over the Plan period was estimated to be around Rs.

950.00 crore during 1997-98 and Rs.1160.00 crore during 1998-99. Against this provisions made in 1998-99 is Rs. 904.00 crore which is less than even the requirement for 1997-98. It indicates how bulk of the budget provision for family welfare programme is used only towards maintenance of infrastructure created in the earlier plan periods. Because of the inadequate budget provision, provision in annual budget for maintenance of infrastructure remains lower than actual level of expenditure. More so the Department has not been in a position to revise the norms, contingencies etc., which were fixed as early as 70s.

The budgeted amount is released during the year to the States. The States naturally incur expenditure on prevailing level of salary, allowances etc. which is in excess of the grants released to the States. Therefore after some gap when the audited accounts are available with the State Governments they prefer claims for the difference. Inability of the Governments due to inadequacy of the budget support to liquidate the dues of the States Governments puts the Department of Family Welfare in unenviable situation vis-a-vis the States for meeting actual cost of the maintenance of the infrastructure.

The Department of Family Welfare however makes all possible efforts to clear the dues of the State Governments by taking up the issues for more funds with the Ministry of Finance and Planning Commission. It was decided in the meeting that Planning Commission while recommended Annual Plan outlay for 1998-99 would take realistic view of the arrears and actual level of expenditure for maintaining infrastructure and provide for these as first charge of the Department. Due to the efforts by the Department the outlay for the programme was in creased from Rs.1829-35 crore in 1997-98 to Rs.2489.35 crore in 1998-99, of this Rs. 660.00 crore the increase in the DBS component was Rs. 410.00 crore. Considering the severity of the problem of arrears and dam age it is causing to RW Programme, all of this additionally has been used by the Department to address this most pressing problem:

A major portion (Rs. 236.00 crore) was used to augment assistance for infrastructure maintenance to States and Rs. 171.00 crore towards liquidation of arrears. In normal circumstances, this sizeable increase in allocation given by the Planning Commission would have solved about 75% of the problem of arrears for future years. But in 1998, the chain of increase in salaries consequent to implementation of Fifth Pay Commission in Centre has started in States. As a result, the problem of arrears remains of the same size because increased allocation has been largely used in the increase salary bill.

The RCH Programme launched during 1997-98 for implementation during 9th Plan period is jointly funded by World Bank, European Commission, UNICEF, UNFPA etc. The World Bank has sanctioned US$ 248.30 million for RCH Phase I Project for a period of 5 years. World Bank has also committed an equal amount for Phase 11 of RCH Project to begin after 2 & 1/2 years for a period of five years. -European Commission has approved an assistance of ECU 200 million (Eq.US$ 250 million) and UNFPA for US$ 100 million. In addition, bilateral assistance have also pledged sizeable assistance for the RCH Programme especially for the Pulse Polio Immunisation (PPI) campaign. British Agency, DFID has pledged assistance of US$ 77 million, DANIDA has pledged assistance of US$ 33 million, KFW (Germany) has pledged assistance of DM 50 million and JICA (Japan) has pledged assistance of JY 760 million and JY 92 million. In all, foreign assistance already pledged for RCH programme is to the extent of US$ 960 million which is more than 500/6 of the foreign assistance received during the VIII Plan period. While such donor agencies will help in giving a generous push to the RCH programme, this increase depends on foreign aid for the RCH programme to the extent of about two-third of the programme. The programme has an approved outlay of Rs. 5112.53 crores for IX Plan period. For the year 1998-99 the programme has an approved outlay (BE) of Rs. 758 crores. The details of estimated external assistance for the year 1998-99 would be as under:-

(i) IDA	—	US$
(ii) EC	—	15 million ECU
(iii) DFID	—	US$ 20 million
(iv) Japan	—	US$ 2.5 million
(v) KFW	—	US$ 15 million
(vi) DANIDA	—	US$ 6.5 million
(vii) UNICEF	—	US$ 12.5 million

For the Ninth Plan, an outlay of Rs. 16750.36 crore of Domestic Budgetary Support (DBS) and Rs. 5296.38 crore for External Assistance (EAP) for implementing the Family Welfare Programme was proposed to the Planning Commission. Out of DBS of Rs. 16750.36 crore, Rs. 10270 crore was planned as the requirement of the ongoing activities of the Department and Reproductive and Child Health Activities. A minimum of Rs. 2000 crore was required for strengthening some of the key programmes. Thus to achieve the targets set on the domestic front, Rs. 12,270 crore is the minimum DBS requirement during IX Plan. Against this, the Planning Commission has indicated a DBS of Rs. 12000.00 crore. The corresponding EPA allocation is Rs. 371700 crore.

The outlay for 1998-99 and actual expenditure during 1997-98 is given in the statement on page 56.

5

Maternal Health Programme

Introduction

Department of Family Welfare has constantly endeavoured to improve the health status women by providing maternal care services through various programme interventions, since its inception. The Child Survival and Safe Motherhood (CSSM) Programme launched by the Honourable President of India on 20th August 1992 had integrated the Safe Motherhood component with the Child Survival interventions for the first time. This programme, by and large, aimed to reduce maternal mortality morbidity and while ensuring child survival.

The NFHS 1992-93 estimated Maternal Mortality Ratio of 4.37 per thousand live births. This means, on an average one woman dies for every 200 to 250 pregnancies. This ratio varies widely from state to state.

The major causes of maternal mortality are ante and postpartum haemorrhage, anaemia, toxaemia, abortions, sepsis and others. This trend has not changed significantly over the years. This is mainly due to a large number of deliveries being conducted at home and lack of referral facilities for high risk pregnancies.

A large number of these causes are preventable through improved maternal care. Promoting safer institutional deliveries and ensuring appropriate treatment of complications can reduce the case fatality rate.

Table.1

Percentage Distribution of Death under Child Birth & Pregnancy (Maternal death) by Specific Causes 1990-1994

Sl.No. Specific Causes	1990	1991	1992	1993	1994
1.Bleeding of Pregnancy Puerperium	23.7	19.5	25.2	22.6	23.7
2.Anaemia	19.4	19.9	19.6	20.3	19.3
3.Toxaemia	15.2	8.8	12.6	12.8	13.1
4.Abortion	11.8	10.8	13.7	11.7	12.6
5.Puerperall Sepsis	8.1	12.7	11.5	12.5	10.6
6.Malposition of Child	7.1	11.6	8.5	5.5	6.4
7.Not classifiable	14.7	16.7	8.9	14.6	14.2
Total	100.0	100.0	100.0	100.0	100.0

Maternal mortality in India is 40 to 50 times more as compared to the developed countries. The socio-economic status including educational status of women influence the maternal mortality and morbidity. Low social status of women compounded with lack of education, cultural misconceptions and limited access to safe motherhood services are some of the causes of high maternal mortality and morbidity in the country. Hospital based data, also reveal that states like Kerala, Goa, Tamil Nadu, Maharashtra and Andhra Pradesh which have relatively better socio-economic and education status have lower MMR than the other states. Thus, besides improving the maternal health-care services, it is necessary to improve the social status of women, including the education standard, to reduce the current level of MMR.

Safe motherhood programme (CSSM)

The safe motherhood package of the CSSM programme had the following components:

- Early registration of pregnancy
- To provide minimum three Antenatal Care
- Universal coverage of all pregnant women with TT immunisation
- Advise on food, nutrition and rest
- Detection of high risk pregnancies and prompt referral
- Clean deliveries by trained personnel
- Birth spacing
- Promotion of institutional deliveries

In 1997, the current RCH programme has been started as part of the 9th Plan, which will continue all the interventions taken up under the CSSM programme. The major interventions include:

Essential obstetric care

Essential Obstetric care intends to provide the basic maternity services to all pregnant women through:

- Early registration of pregnancy (within 12 to 16 weeks).
- Provision of minimum 3 antenatal check-up by the ANM or Medical officers to monitor the progress of the pregnancy and to detect any risk/complications, so that the women could be given appropriate care including referral, on time.
- Provision of safe delivery at home or at an institution.

- Provision of three postnatal care to monitor the postnatal recovery of the women and to detect complications which include appropriate referral.

This component of the RCH programme is more relevant for the states namely Assam, Bihar, Rajasthan, Orissa, Uttar Pradesh and Madhya Pradesh because most of the deliveries are still conducted at home in unclean environment causing high maternal and mortality morbidity. It is therefore, necessary to give some suitable support to this existing practice, which is unlikely to change quickly. To address to this specific problem, the programme has introduced a new item i.e., "Rubber Sheet," in addition to delivery kit, to be distributed to all pregnant women through ANM, which is to be used as a clean delivery surface for women who decide to deliver at home.

Other items which will be made available through the RCH programme are drugs in form of Kits A, B and Ess. O.C, contractual appointment of additional ANM in 8 states namely, Uttar Pradesh, Madhya Pradesh, Haryana, Bihar, Orissa, Rajashtan, Assam, Nagaland and Delhi and contractual appointment of PHN/SN to promote institutional deliveries. In addition provision for equipment for essential obstetric came have also been made. Funds for appointment of additional ANM's have been earmarked for 15 states contractual appointment of PHN/ Staff Nurse.

Emergency obstetric care

Complications associated with pregnancies are not always predictable. There fore, emergency obstetric care is an important intervention to prevent maternal and mortality morbidity. Under the CSSM pro gramme, 1,748 referral units were identified and supported with equipment kits E to P. However, they did not become fully operational due to lack of skilled manpower, adequate infrastructure, equipment and medicines.

Under the RCH Programme, the FRUs will be strengthened through supply of drugs in the form of Emergency Obstetric drug kits, equipment kits as a regular annual programme (E to P kits) (Ref. Table 5.2), skilled manpower an contractual/ hiring basis. Six states have been forwarded proposals for hiring Anaesthetist. Funds have already been released to them.

Hour Delivery, Services at PHCs/CHCs

To promote institutional deliveries, provision has been made under the current RCH programme to give additional honorarium to the staff to encourage round the clock delivery facilities at health centres. This is to ensure that at least one nurse/ medical officer/cleaner is available even beyond normal working hours.

Table 2

Safe motherhood Programme: Supply of Equipment Kits

1. ANM

   Kit A—Midwifery Kit.

2. Sub-centres

   Kit C- Sub-centre Kit

3. PHCs

   Kit D—PHC Kit

4. First Referral Units

- Kit E- Laparotomy set
- Kit G- IUD insertion set
- Kit H- Vasectomy set
- Kit I- Normal delivery set
- Kit J- Vacuum extraction set

- Kit L- Uterine evacuation set
- Kit M- Equipment of Anasesthesia
- Kit O- Equipment and reagents for blood tests
- Kit N-Neonatal resucitation set
- Kit P- Donor Blood transfusion set

Under this provision, funds have already been sanctioned to 15 states namely, Andhra Pradesh, Karnataka, Madhya Pradesh, Maharastra, Meghlaya, Nagland, Orissa, Rajasthan, Sikkim, Uttar Pradesh and Pondicherry.

Referral transportation to indigent families through Panchyat

Time is an important factor for obstetric emergencies. Women, who undergo deliveries at home and develop complication, often find it difficult to be transported to a referral unit.

Under the current RCH programme, provision has been made to assist referral of women from indigent families in 25% of the sub-centres in selected states namely, Madhya Pradesh, Uttar Pradesh, Bihar, Orissa, Rajasthan, Assam and Nagaland, to provide a lumpsum corpus fund to the Panchayat through District Family Welfare Officers. Funds have already been sanctioned for seven states.

Medical termination of pregnancy

Medical Termination of Pregnancy (MTP) is a reproductive health measure that enables women to opt out of an unwanted/ unintended pregnancy in certain specified circumstances without endangering her life and well being.

India legalised medical termination of pregnancy on broad socio-medical grounds through MTP Act, 1971. The aim of the Act was to reduce maternal mortality and morbidity due to illegal/unsafe abortion. To make safe abortion services accessible to all women in the country, The Government of India under the RCH programme is expanding and improving the MTP facilities and their utilisation.

Assistance from the Government of India will be in the form of training, supply of MTP equipment and provision for engaging doctors trained in MTP to visit PHCs to perform MTP on a fixed day, once in a week or once in a fortnight. Assistance in the form of equipment and training will be provided to well run and competent medical clinics in the non-government sectors, if they have functional Operation Theatres and trained doctors/ nurses.

Reproductive Tract Infection (RTI) /Sexually Transmitted Infections (STI)

RTIs and STIs represent a serious threat to the health and well being of Indian women and men. They are exposed to pain and discomfort of acute illness and often experience long-term impairment of their reproductive functions as a consequence of these infections. The presence of RTIs/STIs has been found to facilitate the acquisition and transmission of HIV infection 5-10 times.

Under the RCH programme, the component of RTI/ STI is linked to HIV and AIDs. Therefore, it has been planned and being implemented in close collaboration with National Aids Control Organisation (NACO). Under this programme, NACO will provide assistance for wetting up RTI/STD clinics up to the district level and the Department of Family Welfare will assist in setting up FRUs in a phased manner. The assistance from the Government of India will be in the form of training and drug kits, including disposal equipment. This support will also be made available in the urban areas.

Guidelines on RTI/STI, for paramedical workers, have been prepared in consultation with NACO.

Under the RCH programme, each district will also be assisted to engage two laboratory technicians on contractual basis for doing routine blood, urine and RTI/STI tests at FRUs, if such technicians are not readily available.

6

Information, Education and Communication

The Information, Education, Communication (IEC) component of National Family Welfare programme is mainly to create an effective communication strategy to inform the masses about the means and measures of Family Welfare programme, educate them about the perils of over population and motivate and persuade them to adopt small family norm, using all possible channels of media.

New initiatives and thrusts

During the year under report, IEC activities were organised on priority basis in 135 weak districts. Greater emphasis was laid on a more judicious media-mix based on local specific media forms and need-based inter personal communication schemes. More stress was given at grassroot level and the segments not reached by conventional mass media channels for effectively transmitting population related values and messages. Remote areas were covered by adopting multimedia strategy; song and drama programmes organised and print material designed for neo-literates and semi-literates. From next year, the IEC strategy will be focused on the 'C' category districts as well as the weaker States.

As part of the new IEC strategy in tune with the

Reproductive,& Child Health programme, a professional agency has been selected for making new video spots. It has also been decided to produce a, folk son-based radio programme, through a professional agency, to be broadcast twice a week over national and commercial channels of AIR. Eminent filmmakers like Shyam Benegal and Amol Palekar are being commissioned for feature films. Ten hoardings each are being installed in 13 big cities of the country with messages of Reproductive and Child Health and family welfare issues. Agency for North Zone has been selected.

British Nandy Communications have been assigned the job of conducting interactive panel discussions. This programme will be telecast on Doordarshan once a month.

To make local specific IEC activity more affective, Zilla Saksharta Samitis (District literacy Committee), who are already involved in the literacy campaign programme, are being roped in for chalking out independent District IEC campaign for every district. In this way, Family Welfare IEC will be integrated with Education at the district level.

A national level communication workshop is proposed to be held later this year for chalking out a national communication strategy in tune with the RCH programme.

Concurrent impact evaluation and assessment of the IEC efforts has also been decided for constant review of the programme.

New Initiatives and Activities

A detailed account of the new initiatives and the activities of the IEC Division is given in the following paragraphs.

Population clocks

Five population clocks have been functioning at Inter-State Bus Terminus (Kashmiri gate) and All India

Institute of Medical Sciences intersection in Delhi; Tribune Office, Chandigarh; Main bus-stand, Bangalore and Hazratganj Mahila Hospital, Lucknow. These clocks help in creating awareness about the national dimensions of the problem.

Social mobilisation for P.P.I.

An allocation of Rs. 3379.56 lakh was made to States/UTs for conducting the unprecedented social mobilisation to eradicate polio from the country. In the first phase, (i.e. 6th Dec., 1998) polio doses were provided to 13.61 crore children below five years. Rs. 100 per booth has been allocated for all 6.5 lakh booths, for the student volunteers, drawn from secondary schools, for both rounds.

Production of A.V. material

A number of audio-visual programmes were produced during the year through different agencies such as Doordarshan, Films Division, DAVP and NFDC. These programmes were in Hindi and regional languages. NFDC produced 5 video spots on Pulse Polio Immunisation programme and the film entitles 'Ladkiyan'. Video spots were telecast on Low Power Transmission and National network of Doordarshan.

Films made by Doordarshan network from time to time. Haseen Lamhe and Yeh Bhi Khoob Rahi, 15 minutes Radio sponsored programmes are broadcast in Hindi and 11 regional languages from 30 All India Radio stations of commercial broadcasting services. Both the programmes cover the topics of Family Welfare, and Reproductive Child Health and Population issues in an interesting and absorbing manner.

Activities through Media Units of I & B Ministry

74.1 The Media Units of the Ministry of Information and Broadcasting provide information, education and communication support to the Family Welfare programmes as per requirements and guidelines of the IEC Division. The focus of their activities is on propagation of mother and child health problem, population growth, status of women, Small Family Norm and the Community Needs Assessment.

Doordarshan

Doordarshan telecast the video spots on World Population Day and Pulse Polio Immunisation Programmes on their Hindi and Regional channels. Population figures are flashed regularly during the morning transmission before Hindi news. Doordarshan also telecast various programmes including panel discussions, video films, interviews and cover important functions related to family welfare.

The Kendras provided wide coverage to the observation of World Population Day and Pulse Polio Immunisation Programme 1998-99. Doordarshan has been allocated a number of films in Hindi in the year 1998-99 and in addition to this, the film 'Chetna, 'Baap Re Baap', 'Chuimui Si', 'Angan Ki Chhaon Mein' have been produced and telecast on Doordarshan network.

Besides, a message from the Honourable Prime Minister was telecast on the eve of Pulse Polio Immunisation day. Doordarshan also telecast 26 episodes serial, 'Sheela' for the third time on public demand.

AIR

All India Radio produces and broadcasts in different formats such as group discussions, interviews, spot recordings, feature plays, etc. in different languages and areas. The Commercial Broadcasting Services (CBS) have been broadcasting the programme 'Haseen Lamhe' regularly, as well as one minute spots over various channels in Hindi and regional languages.

One minute audio spots are broadcast twice a day during free time allotted to the Department. Besides, sponsored programme 'Yeh Bhi Khoob Rahi' is- also being broadcast on every Sunday in Hindi and regional languages from 30 CBS stations. This is an entertaining programme, in which the listeners interact a question-answer session on Family Welfare and MCH. It has been estimated that daily, on an average 8 minutes programme is being exclusively broadcast on family welfare issues.

Directorate of advertising and visual publicity

Directorate of Advertising and Visual Publicity produced printed material and issued advertisements on family welfare issues, based on the requirement projected by the IEC Division of the Ministry. It also produced a video spot on breast-feeding for telecast on DD. During the year under review, DAVP developed 3 audio spots for the Pulse Polio Immunisation Programme.

Directorate of field publicity

Directorate of Field Publicity organised 40,000 film shows, 13,000 photo exhibitions, and 3,900 oral communication programmes. Special programmes, plays were organised by the Department to sensitise people about the family welfare programmes and the country-wide Pulse Polio Immunisation Programme, Directorate, of Field Publicity and its state units also organised baby shows, seminars, symposia, debates.

Press information bureau

Press Information Bureau provides media coverage to important occasions, events, activities, policies and programmes of the Ministry of Health & Family Welfare. During the period, PIB arranged for coverage of World Population Day functions, Family Welfare pavilion at IITF, 1998 Pulse, Polio Immunisation Programme and other important events.

Song and drama division

To educate the masses about family welfare issues, Song and Drama Division organised live entertainment programmes like puppet shows, dance dramas, folk recitals, mythological recitals, traditional plays, magic shows, etc. Special Programmes to sensitise people regarding the Pulse Polio Immunisation programme were also being organised by the field units, so that greater number of people can bring their children up to the age of 5 years for the extra doses of Polio drops. More than 15,000 variety shows were organised in 1998-99.

Films division

Films Division produces films on themes relating to Health & Family Welfare and undertakes distribution of films to field organisations and cinema circuits throughout the country for exhibition. A sum of Rs. 145 lakh was allocated to the Film Division during the year 1998-99 and a number of films are under production on various themes like small family norm, age of marriage, spacing method and Pulse Polio immunisation.

This year, 3 films produced by Films Division for the Department of Family Welfare have won National Awards and these films are 'Nirankush', a film on female infanticide, 'The Saviour', a film on immunisation aimed at children and 'Banglar Boul'. 2 films entitled 'Kathghar' and 'Anguri' based on the stage play conducted by Song and Drama Division on the occasion on World Population Day are under production.

As part of the new strategy to utilise the services of eminent film makers, the Ministry has assigned eminent directors, Shri Amol Palekar and Shyam Benegal two feature films, i.e. 'Kairee' and 'Teri Godi Hari Bhari Rahe' respectively. The script of 'Kairee' has been approved, while the script for the other films is being vetted by the Ministry.

Activities in the states/union territories

An integrated IEC strategy mixing interpersonal communication with multimedia contents was developed. Activities were given multidimensional and integrated thrust to increase the outreach and impact of Reproductive and Child Health and Family Welfare messages with the objective of bridging the gap between awareness and acceptance. State IEC annual plans for 1998-99 with an outlay of Rs. 1300.40 lakh were formulated through closer interactions, keeping in view the differential approach.

Following major IEC Activities were reported up to September, 1998 by the States/ Union Territories:

S. No.	Activity	Number
1.	Exhibitions	26,627
2.	Film Shows	9,946
3.	Cultural Shows	3,847
4.	Wall writing	49,960
5.	Printed materials	18,74,201
6.	Press advertisements	22,920
7.	Seminars, workshops organised	1,422
8.	Population education activities	3,14,312

Mahila Swasthya Sangh

Greater emphasis is being laid on interpersonal communication to encourage community participation, particularly for the womenfolk through Mahila Swasthya Sangh (MSS) in villages with a population of over 1000 or 200 households in plain areas, and for population of 500 or more in hilly terrain, including the North-Eastern States. The Auxiliary Nurse Midwife (ANM) is the member Secretary of MSS. The MSS comprise five grassroot level functionaries and 10 prominent women from the village community. The field level functionaries of education are also the members of MSS. MSS are being constituted since 1990-91 at village level. A nominal amount of Rs. 1,200/- per year is allocated for arranging its monthly meetings. This women's group helps the Fe male Health Workers (ANMs) to educate and motivate the community and obtain support from other women colleagues working in the village for the welfare of women and children. The MSS are given short-term training and are supplied with education and information material and guidance by local health workers/BEE/ Block Medical Officers. At present 89,738 MSS, with 13,40,670 members are working in States/UTs.

Workshops for sensitisation of opinion leaders

A Scheme to sensitise Opinion Leaders' by holding one day session on various aspects of family welfare issues, was instituted in 1993-94. Under this scheme, 10421 opinion leaders of various categories including members of Zilla Panchayats, Panchs, private practitioners, teachers, etc. were exposed to family welfare issues. Now, it is proposed to be implemented through State/ Regional Health and Family Welfare Training Centres.

World population day

Like every year, the World Population Day was observed on 11th July, 1998 all over the country. A number of functions and activities were organised at Delhi as well as in States/UTs. Dr. Harsh Vardhan, Delhi's Health & Family Welfare Minister flagged off the "Population Race" at National Stadium, New Delhi, in which over 5,000 School and College children participated. The children who participated in the Race were provided specially designed T-Shirts. A play on family welfare issues was also staged by the artists of Song and Drama Division in a Delhi auditorium.

In addition, a number of functions and activities were organised by various governmental and non-governmental organisations all over the country.

Exhibition in IITF, 1998

The Department of Family Welfare participated in the India International Trade Fair, 1988 in New Delhi and won the bronze medal for its display at the Family Welfare Pavilion. The main theme of the Family Welfare Exhibition was on Reproductive and Child Health and on promoting mother and child care, women empowerment, family planning methods, etc. were depicted. Free health check-up including eye care, AIDS, family welfare counselling for male and female was also arranged with the help of CGHS and other agencies like NACO, National Blindness Control Programme. The Department of ISM participated with a detailed exhibition of its activities. The overwhelming response to the No Scalpel Vasectomy Camp of the Family Welfare Pavilion was the highlight of this year's effort. Street plays, children programmes were also organised through Song and Drama Division and Delhi Administration for awareness about the family welfare issues.

Scheme for health awareness through NYKS

This scheme aims to involve NYKS to propagate the implications of population explosion, need for small family and promote reproductive and child health in demographically weak districts through the Health Awareness Units. Orientation-cum-sensitisation training programme for Youth Coordinators and Population Awareness and sensitisation programme for National Service Volunteers were conducted by NYKS. All the training components of the project has been completed. 135 district Coordinators, 405 National Service Volunteers and 12,900 Convenors and joint Convenors have been trained. Up to August 1998, more than 6071 educational programme have been organised by 6, 750 HAUs involving 6, 04, 730 beneficiaries.

National population education programme

The National Population Education Programme launched in India in 1980 has been making efforts to attain the objective of institutionalisation of population education in the existing education system of the country. During the year 1998-99, the project-wise status of the four UNFPA-assisted projects are as follows:

Population and development education in schools

This project, which completed its third phase (1993-97, extended up to May, 1998), entered the fourth phase (1998-2001) with a new project. The main achievements of the third phase were integration of elements of population education at the primary and upper primary stages of school education; publication of more than 500 titles in 16 Indian languages and in English for facilitating integration of population education in the training of over two million teachers and other educational functionaries, organisation (in all States/UTs) of co-curricular activities and population education week; undertaking evaluation and research studies; and the development of the general theoretical framework of Adolescence Education through national and regional consultancies during the next phase.

The next phase of the project reflects a major change in strategies aimed at shifting the focus of project activities from the 'Population Explosion' approach to: 'Sustainable Development' approach in view of the Paradigm Shift made by the ICPD Programme of Action, 1994.

Population and development education in post-Literacy and continuing education (Phase III)

Population Education project in adult literacy, which was launched in 1986 completed its second phase during the year under reference. In the second phase, the emphasis was laid on institutionalisation of population education in the total literacy campaign. The third phase, which was launched in June, 1998, will concentrate on integration of population and development education in post- literacy and continuing education.

Issues connected with women's empowerment, gender equality, reproductive health and rights, family life education, adolescent's sexual behaviour including HIV/ AIDS etc. will receive added thrust in the third phase.

Population and development education in higher education system (Phase III)

In the third phase of this project (1998-2001) being implemented presently, the main objectives are to develop awareness and positive attitude towards population and development issues leading to responsible behaviour among the students and the community at large and to institutionalise Population Education in the higher education system.

During the second phase of the project, the institutional structure was built up further with the setting up of the Population Education Unit (PEU) in the UGC in 1994. The programme at the end of the second cycle has expanded from 12 to 17 Population Education Resource Centres (PERCs) that cover 186 universities and 1,400 colleges, distributed over 32 States and Union Territories.

Besides, there are 1,400 Population Education Clubs (PECs) reported to have a membership of about 3 lakh students.

The IIIrd Phase (1998-2001) proposes the continuation of the project with an emphasis on national capacity-building, adolescence education and improved management systems to realise the set objectives in tune with ICPD goals.

Population education in vocational training programme (Phase II)

The second phase of the project which was operationalised in July, 1996 continued during the year under reference. The main objective of the project, which is being implemented through D GET, Ministry of Labour, is to make the adolescents and youth aware of the population issues and their impact on them and the community.

IEC activity at district level through ZSS

To make local specific IEC activity more affective, efforts were made to use the services of Zila Saksharta Samities (District Literacy Committee) who are already involved in the literacy campaign programme. The ZSS were requested to co-opt the district level health sector officials viz. Chief Medical Officer, District Medical Officer, District Mass Education and Media Officer etc. and to take on responsibility for IEC for Reproductive and Child Health/Population Control.

ZSS's especially in post-literacy and continuing education phase were requested to prepare a proposal for two years, i.e. 198899 and 1999-2000. In this context, proposals were sought from each district involving the design and display of posters, wall writings, use of folk media, kalajathas, rallies, etc. IEC, through ZSS will facilitate community mobilisation and for the first time, will enable families that are not reached through electronic media, to be reached. To this extent, this is an important initiative having large potential for good.

The response from ZSS is encouraging. Over 100 proposals from 17 states have been received, of which, 69 districts have been sanctioned projects. The state-wise break-up of districts whose proposals have been sanctioned are: 4 (Andhra Pradesh) 1 (Assam), 13 (Gujarat), 6 (Himachal Pradesh), 10 (Karnataka), 9 (Madhya Pradesh), 1 (Maharashtra), 3 (Orissa), 1 (Punjab), 8 (Rajasthan), 4

(Tamil Nadu), 5 (Uttar Pradesh) 2 (West Bengal) and 2 (Tripura).

Print software/publicity

The most intensive print media campaign was for PPI which was made systematically through a series of press advertisements in numerous newspapers in Hindi, English and all regional newspapers on all-India basis on and before both the rounds of the PPI programme. A pictorial D.O. letter was also prepared and sent to District Chiefs for better implementation of the PPI programme.

The Editorial-Design Wing brought out a number of print software viz; single-sheeter on breast-feeding, a special booklet on the RCH programme, and detail books like Implementation Issues for the RCH Programmes, Short field guide for AFP Surveillance, publication on RCH Training, and RCH Scheme for Implementation (Hindi version), etc. for disseminating systematic information for health and family -welfare functionaries at different levels.

In an effort to orient the health providers to the new initiatives, a new quarterly newsletter 'RCH Samachar' is also being published in Assamese, Oriya and Hindi and distributed to seven states to help health functionaries in getting up-to-date information on the RCH programme. In addition, the journals 'Centre Calling' and Hamara Ghar are also being regularly published and despatched to various states, districts as well as to the NGOs. A beautiful theme-based wall calendar was brought out and distributed to health facilities and hospitals all over India.

Mass mailing unit

The functioning of the Printing Press of Mass Mailing Unit has been streamlined now by extensive repairs of HMT and Miller 94 printing machines as well as Stal-Folding Machine. In addition a new Web Offset Printing Machine has also been installed and made functional.

From April, 1998 to October, 1998, in addition to 'Centre Calling' and 'Hamara Ghae, the MMU Press has printed the booklet on RCH Training, AFP Surveillance guide, and the List of Blacklisted NGOS, single-sheeter on breast-feeding, in addition to routine jobs like printing of letterheads, etc.

Distribution of material

The Distribution Wing (MMU) mails Audio-Visual, audio and print software/material to various audience groups all over India working in the Central/ States/ UTs/ Voluntary Organisations; concerned with the field of promoting Family Welfare and Mother & Child Health Programmes.

The Address Library of the Distribution Wing, which has over 75 lakh addresses, is being expanded. By October '98, about 13.83 lakh material has been mailed.

7

Organised Sector and Voluntary Organisations

The Family Welfare Programmes, by and large, remained a Government programme till the end of the 7th Plan. During the 8th Plan, it was realised that involvement of NGOs in the programme will give it the much desired impetus, as the voluntary workers can work in close collaboration with the people and bring about the desired changes in social and personal attitudes, perceptions and behaviour, more than the staff of the Government hierarchy. During the 8th Plan, many steps/initiatives were taken to broad base the involvement of NGOs for promotion of the family welfare programmes.

NGO's involvement during Eighth Plan

A number of model schemes were prepared and notified during the 8th Plan and NGOs were given grant-in-aid under the schemes for promotion of the small family norm and population control. These were implemented in weak areas which have couple protection rate up to 60% or where crude birth rate is over 35 per thousand, or where other indicators like IMR, MMR, CBR, CDR, etc. taken together necessitated such supplemental efforts. A few mother NGOs were also approved for identifying, motivation and assistance of smaller organisations.

In addition, certain funds were obtained under IPP-VII (National Component) for releasing to States for giving assistance to smaller NGOs in those States through a network of State SCOVA (Standing Committee On Voluntary Action) Committees. Family Welfare Projects were also undertaken in the organised and semi-organised sector.

Certain large projects under PVOH-II schemes were also financed with the assistance of USAID funds. PVOH-II scheme sought to reduce morbidity, mortality and fertility among the rural and urban poor in the country. The purpose of the project was to expand and improve basic and special preventive health, family planning and nutrition services for the poor by strengthening support to the voluntary sector with special attention to less served areas and deprived population.

Response to NGO Schemes

In view of efforts made during the 8th Plan, participation of the NGOs in the Family Welfare Programmes has been increasing rapidly. The number of NGOs funded during 1996-97 increased to 600 with financial support of Rs. 18.58 crores from 91 NGOs and funding support of Rs. 3.29 crores in 1990-91.

NGO involvement under reproductive & child health project during the Ninth Plan

It has been realised that the work through the NGO is not by way of an alternative to work through a government system. It is actually complementary in nature. The NGOs have the advantage of flexibility in procedures, rapport with local population and credibility. They are, therefore, better placed to try localised innovations which the government system is not in a position to attempt.

The main thrust of the NGO programme during the 9th Plan is to involve NGOs essentially in innovative programmes and not to use them for implementing routine government programmes. An other major feature of the 9th Plan NGO Programme is that for the first time this Department has taken on hand a major exercise for conferring a large degree of autonomy on the, NGP sector.

Under the Reproductive and Child Health programme the NGOs are being assisted at three levels.

Small NGOs

At the village, Panchayat and Block level small NGOs are being involved basically for advocacy of RCH and family welfare practices and for counselling. However, the individual NGOs at this level are being allowed to propose innovative programmes also. As these small NGOs have limited resources they are being assisted through the mother NGOs.

Mother NGOs

Department of Family Welfare intends to recognise one mother NGO for every 8 to 10 districts. NGOs with substantial resources and proved competence are being approved for mother NGOs. So far 49 mother NGOs have been identified by this Department being given grants by

They are the department directly once in a year at the beginning of the year. In subsequent years the annual grant will be given after taking into consideration the performance report for the previous year and utilisation certificate for the grants given earlier. The mother NGOs are required to screen the credentials of the applicant small NGOs, obtain proposals from them, consider them for sanction, release money and monitor its work and obtain utilisation certificate from the small NGOs.

The mother NGOs are also required to provide training to the staff of the small NGO for both management of the NGO and for management of the programme. The mother NGOs have one nominee of the State government and one of the Government of India on its Executive Committee.

National NGOs

A limited number of National NGOs are being assisted by the department on project basis for innovative programmes. The attempt is not to involve NGOs in repeating the government programmes.

The department proposes to involve NGOs for some specific areas wherever involvement is expected to yield good results e.g. for introducing Baby Friendly Practices in hospitals, for helping in enforcement of Prenatal Diagnostics Technique Act by detecting offending sex determination clinics and collecting evidence for making specific complaints against them to the designated authorities in the state. In addition, some NGOs are to be assisted for involving the hospitals/clinics in urban areas for their involvement in offering facility for contraceptive/ terminal methods and for counselling both in regard to RCH and population control measures.

Meeting with NGOs

During 1998, two important meetings were held, one meeting of mother NGOs and prospective mother NGOs on 12th February, '98 in which the role of the mother NGOs came to be discussed in depth and, the other, a special meeting of *the medical* NGOs, PRCs and States Family Welfare Secretaries of six State, identified for relatively poor performance (UP, MP, Bihar, Rajasthan, Orissa and Assam) on 13th February, '98. In this meeting specific action oriented programmes for improving the quality and expanding the scope of Family Welfare in these six States have been identified.

Innovative projects

Innovative projects have been sanctioned to five NGOs including 3 training projects to Population Foundation of India, New Delhi and SWACH, Panchkula, Haryana and CINI, Calcutta. In addition, the following UNFPA projects have been recommended by the GIA Committee:-

Mahila Sewa Trust, Gujarat: The project aims at promoting essential health services including RTIs and STDs with proper follow-up and back-up referral services for common health problems and dissemination of health and family planning related information to 2.15 lakhs sewa members in Khera, Banskantha and Ahmedabad districts.

Society for Service to Voluntary Agencies, Pane: The project aims at improving the status of reproductive health including family planning by strengthening

Working Women's Forum, Chennai, Tamil Nadu: This is an integrated programme of income generation, reproductive and child health for working women of Tamil Nadu, Andhra Pradesh and Karnataka including transfer of working women's expertise to other institutions.

The Department is getting the antecedents and credentials of NGOs applying under mother NGO scheme and Innovative scheme under RCH project (except well-known NGOs, who have worked with this department earlier and whose performance has been very satisfactory) verified/pre-apprised through National Level NGOs. The Standing Committee for NGOs (Grants-in-Aid Committee in their first meeting, approved the following National NGOs for appraisal work and verification of Mother NGO, NGOs applying under Innovative scheme and for evaluation of work of these as well as of small NGOs:-

i. Family Planning Association of India, Mumbai

ii. Gandhigram. Institute of Rural Health & FW Trust, Tamil Nadu

iii. Voluntary Health Association Of India, New Delhi

iv. SWACH, Haryana

v. Child in Need Institute, Calcutta

Similarly, mother NGOs are required to verify the antecedents and credentials of small NGOs before giving any financial assistance to them.

The departments objective is to promote a true partnership between the NGOs and the government and also to encourage strong NGO participation in areas where the presence of the government has been traditionally weak. In the process, the right of the NGO Sector to manage its own affairs is also being recognised.

Whenever any request is received from an NGO for consideration for mother NGO/ innovative scheme, a copy of the proposal is being sent to the Family Welfare Secretary of the concerned State, and another to the agency entrusted with the work for verifying the antecedents and capabilities of the applicant NGO. The NGO who has submitted the proposal is invited to the meeting of the Standing Committee for NGOs (Grants-in-Aid Committee), where the same would be discussed.

Standing Committee (Grants-in-aid Committee) for NGOs proposals

To bring transparency and speed in NGO's cases, a Standing Committee for NGO Projects (Grants-in-aid Committee) has been constituted under the chairmanship of Secretary (M). The Committee has the Joint Secretary in-charge of the Programme, Financial Adviser, three RCH specialists, three representatives of NGOs and representative of Planning Commission. The committee meets once in 2-3 months to scrutinise the proposal and give its recommendations. The Secretary (FW) of the state and the NGO concerned are also invited in the meeting of the Grants-in-Aid Committee. The Standing Committee for NGO projects is, however, a recommendatory body and actual sanctions are assessed with the concurrence of Internal Finance division.

8

Contraception

The National Family Welfare Programme provides the following contraceptive services:

— Sterilisation as a terminal method

— Intra-Uterine Devices (IUD) for the spacing births.

— Daily Oral Contraceptive Pill for spacing births.

— Condoms for spacing births

The acceptance level of the various methods of contraception during the last four years has been as given in table 1.

. After withdrawal of targets for individual contraceptives from 1.4.96 performance levels in the States had fallen substantially in 1996-97. Partly it was because the cause for over-reporting done by field officers somehow show fulfilment of targets was no longer there and partly withdrawal of targets temporarily led to feeling of complacency in some States. The mechanism of determining local needs by consulting the local community and to focus on meeting such need was explained to the field workers through a sustained training programme in 1996 and 1997 This has reversed the trend and contraceptive use is on the increase. The training effect will be maintained and the Department is hoping to achieve a larger rate of increase in contraceptive use in 1998-99.

According to the National Family Health Survey, the acceptance level of spacing methods in the country is still very low. It is only 2.4% in the case of condoms; 1.9% in the case of IUDs and 1.2% in the case of oral pills. Much of the contribution in contraception is of sterilisation and male sterilisation is less than 4%. For moving towards stable population the coverage by condoms, oral pills and IUDs needs to be increased by 5 to 7 time.~ but that would need much larger resources for the programme, greater efficiency of field workers and much larger community support for the programme. The effort of the Department is to maximise these important inputs.

Table 1

	1995-96	1996-97	1997-98	1998-99 (Apr. '98 to Sept. '98)
Sterilisation	4422319	3870226	4127065	1283402
IUDs	6857882	5680671	6085744	2634363
Oral Pills (Users)	5090850	5250179	6249222	5081306
Condom (users)	172974291	17214327	16730468	12984061

Condom, daily Oral Pill and IUDs are provided free of cost through Sub-Centres, Primary Health Centres, Community Health Centres as well as hospitals throughout the country. The quantities given to the State during the last three years along with the budget utilised are given in table 2 and 3.

Table 2

Quantities supplied to States

	1995-96	1996-97	1997-98
Condoms (Million pieces)	690	753	717
Oral Pills (lakh cycles)	406	397	314
IUDS (lakhs pieces)	84	73	69

Table 3

Budget utilisation

(Rs. in Crores)

	1995-96	1996-97	1997-98
Condoms	49.52	60.00	45.35
Oral Pills	15.03	12.96	10.33
IUDS	21-63	22.00	16.83

In view of the inherent weakness of free distribution of contraceptives arising from wastage and perception of low quantity by the consumer, the National Family Welfare Programme had initiated Social Marketing Programme of condoms in 1968 and that of Oral pills in 1987 Under the Social Marketing Programme, both condoms and oral pills are made available to the people at highly subsidised rates.

The extent of subsidy ranges from 70% and 80% depending on the procurement price in a given year. Both these contraceptives are distributed through Marketing Companies/ NGOs. In the case of condoms the marketing companies/ NGOs are given Deluxe Nirodh variety of condoms at Rs. 1.30 per packet of 5 pieces and this is sold at Rs. 2/- per packet of 5 pieces to the consumer.

In the case of oral pills, one strip of oral pills, which is required for one month, is given to the marketing company/ NGO at Re. I/- and it is sold to the consumer at Rs. 2/- per strip under brand name "Mala-D".

Under the social marketing programme, currently three brands of condoms of the Govt. and eleven brands of condoms of various distributing companies/ NGOs are sold in the market. Similarly for oral pill, one brand of the Govt. and seven brands of various distributing companies/ NGOs are sold.

Various marketing companies/ NGOs are participating in the social marketing programme. Their list and performance is given in Table 4 and 5

The performance of the Social Marketing Programme during the last three years is shown in the table 6

A weekly oral pill called Saheli to prevent pregnancy is also being subsidised by the Family Welfare Programme. The weekly oral pill is the result of indigenous research. It is non-steroidal.

The pill is now available in the market at Rs. 1.50 per tablet. The Government of India provides a subsidy of Rs. 1.60 per tablet (both product and promotional subsidy). It will be part of social marketing during 1999, all over.

Supply of laparoscopes and Tubal Rings

In order to maintain uniform quality of laparoscopes and Tubal Rings, this Ministry under the Laparoscopic Sterilisation programme procures and supplies these items to the States/ UTs. Laparoscopes are being provided to States/ UTs at the rate of 1.5 laparoscopes per team trained in laparoscopic sterilisation technique. Basically two brands of laparoscopic viz. KLI brand from USA and Karl Sorz brand from Germany are approved under' the programme and are provided to States/ UTs as per their preference. During the current financing year 50 laparoscopes of each brand have been procured and supplied in states/UTS.

No Scalpel Vasectomy (NSV)

Project

The UNFPA No-Scalpel Vasectomy project is being implemented in the country to promote male participation in the Family Welfare programme. Under the project, 1500 medical personnel all over the country are to be trained in the technique of No Scalpel Vasectomy.

Table 4

Performance of Social Marketing of condoms

Quantity in m. pcs

	1995-96	1996-97	1997-98
1. Hindustan Latex Ltd., Thiruvananthapuram.	17.49	115.38	169-84
2. World Pharma	-	17.10	31.70
3. Parivar Seva Sanstha, Delhi.	4.03	2.99	20.05
4. Population Services International, Delhi,	59.87	48.16	56.11
5. D.K.T India, Mumbai.	3.00	9.95	12.80
6. F.P.A.I., Mumbai.	-	2.00	-
7. M.P. State Civil Supplies Corp., Bhopal.		3.91	-
8. Janani, Patna.		-	7.29
9. Dey's Medical Store (Mfd) Ltd., Calcutta.			-
10. Eskag Pharma (Pvt.) Ltd., Calcutta.			-
11. Pashupati, Calcutta.			3.99
12. Parivar Kalyan Kendra, Panchkula.		-	3.49
13. R.B.D.F	53.12	63.76	19.15

14. Polar Latex Ltd.	4.984	-	-
15. JK Ltd.	4.966		
16. TTK	8.760		
17. LRC	.9968		
18. Brooke Bond	1.67	-	-
	162.92	263.25	324.40

Table 5

Sales of Mala D achieved by market companies
Under Social Marketing of Oral Pill Scheme 1995-96 to 1997-98

Quantity in Lakh Cycles

S.No.	Name of the Markets Company/ NGO	1995-96	1996-97	1997-98
1.	Hindustan Latex Ltd., Thiruvananthapuram.	18.00	13.70	40.03
2.	World Pharma, Indore	12-00	54.00	82.80
3.	Parivar Seva Sanstha, Delhi.	1.72	1.92	3.53
4.	Population Services International, Delhi.	3.33	2.65	9.87
5.	D.K.T India, Mumbai.	-	7.38	13.74
6.	F.P.A.I., Mumbai.		1.75	1.20
7.	Janani, Patna.	-	4.02	10.73
8.	Dey's Medical Store (Mfd) Ltd., Calcutta	52.57	40.70	48.13
9.	Eskag Pharma (Pvt.) Ltd., Calcutta.	0.36	0.43	2.00
10.	RBDF, Delhi	28.30	28.52	13.40
11.	Hoechst India, Mumbai	3.38	-	-
12.	Rallis India, Mumbai	27.14	7.35	2.97
		145.80	162.42	228.40

Table 6

Performance of Social Marketing Programme

	1995-96	1996-97	1997-98
Condoms (Million pieces)	162	262	324
Oral Pills (lakh cycles)	147	162	228

Ensuring the availability of this new procedure up to the peripheral level will help in crease the acceptance of male sterilisation and lead to increase contraceptive acceptance in the country. The total contribution by UNFPA for the projects is US$ 1,353,255. The contribution of the Government of India will be in the form of technical expertise provided by the Master Trainers in imparting training and making available the necessary infrastructure at the training cities.

No scalpel Vasectomy is one of the most effective contraceptive method for the male with practically no side effects/ complications. It is more effective than the pill or injectable and is an improvement on conventional Vasectomy.

NSV Training

The first training session to promote NSV in the country was held in January, 1998. Till date 53 training sessions have been held in the country. 23,829 acceptors have undergone No-Scalpel Vasectomy operations and 214 doctors trained in the techniques of No-Scalpel Vasectomy. 27 Medical Personnel have been certified as Trainers. These certified trainers are to take over the training of other medical personnel in their respective States.

NSV training has been held in the States of Andhra Pradesh, Orissa, Maharashtra, Haryana, Uttar Pradesh,

Tamil Nadu, West Bengal, Kerala, Sikkim, Himachal Pradesh and Rajasthan. NSV training courses are presently on in the States of Rajasthan.

The response to the No-Scalpel Vasectomy in general has been very good with men coming forward voluntarily to accept No-Scalpel Vasectomy. In Andhra Pradesh specially in Karim Nagar District there has been a reversal of trend from female sterilisation to male sterilisation. There are more cases of male coming forward to opt for sterilisation than female.

According to the information given by the district Medical and Health Officer, Karim Nagar, the number of NSVs done in the regular NSV sessions in the district since April 1998 to October 1998 are 17,759 as compared to 4863 of female sterilisation.

Centres of Excellence (COE)

The scheme was initiated in 1987 as an UNFPA assisted project with the technical guidance from Association of Voluntary Surgical Contraceptives. The objective was to train doctors in standards for Male and Female Sterilisation and to provide recanalisation services to those who require it, 16 COEs have been established under the project from 1987 in two phases.

Funding by UNFPA has since been stopped. For providing recananalisation services at the COEs, a provision of Rs. 20.00 lakhs has been kept for the Scheme during 1998-99. The training is to be carried out by the National Institute of Health and Family Welfare who will be disbursing the funds directly to the various COEs.

Performance of contraception

The performance in respect of the use of different family planning methods at National level during the year 1997-98 is summarised in the table 7.

Table 7

Achievements During 1997-98

(Figures in millions)

Sl. No.	Methods		Achievements 1997-98
1.	Sterilisation		4.13
	a.	Vasectomy	0.07
	b.	Tubectomy	4.06
2.	IUD Insertions		6.09
3.	Condom Users		16.73
	i.	Free distribution scheme	9.39
	ii.	Commercial distribution scheme	7.34
4.	Oral Pill Users		6.25
	i.	Free distribution scheme	3.49
	ii.	Commercial distribution scheme	2.76
	Total Acceptors		33.19$

The total number of acceptors of different family planning methods enrolled in the country during the year 1997-98 as per provisional performance figures available so far was 33.19 million.

Performance during the year 1998-99 (April to September, 1998) 9.6.3.1 From 1st April, 1996, the Family Welfare Programme is being implemented all over India on the basis of Target Free Approach and no targets have been fixed in respect of all the four family planning methods for the years 1996-97, 1997-98 and 1998-99.

Table 8 summarises the position in regard to family planning achievements during the year 1998-99 (up to September, 1998) in relation to the corresponding period of last year.

Table 8

Achievements during 1998-99
(April to September '98)

As compared to the corresponding period of 1997-98

(Figures in millions)

SI.	Methods	Achievement 1998-99 (Apr. to Sept. '98)	1997-98 (Corresponding period)	% Change in performance during 1998-99 over 1997-98
1.	Sterilisation	1.28	1.32	(-)2.5
2.	IUD Insertions	2.63	2.43	(+)8.3
3.	Condom Users (Eq.)	12.98	10.73	(+)21.0
	i. Free distribution scheme	8.07	7.87	(+)2.5
	ii. Commercial distribution scheme	4.91	2.86	(+)72.0
4.	Oral Pill Users (Eq.)	5.08	4.87	(+)4.3
	i. Free distribution scheme	3.04	2.94	(+)3.4
	H. Commercial distribution scheme	2.04	1.93	(+)5.7
Total Acceptors		21.98$	19.35	(+)13.6

Sterilisation Programme: A total of 4.13 million sterilisation operations (provisional figures) were performed in the country during 1997-98. The proportion of tubectomy acceptors to total sterilisation was 98.3%. Provisional figures for the year 1998-99 showed that a total of 1.28 million sterilisation operations were performed during the period April to September 1998.

IUD Programme: During 199798, a total of 6.09 million IUD insertions were done in the country. 2.63 million IUD insertions (provisional figures) were done during the year 1998-99 (April to September, 1998) at national level.

Condom Users: A total of 16.73 million Condom Users were enrolled during the year 1997-98. Under the free distribution scheme alone 9.39 million Condom Users were enrolled during the period under report. A total of 12.98 million Condom Users (Provisional figures) were enrolled during the period April to September 98 of the year 1998-99. Under the free distribution scheme alone 8.07 million Condom Users were enrolled during the period under report.

Oral Pills: A total of 6.25 million Users of Oral Pills were enrolled in the country. During the year 98-99 (April to September 1998) a total of 5.08 million users (provisional figures) of Oral Pills were enrolled in the country. Under the free distribution scheme alone 3.04 million Oral Pill Users were enrolled during the period under report.

Couples Protected: About 75.23 million couples (45.4 percent of the total eligible couples in the reproductive age group 15-44 years) were effectively protected against conception by one or the other approved Family Planning methods as of 31st March, 1998. Of these, 29.3 percent were protected by sterilisation alone. The States/Union Territories of Andhra Pradesh, Gujarat, Haryana, Karnataka, Kerala, Madhya Pradesh, Maharashtra, Punjab, Tamil Nadu, Himachal Pradesh and

Pondicherry have protected higher percentage of couples than the all India percentage (45.4 percent).

Medical Termination of Pregnancy (MTP): In 1997-98, a total of 4.00 lakhs medical termination of pregnancy (provisional figures) were done in the country.

During 1998-99 (up to June 1998) 0.82 lakhs terminations (provisional figures) were conducted at national level.

Since inception of the programme in April, 1972, 11.36 million terminations up to June 1998 were effected under MTP Act.

9

Organisation

In view of the federal nature of the Constitution, areas of operation have been divided between Union Government and State Governments. Seventh Schedule of Constitution describes three exhaustive lists of items, namely, Union List, State List and Concurrent List. Though some items like Public Health, Hospitals, Sanitation, etc. fall in the State List, the items having wider ramification at the national level have been included in the Concurrent List.

The Union Ministry of Health and Family Welfare is instrumental and responsible for implementation of various programmes of national importance like Family Welfare, Prevention and Control of major diseases etc. which form the main plank of our developmental efforts. Apart from these, the Ministry also assists the States in preventing and controlling the spread of outbreaks and epidemics through technical assistance.

In addition to centrally sponsored schemes, the Ministry has formulated and is implementing various World Bank assisted Projects for the control of AIDS, Malaria, Leprosy, T.B. and Blindness in designated areas through the States. The State Health System Projects are implemented through the State, but the Department of Health had facilitated the States in availing of external assistance. These Projects are currently under implementation in Andhra Pradeh, Karnataka, West

Bengal, Punjab and Orissa. All these Schemes aim at fulfilling the national commitment to improve access to health keeping in view the needs of rural areas and where the burden of disease is high.

The Union Ministry of Health & Family Welfare comprise of the following departments, each of which is headed by a Secretary to the Government of India: (i) Department of Health, (ii) Department of Family Welfare, and (iii) Department of Indian Systems of Medicine & Homoeopathy. Organisational Charts of Department of Health, Family Welfare and Indian Systems of Medicine & Homoeopathy are at Annexure I, II and III respectively

The Directorate General of Health Services, a repository of technical knowledge, is an attached office of this Ministry. The Organisational Chart of the Directorate General of Health Services is at Annexure-IV. The DGHS also renders technical advice on all medical and public health matters and in the implementation of various health schemes.

In order to implement the policies and programmes of the Ministry in an effective manner, there are three subordinate offices located at various places in the country which function directly under the Ministry. The Ministry is also administratively concerned with 29 autonomous/statutory bodies. There are also three Public Sector Undertakings under the administrative control of the Ministry.

Department of health

The Department of Health deals with medical and public health matters including drugs control and prevention of food adulteration. It is headed by a Secretary to the Government of India, who is supported by two Additional Secretaries.

Toning up the administration

The department has launched an all-out drive to improve the quality of work by cutting down delays, inefficiency and red-tapism. Efforts made during the previous years were sustained during the year and several steps were taken to ensure that Government policies and programmes are implemented not only in time but also efficiently. Administration has been toned up by enforcing discipline and accountability. Periodical reviews are being undertaken to monitor the quality and speed of implementation of various programmes, schemes etc. In this context Minister of State (Health and Family Welfare) has also taken reviews with all State Governments on a regional basis to monitor the implementation of various national programmes in the field and to obtain a first hand feed back from the States/Union Territories.

The Director incharge of Establishment has also been appointed as Director (Grievances) and Staff Grievances Officer in the Ministry for timely redressal of public grievances including pensioners and employees of the Ministry of Health and Family Welfare.

Towards a more transparent working, a computerised Information Facilitation Centre near Gate No. 5 of Nirman Bhawan was setup on 30.6.97. Information on activities of the Department of Health, Family Welfare, Directorate General of Health Services and Central Government Health Scheme is provided at the Centre. At present, information on the following areas is being provided from the Information Facilitation Centre:

- Status of medical re-imbursement claims under CGHS;
- Information pertaining to officers in the Ministry and their areas of responsibility;

- Citizens Charter for Central Govt. Hospitals;
- Approved Medical & Dental Colleges in the country;
- Programmes for N.G.Os.;
- National Health Programmes;
- Information relating to N.O.Cs to Doctors for studies abroad.

Central health service

The Central Health Service constituted in 1963 and subsequently restructured in 1982 provides medical manpower to various participating units like Directorate General of Health Services, Central Government Health Scheme, Government of NCT of Delhi, Department of Labour, Department of Posts and Assam Rifles etc. In the mean time, a number of participating units / States like ESIC, NDMC, MCD, Himachal Pradesh, Manipur, Tripura and Goa etc. having formed their own cadres, have gone out of this service. Simultaneously, some of the participating units like Central Government Health Scheme have expanded significantly. The Central Health Service now consists of the following four sub-cadres and the present strength of each sub-cadre is as under:

General Duty Medical Officer sub-cadre	3822
Teaching Specialists sub-cadre	626
Public Health Specialists	756
Sub-cadre	+13 (HAG)
Non-Teaching Specialists Sub-cadre	79

Dental Posts

Central Dental Posts Recruitment Rules were notified during the year.

Non-Medical scientists

During the year, out of the 66 cases received for consideration for grant of In-Situ promotion, 29 cases complete in all respects were forwarded to U.P.S.C. Necessary documents (Bio-data and ACRs) in respect of the remaining 37 officers were completed for processing their case for In-Situ promotion 4 officers of Specialist Gr. II of Non-Teaching sub-cadre of Central Health Service were confirmed 148 officers attended different training programmes organised by this Ministry for CHS officers.

Computerisation

Health Informatics Division of National Informatics Centre provides MIS and computer support to the Ministry of Health & Family Welfare and is running a full-fledged computer centre for this purpose in the Ministry of Health & Family Welfare, Nirman Bhavan.

LAN based on CAT5 UTP cabling has been installed in Nirman Bhavan in October,'98. High band width Radio Frequency link had been established and common mail & proxy servers had been installed in Nirman Bhavan for providing E-Mail and browsing the INTERNET for accessing the subject based data from the INTERNET. With the establishing of building-wise LAN, inter and intra-Ministry workflow applications can be made operational.

The computing facility is being provided through 90 dumb terminals- connected in the LAN through Local Terminal Servers and a UNIX based server. In addition, LAN support is provided to 100 Windows-based client systems, thus providing Wide Area Networking facility through NICNET.

The connectivity to NICNET provides all users of the Ministry, access to INTERNET and facility for national and international Electronic Mail. In addition, hardware and software support is provided for timely preparation of various documents of the Ministry. Salient features of the projects handled and their progress during the current year are given below:

Community Needs Assessment Approach in Family Welfare Programme: Community Needs Assessment Approach (CNAA) introduces decentralised planning in consultation with the community at the grass roots level to provide quality services under the Family Welfare Programme. An appropriate MIS at District level had been designed for monitoring and evaluation of the performance under CNAA and software had been prepared for installation in the District NIC Computer Centres.

Video Conferencing Facility: During this year, Video Conferencing Facility had been made available in Nirman Bhavan, for which the system and software had been installed in Room No. 145, A-wing, Nirman Bhavan. Through this facility, Video Conferencing can be done simultaneously with 8 sites. Presently, the facility is available in the Ministries in Delhi or in 14 sites within India including State capitals of major states as well as at the international level.

World Wide Web Page: A home page for the Ministry under URL address www. nic. in/mohfw exists on WWW. Currently, information related to the Department of Family Welfare, Department of Indian Systems of Medicine and Homoeopathy and National Aids Control Organisation is available on this page. Action is being taken to include the information related to the Department of Health.

Y2K compliance: Already this division is taking action for Y2K compliance by appropriate modification of the existing software released by this Division by April, 1999.

Computerisation Support to Department of ISM & H: Windows-NT based server had been installed to provide LAN in the Dept. of ISM & H at Red Cross Building. LAN will be established once the cabling work is over. NICNET connectivity and INTERNET access is being provided through dial-up modem.

MEDLARS Service: "Me Bibliographic Informatics; Division continued to provide bio-medical information from various international databases to the medical community in India, including the MEDLARS databases of National Library of Medicine, USA. A number of medical colleges/institutions have registered as MEDLARS User Centres to access the databases available at NIC. Information was also provided from other MEDLARS databases, CD-ROM databases as well as resources accessible over INTERNET. Information on EPIDEMIC DROPSY, compiled from MEDLINE, BIOSIS and CAB databases as well as full text of journal articles were given to the Minister for Health, Government of NCT of Delhi. This information was also provided to Director General, ICMR and Medical Superintendent, Dr. RML Hospital.

Bio-medical Peridicals: The coverage of the. InDMED database was expanded to include data from 77 Indian journals (1986 onwards) which were not available in international databases of this nature. The Union Catalogue of Bio-medical periodicals has been updated till November, 1998.

Training Activities: The training programmes at the Training Division of NIC Head quarters are extensively being used by the personnel of the Ministry. In addition, regular training programmes are given by this division in training the officers/staff of the Ministry in application softwares as well as in MS-Office software products, E-mail and INTERNET usage.

Accounting organisation

The chief Controller of Accounts heads the departmentalised accounting organisation of all the three Departments viz. The Department of Health, Department of Family Welfare and Department of Indian Systems of Medicine and Homoeopathy. With a network of 11 Pay & Accounts Offices located in Delhi and outstations, 56 Cheques Drawing DDOs and 73 Non Cheque Drawing DDOs located throughout the country, the accounting organisation prepares consolidated monthly and annual accounts of the entire Ministry. During the period upto 9/98, the PAOs cleared 48923 bills, 282 pension cases and 124 GPF final Payment cases.

There are 8 encadred posts of Accounts Officer in the Ministry and its attached and subordinate offices. The Internal Audit Organisation working under the supervision of C.C.A., carried out 122 fields inspections and conducted 2 special audits in JIPMER (Pondicherry) and GMSD (Mumbai). In annual Audit Review, many important points came into light and Divisions/Officers were suggested to imporve maintenance of their records related with money transactions, receipt/payments.

Close monitoring and review of receipt budget of the Ministry led to the recovery of Rs.45.58 crores during the year 1998-99 upto September 1998 against a total provision of Rs.58.88 crore. There is an increase of Rs. 11.37 crore in revenue receipts over the preceding year for the same period i.e. September 1997, which works out to 33.23%. Close monitoring has led to the reduction of pending utilisation certificates from 2199 to 1892 during the said period. The progress of plan expenditure by various divisions is also being monitored by this organisation closely.

10

Health Plans

In the last few decades, significant progress has been achieved in the direction of improving the health status of the people. This has been corroborated from the fact that the life expectancy in the country has increased to 62 years, Infant Mortality Rate has come down to 71 per thousand live births and death rate has been reduced to 8.9 per thousand of the population.

Department of Health is implementing National Health Programmes to control/eradicate major communicable and noncommunicable diseases like Malaria, Tuberculosis, Leprosy, Blindness, Cancer etc. Morbidity and mortality due to these diseases has been reduced substantially. Programmes are also being implemented for prevention and control of HIV/AIDS, control of Iodine Deficiency Disorders, Mental Health, Cardio-vascular diseases, Diabetes and rehabilitation of the medically disabled.

Schemes are also under implementation for strengthening of surveillance and epidemic response systems to prevent outbreak of infectious diseases. Plans for augmenting the emergency services in Central Government hospitals have been drawn up and are at various stages of implementation. Renovation and modernisation of institutions and organisations in the Central health sector have been planned through a project which aims at strengthening drug quality control, food safety, the medical store organisation and vaccine production centres.

The Outlay for Central Sector Health Programmes in the Annual Plan 199899 is Rs. 1145.20 Crore including an external aid component of Rs.524 crore against the total outlay of Rs.920.20 crore (including Rs.400 crore as external aid) for the year 1997-98. A major portion of outlay is for the National Health Programmes for the control of communicable diseases implemented through Centrally Sponsored Schemes. In a number of projects external assistance has been availed of and is being further sought so that in critical areas, the Centre can assist the States in the containment and eradication of diseases. During the Annual Plan 1998-99, following allocations have been made under Centrally Sponsored Schemes.

(Rs. in Crore)

Item	Outlay approved for 1998-99
Control of Communicable Diseases	687.50
Food and Drug Administration	4.50
Total	692.00

Another major component of the Central Sector Health Programme relates to purely Central Schemes through which financial assistance is given to Central institutions engaged in various health-related activities. These institutions are responsible for contribution in the field of control of communicable and non-communicable diseases, medical education, training, research and patient-care. During the Annual Plan 1998-99, following allocations have been made under Purely Central Sector Schemes:

(Rs. in Crore)

Items	Outlay approved for 1998-99
Rural Health Training Centre, Najafgarh	0.80
Institutions for Control of Communicable Diseases	24.97
Control /Containment of Non-Communicable Diseases	39.35
Hospitals and dispensaries	57.14
Institutions dealing with Medical Education, Training and Research	254.61
Other Programmes	76.33
Total	453.20

Financial assistance to voluntary organisations

In order to promote outreach services in rural and high density urban slum population of the country, the Government of India have been giving financial assistance to the voluntary organisations for encouraging them to set up new hospitals/dispensaries in rural areas or to expand and improve the existing hospital facilities. Financial assistance is available under the following grant-in-aid schemes:-

- Scheme for Improvement of Medical Services;
- Promotion and Development of Voluntary Blood Donation Programme; and
- Special Health Scheme for Rural Areas.

The upper ceiling of grants available under the grant-in-aid schemes are as follows: -

- Improvement of Medical Services (w.e.f. 1-4-1992): Rs. 4.00 lakh for purchase of hospital equipment and/or for construction.
- Promotion & Development of Voluntary Blood Donation Programme. (w.e.f. 29.3.1989): Non-recurring-Rs. 1.00 lakh for purchase of mobile van.. Recurring—Rs. 15,000/- in the first year and Rs. 10,000/ in subsequent years.
- Special Health Scheme for Rural areas (w.e.f. 1.4.1992): Rs. 8.00 lakh for construction of hospital building, O.T. etc. and Rs. 4.00 lakh for purchase of hospital equipment.
- Grant-in-aid amounting to Rs. 17.74 lakh have been released to 7 Voluntary Organisations during 1997-98. During the current financial year, i.e. 1998-99 upto October 1998 an amount of Rs. 2.00 lakh has been released to one voluntary organisation.

Audit inspection report

As per information received upto 31st March 1998 from various Accountant General and Director General of Audit, Central Revenues, the number of audit objections, and the no. of paras from the Audit Inspection Reports on the accounts of the Department of Health and its attached and subordinate outstanding as on 31.3.1998 were as under:

(a) Inspection Reports	425
(b) Audit Paras	2508

All efforts are continued to be made to settle the outstanding objections and audit Inspection report paragraphs.

Utilization Certificates:

The Certificate of Utilisation of Grants is required to be furnished in respect of giants released to the two statutory bodies, non-government organisations etc. The purpose of furnishing the utilization certificates is to ensure that grants have been properly utilized for the purpose for which they were sanctioned and where grants released were conditional, the prescribed conditions have been fulfilled. The certificates are required to be submitted by the sanctioning authorities not later that 18 months from the date of sanction of the grant.

Close monitoring has led to submission of 429 utilisation certificates of composite amount of Rs. 58.85 crore in respect of Department of Family Welfare and 266 utilisation certificates of composite amount of Rs. 222.38 crore in respect of Department of Health during 1997-98.

Health minister's discretionary grant

Financial assistance to the poor and indigent patients is given from the Health Minister's Discretionary Grant to defray a part of the expenditure on hospitalisation/ treatment in cases where free medical facilities are not available. During 1997-98, assistance totaling Rs. 47.00 lakh was given to 300 individuals. A provision of Rs. 50.00 lakh has been made during the financial year 1998-99. The upper ceiling of grant under the scheme has been raised from Rs. 10,000/- to Rs. 20,000/- in each case. A sum of Rs. 21.69 lakh has already been released upto 31st October, 1998 to 139 patients.

National Illness Assistance Fund

National Illness Assistance Fund has been set up vide Resolution No. F.7-2/96-F.II dated 13.01.97 with an initial contribution of Rs. 5 crore. Some of the State Govts.UTs, viz., Karnataka, Madhya Pradesh, Tripura, NCT of Delhi, Andhra Pradesh, Tamil Nadu, Himachal Pradesh and Jammu and Kashmir have also set up State Illness Assistance Funds during 199697, 1997-98 and those

States/UTs were released grant-in-aid as admissible to them.

The scheme was reviewed during January, 1998 and it was decided that Medical Superintendents of 3 Central Government Hospitals in Delhi and 3 Institutes of national repute, viz., ARMS, New Delhi, PGIMER, Chandigarh and JIPMER, Pondicherry may be sanctioned an Amount of Rs. 10 lakh each from NIAF to provide financial assistance to patients availing treatment in these hospitals/institutions and living below the poverty line, of an amount not exceeding Rs. 25,000/ in each case.

Grant-in-aid has been released to the following States during 1998-99:

West Bengal	Rs. .5 crore
Maharashtra	Rs. 2 crore

Financial assistance of Rs. 50 lakh were~ also sanctioned to the following UTs (without legislature) during the year. (i) U.T. of Lakshadweep (ii) U.T. of Daman & Diu (iii) U.T. of Dadra & Nagar Haveli

Other States/Union Territories have been requested to set up the Fund, as early as possible. The first meeting of the Managing Committee of NIAF was held on 21.10.98 under the Chairmanship of the Union Health Minister.

11

Food Processing Industries

Education was one of the goals of the India's freedom movement and Mahatma Gandhi, even while leading the epic struggle against colonial power, evolved an alternative, community based system of education. Rooted in the struggle for Independence, several articles in the Constitution of India bring into focus the general principles governing educational development in the country. At the time of Independence in 1947 India inherited an educational system which was not only quantitatively small but was also characterized by striking regional and structural imbalances. Only 14 per cent of the population was literate and only one child out of three had been enroled in primary school. The low levels of enrolment and literacy were compounded by acute regional and gender disparities. Recognizing that education is vitally linked with the totality of the development process, the reform and restructuring of the educational system was accepted as an important area of state intervention.

Accordingly, the need for a literate population and universal education for all children in the 6-14 age group was provided with a precisely defined and delineated framework in the Indian Constitution as well as in successive Five Year Plans. The Constitution makes an elaborate legislative, administrative and financial distribution of powers between the state governments and the union government. Decisions regarding the organisation and structure of education are largely the concern of the states. Within the overall policy framework, each state determines independently the educational structures to be adopted. However, the Union GOvernment has clear responsibility regarding the quality and character of education.

The Central Advisory Board of Education (CABE), set up during the pre-Independence period in 1935, continues to play a lead role in the evolution and monitoring of educational policies and programmes, the most notable of which are the National Policy (NPE), 1986, Programme of Action (POA), 1986, and a revised NPE and POA (1992).

In addition to policy formulation, the Department of Education shares with the states the responsibility for educational planning. Till the Sixth Plan, education was taken to be a social service rather than an imput in the development process. But now education is considered pivotal in social and economic development through development of human resources.This is reflected in the National Policy on Education, 1986 and in the budgetary allocation of resources. The Eighth Plan outlay for education (Centre and states) at Rs. 19,599.7 crore is higher than the Seventh Plan expenditure of Rs. 7,633.1 crore by 2.6 times. In keeping with this set up, the Central plan outlay for education has been substantially increased from Rs. 1,541 crore in 1994-95 to Rs. 1,825 crore in 1995-96. There has also been an *inter se* shift in the allocation of resources within the education sector from higher education to elementary education. The outlay on elementary education is up by 24.5 per cent to Rs. 651.04 crore in 1995-96. Further the outlay consists of Rs. 409.11 crore for secondary and physical education, Rs. 245.55 crore for university and higher education, Rs. 234 crore for adult education and Rs. 253.41 crore for technical education. Plan expenditure on different sectors of education (percentage) is given in table 1.

The National Policy on Education (NPE) 1986, a landmark in the educational development of the country was reviewed by a committee under the Chairmanship of Acharya Ramamurthi in 1990. Its recommendations were considered by the Central Advisory Board of Education (CABE) Committee on Policy under the Chairmanship of Shri N.Janaradhan Reddy, then Chief Minister, Andhra Pradesh which submitted its report on 22 January 1992. The Report was considered by the CABE which recommended certain modifications. Consequently, a Revised Policy Formulations containing the modifications recommended by the CABE were tabled in the Parliament on 7 May 1992. Subsequently, a revised Programme of Action (POA) was prepared to opertionalise the policy and the revised POA, 1992 was tabled in the Parliament on 19 August 1992.

Five thrust areas viz,. adult literacy, primary education, decentralisation of management of education, vocational education and technical education, have been identified to achieve Universalisation of Elementary Education to make education relevant to the needs of the community and also to meet new challenges of liberalisation and globalisation of the economy.

Education

- Our system of elementary education is the second largest in the world with 151 million children enrolled in 1994-95 in the age group of 6-14 years covering about 91 per cent of the children in this age group.

- The number of primary schools increased substantially from 2.10 lakh in 1950 51 to 5.90 lakh in 1995-96. During the same period, the number of upper schools rose from 0.14 lakh to 1.71 lakh. The Gross Enrolment Ratio (GER) in the primary stage (classes I-V) increased from 42.6 per cent in 1950-51 to 104.3 per cent in 1995-96 and in the upper primary stage (classes VI-VIII) from 12.7 per cent to 67.6 per cent. These changes have contributed in raising the overall literacy rate from 18.3 per cent in 1951 to 52.2 per cent in 1991.

- What is equally important at this stage is that concerted efforts are required for raising the GER at the primary stage in States like Bihar, Haryana and Uttar Pradesh which are having GERs of less than 90 per cent. This would help in raising the literacy levels in these States.

- The affirmative policies of the Government have helped in raising the enrolment of Scheduled Castes (SCs) and Scheduled Tribes (STs) considerably as was mentioned in the Economic Survey 1995-96. The participation of SCs and STs in now more or less primary level. Dropouts, though declining over the years, are significantly large. Gender disparities are also very conspicuous among SCs and STs.

- The total Literacy Campaign has become the principal strategy of the Naitonal Literacy Mission (NLM) in the eradication of illiteracy throughout the country. The target for achieving the total literacy is now 2005 A.D. As December 1996, 417 districts have been covered either fully or partially under the Total Literacy Campaign. Similarly, 178 districts have also been covered under the Post Literacy Campaign. Under all the schemes of NLM, 57.96 million persons have so far been made literate as per NLM norms against an enrolment of 96.80 million. The new scheme of Continuing Education for neo-literates (approved in December, 1995) is now under implementation.

- In view of the importance of the National Programme of Nutritional Support to primary education (Mid-Day Meal Programme) which was launched from 15th August, 1995 for boosting universalisation of education and improving the nutritional level of students in primary classes (I-VI), the Central Plan allocation has been raised from about 612 crore in 1995-96 (RE) to Rs.1400 crore in 1996-97 (BE). The Central support under this programme is on the following:

— Provision of foodgrains free of cost to the implementing agencies.

— Reimbursement to District authorities for transportation cost for moving of foodgrains from Food Corporation of India's godowns to schools/ villages at the rate of Rs.25 per quintal as applicable under Revamped Public Distribution System.

— Remuneration for conversion of foodgrains into cooked food as well as expenditure on construction of kitchen sheds will be eligible for coverage under the poverty alleviation schemes being administered by the Ministry of Rural Development.

- The Mid-Day Meal Programme has commenced in all the States/UTs. Seven States, namely, Gujarat, Haryana, Jammu & Kashmir, Kerala, Madhya Pradesh, Orissa and Tamil Nadu and UT of Pondicherry are serving cooked meals. In rest of the States/UTs foodgrains are being distributed.

- The District Primary Education Programme (DPEP) introduced in 1994 is the most intensive effort by the Central Government to operationalise the strategy of deccentralised planning for Universal Elementary Education (UEE) as envisaged by the National Policy on Education, 1986. This has been in operation in 59 districts of eleven States of Andhra Pradesh, Assam, Gujarat, Himachal Pradesh, Haryana, Karnataka, Kerala, Madhy Pradesh, Maharashtra, Orissa and tamil Nadu, DPEP is funded by multiple external agencies including the World Bank and the European Commission.

- The Central Plan outlay for DPEP has been raised substantially from Rs.25 crore in 1995-96 (Be) to about Rs.239 crore n 1996-97(BE).

- With a view to bringing the benefits of Techno-Economic advances and large scale investments in the Technical Education Systen to the poorest of the poor in the country, the Government has been running an institutionalised and structured scheme of Community Polytechnics functioning all over the country. This alongwith its extension centres in remote/inaccessible areas provides a delivery capacity comparable to that of the committed voluntary organisations. The network of Community Polytechnics. A large number of villagers have also been benefitted through transer of technology these institutions.

- The share of both Central and State Governments including local bodies, etc. in financing educational institutions to be quite high. It accounted for 92.9 per cent of the total income of educational institutions in 1990-91, whereas the share from fees and endowments and other sources of educational institutions declined sharply.

- While the Central Government plays an important role for overall policy directions in education and funding of centrally sponsored plan schemes, the State Governments provide most of the funding for education system. There is, therefore, an urgent need for State Governments to re-prioritise expenditure and tighten fiscal discipline. Private initative s in education may be encouraged for supplementing the public resources. Further, resources must be mobilised by revising fees and other user charges especially for higher levels of education.

According to the 1991 Census, the national literacy rate

for the population aged seven years and above, increased form 43.56 per cent in 1981 to 52.21 per cent in 1991 registering an increases by 8.65 percentage points. While the male literacy increased by 13.10 per cent, the female literacy rate increased by 6.45 per cent. The number of literates aged seven and above in 1991 at 3,593 lakh compares very well with the number of literates at 2,357 lakh in 1981. The number of illiterates in 1991 was 3,289 lakh which is a marginal increase form the 3,053 lakh in 1981. The increase in the number of literates in 1991 over 1981 was 1,236 lakh whereas the corresponding increase in the number of illiterates was 236 lakh only. Kerala (89.81 per cent) tops the literacy rate followed by Mizoram (82.27 per cent), Lakshadweep (81.78 per cent) and Chandigarh (77.81 per cent). At the end of the ladder are Bihar (38.48 per cent), Rajasthan (38.55 per cent) and Dadra and Nagar Haveli (40.71 per cent). The increase in female literacy rate has been very significant in the states/union territory–Sikkim (19.29 per cent), Lakshadweep (17.59 per cent), Nagaland (14.45 per cent), * Manipur (13 per cent), Andaman and Nicobar Islands (12.26 per cent), Pondicherry (12.63 per cent), Tripura (11.65 per cent) and Kerala (10.47 per cent). The literacy rate is above the all India level of 52.21 per cent in case of 22 states/union territories but nine states/union territories *viz.*, Bihar, Rajasthan, Arunachal Pradesh, Madhya Pradesh, Uttar Pradesh, AndhraPradesh, Meghalaya, Orissa and Union Territory of Dadra and Nagar haveli are still below the threshold level of literacy i.e. 50 per cent. All these states/ union territories except Meghalaya are also below the all India level in case of female literacy.

The National Policy for Education document recognised that the educational structure had not been able to address traditional gender imbalances on educational achievement and that women and girls continued to have low levels of literacy and be marginalised form development. The NPE document made a strong commitment to 'a well conceived edge in favour of women' as 'an act of faith and social engineering'. These commitments have been translated into concrete guidelines, and have resulted in a number of interventions which focus on the empowerment of women as the critical precondition for their participation in the educational process. The impact of these programmes is reflected in the decennial growth rate in female literacy of 9.54 per cent (Census 1991) which is significantly higher than the corresponding figure for males (7.76 per cent).

The following special provisions for women have been incorporated in the existing schemes: (i) The Operation Blackboard scheme now provides that atleast 50 per cent of the teachers recruited in the future should be women. Out of the 1,13,259 posts of the teachers filled under the OB scheme, 48.60 per cent are by women; (ii) An innovative approach taken up in Rajasthan to improve access to education is the Shiksha Karmi Project. It envisaged substitution of the primary school teacher in single teacher schools by a team of two locally resident educational workers called *Shiksha Karmis*, of whom 10.2 per cent are women; (iii) Under the scheme of Non-Formal Education, 90 per cent assistance is given for NFE centres exclusively for girls. The scheme has recently been revised so as to provide more facilities for educating girls by increasing the ratio of NFE Centres exclusively for girls from 25 per cent to 40 per cent of the total; (iv) Efforts are being made to ensure that at least one third of the students in each Navodaya Vidyalaya are girls. In Navodaya Vidayalayas and Kendriya Vidyalayas, free education is imparted to girls up to class XII; (v) Free education is provided to girls upto class VIII in Punjab (Government schoold), Manipur, Rajasthan (Government schools), UP, Delhi, Meghalaya and Chandigarh and upto secondaryd stage in Andhra Pradesh, Assam, Bihar (Government schools), Himachal Pradesh (Government schools), Karnataka., Tamilnadu (Government schools),

Mizoram and Lakshadweep and upto senior secondary stage Class XII in the states of Arunachal Pradesh, Goa, J&K, Kerala, Sikkin (Government schools), Tripura, West Bengal, A&N Islands, D&N Haveli, Daman and Diu, Pondicherry, Gujarat and Madhya Pradesh; (vi) Under the Centrally-sponsored programme at +2 level vocational programmes with emphasis on enterpreneurhsip are being designed to cater to the needs of girls who drop out of schools. Efforts are also on to consciously encourage participation of girls in the nontraditional and emergent technologies; (vii) Womwn's education at the university and college levels have been diversified and reoriented in tune with the changing requirement of society, industry and trade. The number of women enrolled in institutions of higher education increased from 40,00 in 1950-51 to about 16,64,000 in 1993-94, an increase of more than 41 times over the 43 year period; (viii) The enrolment of women students at the beginning of the year 1993-94 was 15.90 lakh as against 15.12 lakh in the previous year. At the post-graduate level the enrolment of women was 34.09 per cent of the total enrolment; (ix) The UGC has been providing assistance to universties for undertaking research projects in women's studies; a number of research projects have been approved for assistance. Also assistance has been provided to 22 universities and 11 colleges for setting up women's studies/ cells. The UGC has also created * and (x) The participation of women in technical and professional streams has also showna marked increase from a little over 6,000 in 1950-51 to 1.46 lakh in 1986-87, an increase of 23 times. There was also noticeable growth in the number of women students in the engineering an technology streams (in IITs and Polytechics). As against 40 women students in 1950-51 (0.3 per cent) it rose to 16.67 thousand in 1986-87 (7.7 per cent) and 78.3 thousand in 1993-94 (13.1 per cent).

Mahila Samakhya Programme (Education for Women's Equality) is a Dutch assisted project which is spread over

14 districts of Uttar Pradesh, Karnataka, Gujarat and Andhra Pradesh. Mahila Samakhya is a women's empowerment project which does not aim at service delivery but seeks to bring about a change in women's perception about themselves and that of society in regard to women's traditional roles. It endeavours to create an environment for women to seek knowledge and information in order to make informed choices and create circumstances in which women can learn at their own pace and rhythm. The centrality of education in the struggle to achieve equality is an important focus of Mahila Samakhya.

The Cabinet has approved the continuation and expansion of the Mahila Samkhya Project during 1992-97. The total outlay over 1992-97 is Rs. 51.29 crore.

Sainik schools prepare boys academically and physically for entry into National Defence Academy. There are 18 sainik schools in the country, one in each state, except in Nagaland, Meghalaya, Tripura, Sikkim, Arunachal Pradesh, Mizoram and Goa. These schools are affiliated to the Central Board of Secondary Education and follow the 10+2 pattern, in science stream.

Admission is made to class VI on the basis of an all-India entrance examination held every year in February, in which boys in the age group of 10-11 years are eligible to appear. From 1992-93 academic session lateral admission to class IX has also been started for which the boys have to be 13-14 years of age on 1st July of that year. Since its inception, a total of 4,647 boys from these schools were selected for admission to the National Defence Academy, Naval Academy, Armed Forces Medical College etc.

The National Defence Academy (NDA), Khadakwasla, is a Joint Services Training Institution which imparts academic as well as service training.

The NDA has been brought in step with the national education format of 10+2+3. The syllabus of the Academy was reviewed to meet these requirements and has been approved by the Jawaharlal Nehru University for the grant of BA/B.Sc degree, at the time of passing out from Academy. the first course commenced training on revised syllabi in January 1989. After passing out from the NDA, the cadets go to their respective service acadmies for further training before being commissioned as officers in the Armed Forces. The present authorised training strength of the Army, Navy and Air Force cadets at the Academy is 1,800. This includes cadets from Bhutan and other friendly countries on as required basis.

The Indian Military Academy (IMA), Dehra Dun caters for training of cadets for commission into the Army. Cadets join the Indian Military Academy as per the following modes of entry: (a) on passing out from NDA, (b) on graduation from the Army Cadet College which is a wing of the IMA itself, (c) Direct entry graduate cadets who join on qualifying at the Union Public Service Commission Examination and the Services Selection Board, and (d) Technical graduates and University Entry Scheme. The present authorised strength of trainees at the IMA is 1,200 which includes cadets from Bhutan, Shri Lanka, Maldives, Mauritius and Nepal. The authorised training strength of Army Cadet College is 450.

The Officers Training Academy (OTA), Madras imparts pre-commission training for the following type of courses, (a) Short Service Commission Course of 44 weeks for university graduates who quality in the Union Public Service Commission; (b) course of six months for lady cadets (Women Special Entry Scheme); (c) Permanent Commission on Special List (PC) (SL) to selected service candidates, who qualify after a training of four weeks and (d) Regimental

Commission Course for selected service candidates, who qualify after a training of 13 weeks duration. Authorised training strength of the Academy is 500. So far 50 lady cadets have been granted Short Service Commission.

Education on public school lines is imparted at the Rashtriya Indian Military College (RIMC), Dehradun principally for the boys who subsequently desire to join the NDA with a view to obtaining a commission in the Armed Forces. The College runs classes from eighth to 10+2 class. Selection for the RIMC is through a written examination cum *viva voce* conducted through the state governments. Seats for the respective states are reserved, based on population. Intake into the RIMC is bi-annual.

Inaugurated by Pandit Nehru in 1960, the National Defence College is an Inter-Service Organisation functioning under the Ministry of Defence. The NDC is the highest defence institution in India imparting instructions on all elements of national security and strategy to officers due to become Major Generals and equivalent and attain similar status in the Civil Service. The aim is to equip these policy makers with the necessary background and understanding of the total system of economic, political, military, scientific, international relations, national organisational aspects and the planning necessary for national security, both in its internal dynamics as well as the external comulsions. The head of the College is the Commandant, with five faculty members from the Army, Navy, Air Force, IAS, IFS and an administrative staff.

Army Cadet College is a Wing of IMA which caters for the training of service cadets selected for commission. The academic format is similar to the NDA on the lines of 10+2+3, and the syllabus is common. On completion of the course these cadets also qualify for a BA/BSc degree recognised by the Jawaharlal Nehra University.

The College of Combat, Mhow conducts the higher command, senior command and junior command courses for Army officers. It also conducts a Combined Operational Review and Evaluation (CORE) programme for selected senior officers of the rank of Major General and equivalent of the three Services once every year. College of Military Engineering, Kirkee (Pune), imparts training to the officers and other ranks in all aspects of military engineering. Long courses of over two years duration are also conducted to train officers up to degree standards. Military College of Telecommunication Engineering, Mhow imparts basic and advanced technical training in telecommunications and signal tactics. Armoured Corps Centre and School, Ahmednagar, conducts training in tactical handling of armoured fighting vehicles, driving and maintenance. School of Artillery, Deolali, provides training in field branch artillery. The Air Defence Guided Missiles School at Gopalpuron-sea trains personnel of the Air Defence Artillery. The High Altitude Warfare School located at Gulmarg and Sonmarg train personnel in the art of mountain warfare including rock, snow and ice-craft. The Counter Insurgency and General Warfare School, Viairengate, trains officers and men in the art of combating insurgency.

Mechanised Infantry Regimental Centre conducts basic and technical training for recruits of mechanised infantry. In addition, it runs basic and instructor courses on anti-tank guided missiles for officers, JCOs and other ranks of mechanised infantry. It also carries out conversion training of units when they are converted to mechanised infantry or when change in equipment is involved. College of Materials Management, Jabalpur, imparts specialised training in materials management including ammunition and explosives and also in contemporary materials management techniques. Some of the other Army training centres and schools are Army Service Corps School, Bareilly; EME School, Vadodara; Military College of Electronics and Mechanical

Engineering, Secunderabad; College of Defence Management, Secunderabad; Remount and Veterinary Corps Centre and School, Meerut; Army Eucation Corps Training College and Centre, Pachmari; Army School Physical Training, Pune; Army/Air Transport School, Agra; Military Intelligence Training School and Depot, Pune; Army School of Mechanical Transport, Bangalore; Corps of Military Police Centre and School, Bangalore; Institute of Military Law, Kamptee; Armed Forces Medical College Pune; Institute of National Integration, Pune and Army Medical Corps Centre and School, Lucknow.

There are more than 60 million youth out of schools and an additional 30 million youth in the age—group of 18 to 30 yearrs who had missed an educational opportunity. A large number of girls, children and youth from SC, ST and minority communities, specially from the rural areas, drop out of schools due to poor economic condition, social tabbos or their inability to cope up with the rigid demands of the formal education. These school drop—outs take to unskilled wage employment or become engaged in house—hold work. Only a flexible, life related programme of education delivered at the door steps can provide a fresh learning opportunity for them.

There has been a significant increase in the number of Secondary and increase in the number of Secondary and Senior Secondary schools and in enrolment during the period from 1987—88 to 1990—91. During this period enrolment at Secondary stage increased by 16.8 per cent and at the Senior Secondary stage by 17.6 per cent. The number of Secondary schools increased from 54,845 in 19987—88 to 59,468 in 1990—91; corresponding figures for Senior Secondary schools are 16,460 and 19,151 respectively. The ratio between Secondary schools and Primary schools had declined from 1:1.98 in 1987—88 to 1:1.86 in 1990—91.

Still there are unserved areas in the country where there is no school for 10 to 20 kms. like in some tribal areas, desert or hilly areas. An area may also be unserved due to geographical barriers like river or mountain. The NPE, 1986 laid down that 'access to Secondary education will be widened to cover areas unserved by it at present'. The target is by 2000 A.D. the unserved areas will be fully served.

Gender disparities in enrolments are significant. In 1990–91 girls accounted for 33.4 per cent of the enrolment at the Secondary stage and 32 per cent at the Senior Secondary stage. SCs accounted for 11.85 per cent at the Secondary stage and 9.7 per cent at the Secondary stage and 9.7 per cent at the Senior Secondary stage; corresponding figures for STs were 4.21 per cent and 3 per cent respectively. The girls, SCs and STs lag behind in enrolment to Secondary and Senior Secondary schools.

Inspite of spending an average of 22 per cent of the State budget on education, the formal schools can accomodate only about 35 per cent youth. Improvement in literacy rates has brought about a significant increase in enrolment in Elementary schools. A few years from now, the doors of Secondary schools too would be knocked. The States, even with an enhanced budget would not be able to expand the numbers of schools for the remaining 65 per cent. It is only open schooling then can serve marginalised groups, rural and urban poor and people in dispersed habitations. National Open Schooling (NOS) has been set up to design, develop and offer a flexible, life—oriented programme through distance education, in 1989 by the Government of India, Ministry of HRD, in pursuance of the NPE 1986, as an autonomous instituion. The task of NOS is universalization of education and special concern is the education of girls and women, rural youth, working men and women, SC and ST, handicapped and other disadvantaged groups.

The NOS provides the following programmes:

— Foundation Programme—This course is for those who have discountinued education after 4 or 5 years of primary education. The course is equivalent to VIII standard and serves as a foundation or 'bridge' course for Secondary education. It comprises subjects such as Hindi, English, Mathematics, Science and Social Science.

— Secondary Education Programme—This course is offered to those who are desirous of completing 10th level education. The course comporises subjects like Hindi, English, Mathematics, science, Social Sciences Economics, Commerce, Home Science and Typewriting.

— Senior Secondary Education Programme—This course is offered to those who like to complete 12th level education. It includes wide range of subjects such as Hndi, English, Mathemetics, Physics, Chemistry, Biology, History, Geography, Political Science, Economics, Commerce, Accountancy, Home Science, Typewriting, Stenography and Secretarial Practice.

— Vocational Education Programme—Several vocational courses such as Refrigeration & Air Conditioning, Electrical Technician, Radio & TV repairing, Plumbing, Library Science, Tailoring, Beauty Culture either independently or in combination with the subjects in Secondary and Seniior Secondary courses.

— Life Enrichment Programmes—A few life enrichment programmes in Women's development, Community Health, Educational Technology, Institutional Management, Interactive Learning, Computor Applications, etc., are being planned to teachers, principals, executives in public and private sectors.

The distinctive feature of NOS are as follows:

— Students can learn at one's own speed and will

have a period of 5 years and 9 chances to complete. He/she can also pass one subject at a time.

— Students can choose any subject combination like Science and Business Studies at Secondary level: History, Chemistry and Accountancy at Senior Secondary level.

— Student can earn credit collectively in all subjects for final certification.

— Student can know his/her continuous progress through Tutor Marked Assignments (TMAs).

— NOS offers programmes through distance education mode involving printed self learning materials, audio and video programmes, personal contact programmes in Accredited Institutions (AIs) or Study Centres.

— After the completion of NOS one can seek admission to the regular Colleges or Universities that have recognized its certificate. He/she can also take graduate course from open universities in Maharashtra, Andhra Pradesh, Rajasthan or IGNOU.

— Standard of education in NOS has been recognized by 12 State Boards okf Secondary Education. Its Senior Secondary Certificate is recognized by Association of Indian Universities and 73 Universities including IITs and Agricultural Universities.

There are regional variations in NOS enrolment. From Delhi and other northern states, it is 65 per cent. The enrolment from the eastern region is about 18 per cent while from north—eastern states it is 7 per cent. The enrolment from western and southern regions are 7 per cent 3 per cent respectively.

Nearly 57 per cent of NOS students are from marginalised groups, of which 38 per cent are girls and women and 19 per cent are SCs and STs.

Admission is open to all, twice during the year. There is no upper age limit in NOS. There are 353 Study Centres/ accredited Institutions (AIs) all over the country.

A student in NOS is a self–learner. For this specially printed self–instructional materials will be provided on different subjects. Also other support materials like audio cassettes, practical manuals, glossaries and study guides will be provided. Medium of instruction will be Hindi or English. Students are required to get pass marks is in 5 subjects with 1 or 2 languages for both Secondary and Senior Courses.

Contact sessions will be organised in the Accredited Institutions (AIs) on weekends and holidays. About 30 such contact sessions will be organized per subject in one academic year.

In these sessions students are expected to:

— Clear doubts and problems that they have faced while covering the syllabus.

— listen oto audio tapes;

— view video films;

— perform practicals in Science and other related subjects;

— get tutoring in specific and difficult concepts/areas;

— get assignments corrected by the AI teachers;

— discuss study problems, assignments with other students in groups; and

— meet other learners and form study groups.

The AIs will serve as study centre. Students have to go to AIs for—

— submitting application form with admission fees/ documents;

— receiving study materials and identity cards;

— attending contact classes;

— finding out the dates of payment of fees, examination date sheet;

— knowing results of public examination;

— collection of marksheet, pass certificate and migration certificate;

— change of subject(s) or additional subject;

— corrections in names, subjects and other particulars, etc.

NOS is authorized by; the Government of India to conduct Secondary and Senior Secondary examinations and issue certificates. The examinations are conducted twice a year in more than 250 centres spread all over the country.

Of the total 100 marks in each paper, 20 per cent weightage is given to continuous assessment in the form of Tutor Marked Assignments. Another 15 per cent marks are allotted to practical examinations in certain subjects. The remaining marks are for the end—of—the course public examinations.

Students are free to appear in one or more subjects at a time. The marks are retained in the computerized credit banks. He/she gets the certificate on earning the total requisite credit in 9 examinations over 5 years. NOS will also allow for improvement of performance in already passed subject, but only once.

Students pay a fees of Rs. 150, Rs. 650 and Rs. 775 to the Foundation, the Secondary and Senior Secondary courses respectively. To encourage education of girls, SC, ST and handicapped students a special concession is allowed. The fee includes the cost of the study materials, about 30 classes in each subject, audio and video programmes and a year's subscription to the magazine. When compared to the estimated cost of Rs. 3000 per student for Secondary and Senior Secondary courses in formal school, the education in NOS is cost effective. For every one student in the formal system, 4 to 5 students can be served by the open learning system.

NOS has an annual budget of more than ten crore. It generates about 95 per cent of its revenue through students' fees. The Government of India provides recurring cost (5 per cent) and full development cost. The Government share is about 30 per cent of the total budget compared to more than 90 per cent salary cost in formal education, the total administrative cost in NOS is about 15 per cent the rest is spent on academic activities.

In order to disseminate Foundation and Secondary education, it is necessary to impart education through regional languages. In a recent need assessment survey, 20 open schools have been suggested. These open schools have come up in A.P., Haryana, T.N., and Karnataka. Proposals from several other States are in active consideration. NOS will provide academic and technical support to such open schools.

NOS is a national apex institution in open learning. A network of 20 to 25 State Open Schools along with NOS can provide education to 2.5 crore youth and adults. The multichannel learning, maintenance of quality of instructional process and the inherent flexibility make open schooling an acceptable complement to formal education, and a strategy in universalization of education. Open schooling would, thus, udoubtedly schooling would, thus, undoubtedly trigger new hopes in the lives of those who have lost hope.

We in India have to re-structure education at all levels by introducing the credit and semester system which will offer the kind of flexibility and choice for students to opt for particular subjects. This freedom to choose from a list of course offerings will give students a chance to learn many optional subjects and achieve all-round knowledge essential for a fulfilling life.

The vast variety of courses offered a t a college under the CSS will enable the student s to choose whatever course units they really like. For example, those who graduate in physical sciences today do not have any exposure to the arts or humanities, social sciences or even natural sciences. The biggest drawback of our present system is that most college graduates are unconnected with the socio-economic realities in the country and the world. They are not even aware of the problems of their locality. Their books and their annual exams will be followed in a dull and mechanical fashion. The CSS will give that flexibility essential for making higher education more up-to-date and relevant. It will reduce the tendency among scholars to learn by rote for selective learning from an examination angle.

Today's higher education of India is wholly exam-centred-annual-exam-centred, ehereas it ought to be divided into assimilable segments which are to be evaluate on a continous basis. Instead of the annual system, we should have the semester (half -yearly) system. Instead of taking a vst area of knowledge, logical sections of the area should be offered as course units. The instruction and evaluation in a particular course unit should be completed 14 or 15 weeks.

Each course unit is given credits depending on the number of hours of teaching; for example, a course that is taught for one hour a week for a semester of 14 or 15 weeks will be given a one-credit curse. A student who completes the requirements of a course offering through one hour of instruction a week for a semester of 14 or 15 weeks will get one credit. Most courses are 3-credit course.

Both the course instructor and the student will be on their toes throughout the semester because the method of instruction is different from that in the annual/conventional system. Teachers are expected to guide the students to new knowledge thrugh constant updating. The students cannot depend solely on textbooks, lecture notes or the ubiquitous "guides", or bazaar notes. In the CSS, the teachers are the guides and not commercal notewriters. Since knowledge is constantly expanding, the market notes are not of much use to the students. Students have to depend more on their own library search and interactions with the teachers in and out of classrooms and seminars with fellow students and guest lecturers. Unfortunately this system does not find much favour withthe teachers in the present set-up.

Students get an opportunity to prove their worth by facing boldly what Jawaharlal Nehru called the 'adventure of ideas'. Gandhiji's hope that higher education should make them discover their own all-embracing personality can also be realized if colleges and all institutions of higher learning introduce the SCC.

But the biggest advantage is the freedom for the teachers to innovate and thereby help the students. The present system of teachers and students following a rigid three-subject and two-language pattern where instruction and evaluation do not go side by side has led to an insipid system of higher education. teachers depend on an outmoded syllabus (as old as their own college days, perhaps!) and students do not have read either at home or at the library and cut classes conveniently. (Even without such cutting, the average number of working days is below 100, certainly in Kerala, supposedly the most advanced state in India, educationally, as opposed to 200 or 180 days generally stipulated by the UGC and students can pass their annual exams.) If this is the case, why attend colleges? Why not depend solely on an outmoded exam system whose responsibility rests solely on the university—an anonymous exam-conducting body and nothing more? Precious working days are lost for strikes, bandhs, protests, sit-ins and what not? But working days, to be honest, are not working days, but non-working days. There are undeclared holidays in addition ot the large number of holidays declared by each State government in advance. Ours is a country that enjoys the largest number of holidays. Our young people are given the impression that they can become educated without any effort. Our teachers are setting a model for their young wards by coming to work late and leaving early. Where is the opportunity for them to sit in the library for at least an hour everyday to augment their own knowledge and thereby enhance the knowledge of their words. Are they endeavouring to transfer such newly acquired knowledge to their students?

It is very unfortunate that despite the tremendous growth in the number of colleges and universities in India, education that should conscientize the educated about their national socio-economic and political condition help liberate the nation from the shackles of old systems and ways of thinking is still a dream. Neither universalization of primary education nor vocatinoalization of primary education nor vocationalization of higher education has been achieved. It is sad that large sums of money spent on education (whether it be 3% or 6% of GNP) are not helping anyone to draw out the best in the educated (literally education means such drawing out).

The very basis of Gandhiji's educational vision was his belief that manual work was equal to mental work. Dignity of labour was given a high place in his scheme. But what do we see today? the "educated" refuse to work with their hands. Those who have high degrees apply for lower level jobs and then refuse to work or offer unsatisfactory work.

Education introduced in the colonial period is still continuing in free India despite all the educational commissions and their recommendations. The Radhakrishnan Commission, the Kothari Commission, the Adiseshiah Commission, the Punnayya Commission and the host of UGC committees and special task forces have made many recommendations which, if implemented, would have raised the level of higher education. Unfortunatley these recommendations were not implemented, although newer commission and committees came into being. No structural changes were introduced and therefore the old systems continue even today with almost no basic change.

The National Policy on Education, 1986 accorded high priority to vocationalisation of education at the secondary stage. The NPE as revised in 1992, set the target of achieving diversion of 10 per cent of the students at the +2 level to the vocational stream by 1995 and 25 per cent by 2000 AD. Accordingly, a Centrally-sponsored scheme of Vocationalisation of Secondary Education was launched in February 1988 with these objectives: Providing diversification of educational opportunities so as to enhance individual employability; reducing mismatch between demand and supply of skilled manpower and providing an alternative for those pursing higher education without particular interest or purpose.

Under the scheme, substantial financial assistance is provided to states/UTs for introduction of vocational courses in classes XI and XII of the school system. Its components include; (i) creation of separate management structure at the Directorate/SCERT/district and school levels for planning and monitoring of the programme; (ii) strengthening of the technical support system for research, development of curriculum/instructional material/ textbooks, training of teachers, etc,; (iii) conducting of district vocational surveys for assesment of labour market demand and (iv) provision of basic facilities for practical training in the school itself. So far all states/UTs except Lakshadweep have joined the programme. In all 18,055 vocational sections have been sanctioned in 6,280 schools all over the country thereby creating capacity for diversion of about nine lakh students to the vocational stream which is 11.46 per cent of the enrolment at the +2 stage.

A Centrally-sponsored scheme of pre-vocational education was launched in 1993-94 with the objective of imparting simple marketable skills to the students of classes IX and X. So far assistance has been provided to nine states/ UTs for introduction of pre-vocational cources in 428 schools.

Assistance is also-provided to non-governmental organisations for conducting innovative and non-formal programmes of vocational education. So far 37 such organisations have been assisted under the scheme.

A joint Council for Vocational Education (JCVE) was set up in April 1990 for policyformulation and coordination at the national level. A standing committee of JCVE was also set up in April 1990 to follow up on the decisions taken by JCVE and a Central Institute of Vocational Educational (CIVE) was set up at Bhopal in July 1993 to provide technixcal and academic support to the programme. About 18 vocational courses have been introduced in six major areas i.e. agriculture, business and commerce, engineering and technlogy, health and paramedical, home science, humanities and others while 60 vocational courses have been notified under the Apprenticeship Act.

Collaborative arrangements have also been made with some government departments, undertakings like Ministry of Railways, Ministry of Health, GIC, LIC, etc. Currently the emphasis * the quality of the programme States have thus been advised to strengthen the management structure at various levels, induct experts to infuse professionalism in programme, introduce need-based courses and to strenghten linkages with the industry on the job and apprenticeship training. An amount of Rs. 410 crore has been earmarked for the Vocational Education Programme during the Eighth Plan period. The budget estimate for 1995-96 is Rs. 82 crore.

Higher education is imparted through 197 universities in the country. Of these, there are 12 Central universities and the remaining are functioning under the state Acts. Total number of colleges in the country is 8,210. Besides, there are 34 institutions declared as deemed-to-be-universities under the University Grant Commission Act, 1956. The enrolment of students is 50.07 lakh while the number of teachers is 2.86 lakh.

Indian Council of Historical Research, New Delhi, set up in 1972, enunciates and implements a national policy on historical research and encourages scientific writing of history. It operates research projects, financial research projects by individual scholars, awards fellowships and undertakes publication and translation work.

Indian Council of Philosophical Research, which started functioning from 1981 with offices in New Delhi and Lucknow, reviews the progress, sponsors or assists projects and programmes of research in philosophy, gives financial assistance to institutions and individuals to conduct research in philosophy and allied disciplines.

Indian Institute of Advanced Study, Shimla, set up in 1965, is a residential centre for advanced research on humanities, social sciences and natural sciences. It is a community of scholars engaged on exploring new frontiers of knowledges aimed at conceptual development and offering interdisciplinary perspectives on question of contemporary relevance.

Indian Council of Social Science Research, New Delhi, is an autonomous body for promoting and coordinating social science research. Its main functions are to review the progress of social science research, give advice on research activities in government or outside, sponsor research programmes and give grants to institutions and individuals for research in social sciences.

Coordination and determination of standard of higher education, a subject of the Union List and as a special responsibility of the Central government is discharged mainly through University Grants Commission (UGC). The UGC was established in 1956 under an Act of Parliament to take measures for promotion and coordination of university education and determination and maintenence of standards in teaching, examination and research in universities. To fulfil its objectives the Commission can enquire, among other things, into financial needs of universities, allocate and disburse grants to them, establish and maintain common services and facilities; recommend measures for improvement of university education and give advice on allocation of grants and establishment of new universities. UGC has approved 111 colleges for autonomous status, 23 in Andhra Pradesh, 44 in Tamil Nadu, 30 in Madhya Pradesh, five each in Rajasthan and Orissa, two each in Gujarat and Uttar Pradesh.

Indira Gandhi National Open University (IGNOU) was established by an Act of Parliament in September 1985 for the introduction and promotion of open university and distance education system in the educational pattern of the country and for the coordination and determination of standards in such systems. The major objectives of the University include widening access to higher education to larger segments of the population, organising programmes of continuing education and initiating special programmes of higher education for specific targets group like women, people lliving in backward regions, hilly areas, etc.

The IGNOU provides an innovative system of university level education, flexible and open in regard to methods and pace of learning, combination of courses, eligibility for enrolment, age of entry, methods of evaluation, etc. The University has adopted an integrated multi-media instructional strategy consisting of printed materials and audio-video aids, supported by counselling sessions at a network of study centres throughout the country. It conducts both continous evaluation as well as term-end examinations.

The IGNOU introduced its academic programmes in 1987 and has so far launched 58 programmes. These include a certificate course in guidance for primary school teachers, food and nutrition in seven languages and rural development, the preparatory programmes for the bachelor's degree, diploma programme in management, rural development, higher education, distance education, creative writing in English and Hindi, computers in office management and operations management, the bachelor's degree programmes in arts/science/commerce and library and information sciences as well as the master's degree in business administration and distance education.

The total number of students registered for various programmes of study during 1995 is over 91,000. The University has established an extensive students support services network consisting of 16 regional centres and 244 study centres situated in different parts of the country. A Distance Education Council (DEC) established bythe University as a statutory authority is an apex body for coordination and determination of standards in distance education.

Doordarshan commenced telecast of IGNOU'S programmes in May 1991 while the Bombay and Hyderabad stations of All India Radio started broadcasting selected audio programmes of the IGNOU from early 1992. At present there are six other open universities in the country viz., B.R. Ambedkar Open University in Hyderabad (Andhra Pradesh), Kota Open University, Kota (Rajasthan), Nalanda Open University (Bihar); Yashwant Rao Chavan Maharashtra Open University, Nasik (Maharashtra), Madhya Pradesh Bhoj Open University, Bhopal (Madhya Pradesh) and Ambedkar Open University, Ahamadabad (Gujarat).

The National Literacy Mission (NLM) which was launched in 1988 with the objective of imparting functional literacy to 800 lakh adult illiterates in the age-group of 15-35 by 1995 now aims to impart functional literacy to 100 million adult illiterates in the age group of 15-35 (including age-group of 9-14 where NFE is not in operation) by 1997. The implementation of programmes under the NLM has showed that eradiction of illiteracy is not a uptopian idea but is possible, feasible and achievable. The most important development that has taken place under the NLM is the near ascendancy of the campaign mode in the adult education programmes in the country.

On the heels of success of Ernakulam and Kerala experiments for achieving full literacy, these campaigns for total literacy have generated certain characteristic feature which make them unique and distinguished them from other programmes. They are area-specific, time-bound, volunteer-based, cost-effective and outcome-oriented. Total Literacy Campaigns have been launched in 336 districts of the country covering over 81 lakh illiterate persons and 134 districts have commenced post literacy campaigns to consolidate the gains of literacy. It is proposed to cover 345 districts by TLC campaigns by the end of the Eighth Plan period. The focus of the campaign is now on the four major Hindi dpeaking states of Bihar, madhya Pradesh, Rajasthan and Uttar Pradesh where bulk of the illiterate populations resides.

Education should be looked upon as a national investment in the development of human resources. Educational development, however, must be based upon national priorities, national ethos and an international outlook. Perhaps with the exception of China, no other country in the world has got such a massive structure for higher education as India has. And the demand for education in India is expanding at an exponential rate because of the rapidly increasing population and the huge plans for socio-economic development launched by successive governments based on the principles of equality and social justice.

The magnitude of the growth of higher education in free India can be gauged better when we look at the status of education during the British period. Even as late as 1947, the number of students in colleges and universities could be counted in their thousands as against today's millions in the institutions of higher learning. The number today is about six million by 2010 A.D. Where the number of the universities in India stood at 20 in 1947, the number today is 220 (including deemed-to-be universities), an eleven-fold increase in fifty years. No other country has witnessed such a phenomenal growth. But based on population and based on the type of educational system prevalent today, India needs at least a thousand universities and a hundred thousand colleges (as against today's 8000 odd-colleges). The student population in the higher education sector alone in India is greater than the total population of Sweden or Switzerland or the Netherlands.

This problem of number ought to make our educational experts and planners think and act in a manner that is different from that in countries with small populations and high resoureces.

Education has to be looked upon as a national investment. The question of accountability needs very special attention from planners and funding agencies in India because the inputs are huge but the output is low. State and central government agencies, planning boards, private and public management, philanthropists, student, teachers, administrative staff and the general public ought to be concerned about returns on investment, not only on monetary considerations but certainly on the scale of human resource development. Otherwise, all that is investment will not only not generate excellence but create mediocrity and even patently dangerous intellectual evil.

The question of quantity versus quality assumes national importance in contemporary India because of goals of education in pre-Independence India were different. The British rulers did not finance higher education in any big manner but there was ample governmental policy support to individuals and trusts, religious and social groups for organizing, maintaining and developing colleges. The objectives of higher education during the British period were very limited and they mostly served the Macaulayan vision of creating "a class of people Indian in blood and colour but English in tastes, manners and intellect". In other words, the educated class had to think British rather than Indian and cater to the economic and political needs of governance in a country where the large majority of the governed were culturally far removed from the governors.

For higher education, the British establish three universities in the big cities of Calcutta, Bombay and Madras which were the provincial capitals of three British provinces directly under the responsibility first of the East India

Company and then of Britsh Crown. The three universities were established in 1857 after the model of the London University. The responsibility of expanding higher education was lwft with the colleges affiliated to each university and they were run by private management.

The elilte in pre-Independence India were exposed to the liberal traditions, legal principles and the history of democratic and egalitarian movements in the West, particularly Europe through the syllabi prescribed for higher education. The economic aspect of life in India, the political imperatives that led to suppression of democratic aspirations of the people and the large-scale drains of wealth from the country did not receive any attention in the syllabi. This resulted in the creation of a very huge number of educated young people who lost touch with the reality of Indian political, economic and social life, particularly in the rural areas.

In keeping with the National Policy on Education (NPE), 1986 (as updated in 1992) and its Programme of Action (POA), a new initiative to achieve Universalisation of Elementary Education (UEE) has been evolved titled, "District Primary Education Programme (DPEP)". It seeks to operationalise the strategy for UEE as enunciated in the POA, through decentralised planning and disaggregated target setting.

The DPEP is a beachhead for effecting improvements and full-scale development of the entire elementary education sector. Its fundemental principle is capacity-building at national, state and local levels and to evolve strategies which are replicable and sustainable. The DPEP, approved as a Centrally-sponsored scheme, is a major and multi-faceted programme seeking to overhaul the primary education system in the country. Infact, it is envisaged that DPEP will be transformed to a National Mission for Elementary Education, thus meeting a major commitment of POA 1992.

The objectives of the programme are:

— to reduce diference in enrolment, dropout and learning achievement among gender and social groups to less than five per cent;

— to reduce overall primary dropout rates for all students to less than 10 per cent;

— to raise average achievement levels by at least 25 per cent over measured baseline levels and ensuring achievement of basic literacy and numerous competencies, by all primary school children;

— to provide, according to national norms, access for all children, to primary education classes (I-IV), wherever possible, or its equivalent non-formal education. The programme would also strengthen the capacity of national, state and district institutions and organisations for the planning, management and evaluation of primary education.

The coverage of the programme will be gradually extended to all the districts which satisfy one of the twin criteria, viz., (a) educationally backward districts with female literacy below the national average and (b) districts where TLCs have been successful, leading to enhanced demand for elementary education.

The programme which lays greater emphasis on participatory processes for planning and management, has a marked gender focus and seeks to enhance school effectiveness through inputs in teachers' training and decentralised management. DPEP lays great emmphasis on people's participation and mobilisation of communities to assist in programme implementation. VECs play a key role in the implementation of the programme at the village level.

As of now the programme is being implemented in 42 districts of Madhya Pradesh, Assam, Karnataka, Haryana,

Maharashtra, Tamil Nadu and Kerala. The planning process has been initiated in five districts each in Andhra Pradesh and West Bengal where it would be funded by ODA. Nineteen districts of Madhya Pradesh are funded by European Community's Programme assistance while the remaining 23 districts are funded by IDA. The Financing Agreement with European Community has been signed for an amount of ECU 150 millon (Rs. 585 crore). First tranche of 19.37 ECUs have already been credited to the Government of India's accounts.

The Computer Literacy and Studies in Schools (CLASS) and is being implemented as a Centrally-sponsored scheme from 1993-94. To be eligible for assistance under the modified scheme, the following conditions are to be satisfied by the states/UTs: (a) The coverage of the scheme for new schools will be restricted to senior secondary schools; (b) In selected schools, instructions in computer literacy will be compulsory for all students of classes XI and XII, these instructions will be part of the school time-table with the evaluation in the subject taking place with/without formal examination; and (c) infrastructure such as a *pucca* room with electricity and other fittings will have to be made in the schools to be covered under the project initially by the state government concerned.

The National Steering Committee under the Chairmanship of Education Secretary is responsible for monitoring and supervision etc. At state/UT levels, Cells have been set up, which are to discharge the dual responsibility of monitoring and actual implementation of the scheme in the schools and of releasing the funds to the implementing agencies. The National Informatics Centre (NIC) which was assigned the responsibility of identifying vendors for hardware had short-listed the names of two vendors which have been circulated to the states/UTs/ autonomous body institutes concerned. On the recommendation of National Steering Committee the guidelines for selection of Implementing Agencies as well as course material to be adopted have also been circulated to all concerned. Rupees 146 crore has been provided for implementing the scheme during the Eighth Plan. This amount is for maintaining 2,598 schools already covered under the old scheme as well as for including 1,320 additional schools during the Eighth Plan.Two hundred and eighteen additional schools were covered during 1993-94 and 449. During 1995-95, it isproposed to cover 500 additional schools.

In order to improve the quality of science education and promote scientific temper, as envisagedin NPE, a Centrally-sponsored scheme, 'Improvement of Science Education in Schools', was started during the last quarter of 1987-88. Under this scheme, financialassistance is provided to states/ union territories for provision of science kits to upper primary schools, upgradation and strengthening of science laboratories in secondary and senior secondary schools, supply of books on science* and training of science and mathematics teachers. Government as well as aided schools qualify for assistance under the scheme. It also provides assistance to voluntary organisations active in the field of science education for undertaking innovative projects and resource support activities in science education.

With a view to identifying and nurturing talent in mathematics at the school level, the International Mathematical Olympiad (IMO) is held every year. India has been participating in this Olympiad since 1989. Aneight-member delegation including six student contestants, leaders participated in IMO held in Hong Kong in July 1994. India ranked 16th out of 69 paticipating countries and own three silver and three bronze medals.

In order to promote integration of educational programmes in the schools with environmental conditions, a Centrally-sponsored scheme, Environmental Orientation to School Education, was started in 1988-89. Under the scheme, cent per cent assistance is provided to the states/ union territories and voluntary agencies on project basic. States/UTs are also assisted for review and development of curricula of various disciplines at primary, upper primary, secondary and senior secondary levels with a view to infusing environmental concepts therein; review and development of textbooks of 'Environmental Studies' at primary and upper primary levels; review of strategy for imparting environmental education at upper primary level; development of teaching/learning material; organisation of suitable innovative work experience activities etc. Voluntary agencies are assisted for taking up of various kinds of experimental and innovative programmes in the field.

In order to provide good quality modern education to the talented children predominantly from the rural areas, Government of India launched in 1985-86 a scheme to establish Navodaya Vidyalaya on an average one in each * admission to Navodaya Vidyalayas is at the level of class VI based on an admission test conducted by NCERT. The medium of test is the mother tongue or regional language of the children. The test is largely nonverbal in nature, class neutral and so designed as to ensure that the talented children from the rural areas are able to compete without suffering any disadvantage.

The Vidyalayas are fully residential and c0-educational in which addmission to the children from urban areas is generally restricted to 25 per cent of the seats. Efforts ae made to ensure that atleast one third of the students in each Vidyalaya are girls. Reservation of seats in favour of children belonging to SCs and STs is provided in proportion of their population in the concerned district provided that in no district such reservation is less than the national level.

The Vidyalayas provide education in the streams of Humanities, Commerce, Science and Vocational upto +2 level and are affiliated to CBSE. There are at present 359 sanctioned Vidyalayas in the country operating in 30 states/ UTs.

The scheme for establishment of Central Schools was approved by the Government of India in 1962 and its implementation was started by the Ministry of Education in 1963 when 20 regimental schools run by the Ministry of Defence were taken over and converted into Central Schools or Kendriya Vidyalayas. Later on the Kendriya Vidyalaya Sangathan, an autonomous body was set up by the Ministry of Education and was registered as a Society in December 1965. The main objectives of Kendriya Vidyalayas are: (i) to cater to the educational needs of the children of transferable Central Government employees including Defence and paramilitary personnel by providing a common programme of education; (ii) to pursue excellence and set pace in the field of school education; (iii) to initiate and promote experimentation and innovativeness in education in collaboration with other bodies like the CBSE and NCERT etc. and (iv) to develop the spirit of national and create a sense of 'Indianess' among children.

During the academic year 1994-95 there were 818 Kendriya Vidyalayas with a student population of approximately seven lakh. There are two Vidyalayas abroad one each in Kathmandu and Moscow. The number of staff sanctioned as on 30 April 1994 was 42,950. During the academic session 1995-96, 21 Kendriya Vidyalayas have been sanctioned out of which two are in defence, 16 in civil and three in public sectors.

Kendriya Vidyalayas are opened in Defence establishments on the recommendation of the Ministry of Defence and in the civil sector on the recommendation of the various ministries/departments * employees welfare associations. The sponsoring agency has to provide a piece of land measuring 15 acre for the construction of permanent building for Kendriya Vidyalaya. The Kendriya Vidyalays are opened in the campuses of public sector undertakings if they are ready to bear all the recurring and non recurring expenditure on the proposed Kendriya Vidyalaya. The children of the employees of such undertakings get priority in admission in Kendriya Vidyalayas However, for admission in Kendriya Vidyalayas under civil and defence sectors the transferable Central Government employees including defence personnel get the priority. The reservation of 15 per cent and 7.5 per cent of fresh admissions is available in all Kendriya Vidyalayas for the children of SC and ST respectively.

All kendriya Vidyalayas follow the same textbooks and medium of instruction which is in Hindi and English, the ultimate object being to enable pupils to achieve proficiency in both the languages. The Kendriya Vidyalayas are having classes Ist to XIIth. Introductory computer science has been introduced as an elective subject in Kendriya Vidyalayas from this year for the XIIth class students.

The first "Education for All" project in India, the Bihar Education Project (BEP) is in operation in Bihar since 1991-92. Its basic objective is to bring about quality improvement in the elementary education system in the state. With an estimated outlay of Rs. 360 crore, it envisages to cover 150 blocks spread over 20 districts over the project period spanning 1991-96. UNICEF would contribute Rs. 180 crore, the Government of India Rs. 120 crore and the Government of Bihar Rs. 60 crore. Participatory planning and community participation are the important characteristics of the project which lays special emphasis on the education of SC/ST and the women. A state level registered society has been set up for its planning and implementation. As of now, seven districts of Ranchi, West Champaran, Rohtas, Muzaffarpur, Sitamarhi, Chatra and East Singhboom are covered. The Unicef cooperation in May 1993 noted the major impact the project ;has had on the attitudes in Bihar towards education at political, administrative and community level. The project has also played a major role in mobilising greater national and international interest in basic education. * The UNICEF-Government of India Joint review in July 1994 noted certain positive features such as *Mahila Samakhaya*, management structures, village education committees and non-formal education through NGOs. The review, inter alia recommended consolidation of the programme and strong linkages between BEP and the education system in Bihar. Against the total releases of Rs. 84 crore so far, the total expenditure including supplies is Rs. 48 crore.

The National Book Trust (NBT) India, an autonomous organisation established in 1957 by the Government of India discharges these functions: (i) publishing; (ii) promotion of books and book-reading; (iii) promotion of Indian books abroad; (iv) assistance to authors and publishers and (v) promotion of children's literature.

NBT publishes general reading material for all segments of society and for all age groups, including books for children and post-literacy reading material for neoliterates. Moderately priced books, fiction and non-fiction in English, Hindi and 11 other major Indian languages viz., Assanese Bangla, Gujrati, Kannada, Malayalam, Marathi, Oriya, Punjabi, Tamil, Telugu and Urdu and also in Konkani, Nepali, Manipuri and Sindhi are brought out under different series. Five hundred and eighty four titles were brought out during 1994-95 including reprints and enrolled 91 new bookdellers as registered dealers of its publications, raising their total number to 460. The gross value of books sold was Rs. 250 lakh.

During 1994-95, three book fairs in Nagpur, Jalandhar and Goa and 124 exhibitions all over the country were organised. Every alternate year, NBT organises the New Delhi World Book Fair which is the largest in Asia and

Africas. The next World Book Fair will be held in February 1996 at New Delhi. To help the book industry grow, NBT organises seminars and workshops in the country and every year from November 14-20 National Book Week is celebrated. On the demand of readers for the availability of books on a permanent basis, NBT has decided to launch pilot project to construst 12 book stalls in Delhi and five in states of the Hindi speaking region.

NBT participated in international book fairs and made arrangements for special exhibitions for display of select titles brought out by Indian publishers in China, Germany, Italy, Male, Nepal, South Africa and Sri Lanka.

NBT gives financial assistance to authors and publishers for bringing out reasonably priced books for higher education. Under its scheme, for the subsidised publication of books only such books are subsidised for which a definite need is felt and which relate to subject areas where books of an acceptable standard are either not available or so highly priced as to be beyond the means of students. So far NBT has subsidised the publication of 830 titles, including 13 in 1994-95 mostly in English.

NBT has established the National Centre for Children Literature to monitor, coordinate plan and aid the publication of children's literature in various Indian languages. The Centre organises workshops and exhibitions and promotes the habit of reading at school level by encouraging the setting up of Reader's Clubs. It is also compling a catalogue of select books for children published in Indian languages.

Under the present policy, as announced by the Ministry of Commerce for the period April 1992 to 31 March 1997, as amended upto 31 march 1995 any person/organisation is free to import all categories of books including journals, magazines and newspapers under open general licence except in case of children's literature.

Copyright protection governed by the Indian Copyright Act, 1957 and has been amended from time to time was last amended in 1994 as Copyright (Amendment) Act, 1994 came into force on 10 May 1995. A notification in this regard was published in the Official Gazette, extra-ordinary dated 5 May 1995. Consequential amendments in the Copyright Rules, 1958 necessitated by the amendments to the Copyright Act, have also been notified simultaneously in the same issue of the gazette as mentioned above.

The copyright office was established in January 1958 in pursuance of Section 9 of the Copyright Act, 1957. The Act, *inter alia* provides for registration of copyright under six different categories, *viz.*, (a) Literary works other than computer programmes, tables and compilations including computer data bases and dramatic works, (b) musical works, (c) artistic works, (d) cinematograph films, (e) sound recordings and (f) computer programmes, tables, compilations including computer data bases. Further, the Act also provides for registering changes in the particulars entered in the Register of Copyright, issue of certified copies of extracts from the Register of Copyright as also of the public documents in the custody of the Registrar of Copyright besides facilitating inspection of the Register of Copyright/Index by the interested persons.

The Copyright Board, a quasi-judicial body, was constituted initially in September 1958. The jurisdiction of the Board extends to the whole of India. It hears cases regaring rectification of copyright registration, disputes in respect of assignment of copyright appeal against the Registrar of Copyright and granting of licences in certain specified works and other miscellancous matters instituted before it under the Copyright Act, 1957. The Secretariat to the Board is provided by the Copyright Office.

The International Standard Books Numbers (ISBN) System aims at boosting the export of indigenous publications at the international business areas. It is an international system by which a distinct identifying number is assigned to each book. In addition to the book trade, the system is very helpful to the libraries and information systems and to research scholars. From 1 January 1985 to 31 March 1995, 2,672 big and small publishers and authors have become the members of the System.

The Department of education funds several scholarship/ fellowship programmes for Indian students for school and higher education. They include the National Scholarship Scheme, a scheme of scholarships to help students of non-Hindi speaking states studying Hindi, research scholarships for Indian classical languages and scholarships to enable talented rural children to continue secondary education. These programmes are administered through the state governments. A new programme of prestigious fellowships for post-graduate studies in India and abroad,named Jawaharlal Nehru Fellowship, has recently been introduced which is now administered by Jawaharlal Nehru Memorial Fund, Teen Murti House, New Delhi.

Scholarships for advanced or specialised studies are offered under the provisions of cultural programme, bilateral agreements, Commonwealth scholarships/fellowships plan and *ad hoc* scholarship offers received from different countries. These scholarships are mostly for Ph.D (Doctoral) and post-doctoral specialisation for which the minimum eligibility * countries like Germany, France, Ireland, Korea (South), Australia, UK, Japan, China, Austria, Norway, Italy, israel, Spain, Czech., Mexico, Egypt and Indonesia.

Since the services sector contributes nearly 40 per cent to the GDP, Mr. Chidambaram has proposed to extend the service tax to six more sectors, including transportation of goods by road, consulting engineers, out—door caterers, man–power recruitment agencies, etc. He expects that this proposals would give him Rs. 900 crore in the coming year and he has promised that the "bulk of the proceeds from service tax on transportation of goods by road" would be utilised to augment the resources of the National Highway Authority.

Revision of postal tariffs was long over—due and increases have been effected in theprices of ordinary post card, printed card, inland letter and envelope.

Among other highlights of the Finance Minister's proposals are the increase in the rate of contribution to Employees Provided Fund in all industries from 8.33 per cent to 10 per cent for both employees and employers, and from 10 to 12 per cent in scheduled industries.

Keeping in mind the common minimum programme (CMP) promise that "the United Front government will identify public sector companies that have comparative advantages and will support them in their drive to become global giants." Mr. Chidambaram said that nine well—performing public sector giants (the "Navaratnas" as he calls them) have been identified for such special attention. These are: IOC, ONGC, BPCL, IPCL, HPCL, VSNL, BHEL, SAIL and NPTC. The industry Minister is to unveil a package of measures that will help these public sector units.

Another area where merit and performance is being rewarded is in respect of outstanding scientists who will be assisted to attain and sustain world class level in science. For this purpose, "Swarnajayanti" fellowships are being launched for outstanding scientists below the age of 45. A sum of Rs. 50 crore in the Department of Education's budget will be used to create a corpus to provide such fellowships. A small beginning, but well worth the effort.

Opening up the insurance sector is a sensitive issue, with some vocal partners in the coalition opposed to such a move. Yet, Mr. Chidambaram has made a cautious move.

He has proposed necessary amendments to enable GIC to float joint ventures and also to allow entry of selected Indian players in the health insurance sector. He has made it clear that "only a few Indian companies, that are Indian—controlled and with majority Indian ownership" will be permitted to enter the health insurance business. In addition to opening the health insurance sector to selected Indian players, he has also allowed UTI and LIC to promote joint ventures in the pension business.

With the country's demand for petroleum products growing at about 8 per cent per annum and with a view to augmenting domestic supplies, Mr. Chidambaram has outlined the highlights of a new exploration licensing policy (NELP). Some highlights of NELP are: companies, including ONGC and OIL, to be paid the international price of oil for new discoveries made under NELP; royalty payments to be fixed on an *ad valorem* basis; freedom to market crude oil and gas in the domestic market; ONGC and OIL to get same duty concessions on import of capital goods under NELP as private production sharing contracts; cess levied under the Oil Industry Development Act 1974 to be abolished for new exploration blocks and a separate petroleum tax code to be put in place as in other countries to facilitate new investments.

Simultaneous with his announcement that "there is no change in the budget estimate of the fiscal deficit which would remain at 5 per cent of GDP" in 1996—97 and that he hoped to contain it at 4.5 per cent of GDP in the coming financial year, the Finance Minister has stated that he proposed to discontinue the system of *ad hoc* treasury bills t finance the budget with effect from April 1, 1997. Instead, a scheme of ways and means advances (WMA) by the RBI t the Central Government is being introduced to accommodate temporary mismatches in the government's receipts and payments. How far this new method will bring in more fiscal discipline remains to be seen.

Affirming the United Front's belief that th polity of India "requires a strong Centre and strong States, and, if I may add, strong local bodies," Mr. Chidambaram has acdepted the recommendation of the Tenth Finance Commission (TFC) t form a single, divisible pool of taxes to be shared between the Centre and the States. To begin with, "we shall adopt the proportion of 29 per cent recommended by the TFC," he has said. The States should welcome this measure, as the new formula would mean devolution of more resources from the Centre to the States.

Education about India's common cultural heritage has been identified in National Policy on Education as one of the core areas under the national system of education. While spelling out the cultural perspective in education, the policy has stressed on the need to bridge the schism between the formal system of education and India's rich and varied cultural traditions. It has called for enriching the curricula and processes of education in as many manifestations as possible and laid considerable emphasis on value education by highlighting the need to make education a forceful tool for cultivation of social and moral values.

Within these overall objectives, a Centrally-sponsored scheme of Assistance for Strengthening Culture and Values in Education has been designed for providing assistance to Government agencies, educational institutions, *Panchayat Raj* institutions, registered societies, public trusts and non-profit making companies. The scheme has two broad components (i) strengthening cultural and value education inputs in the school and non-formal education system and (ii) strengthening the in-service training of art, craft, music and dance teachers. A total grant of Rs. 98 lakh has been approved for sanction to 33 organisations during 1994-95.

National Open School (NOS) was established in November 1989 as an autonomous organisation with the objective to provide quality education through distance education mode upto secondary stage for the school dropouts and children who cannot attend formal schools. This school is vested with the authority to examine and certify students registered with it upto pre-degree level courses. The certificates issued by this school are recognised for admissions for pursuing higher education and also for employment. The students have the freedom to choose the set of subjects according to their needs, interests and abilities and are also encouraged to choose vocational subjects in combination with academic subjects. The marginalised groups, viz., rural youth, girls and women, SC and ST, handicapped, ex-servicemen are given priority by NOS.

The NOS provides student support services through a network of study centres known as accredited institutions (AIs) for academic courses and accredited vocational institutions (AVIs) for*. As on 31 March 1994, 306 AIs were functioning under NOS.

The number of students enrolled by the National Open School during the years 1992-93, 1993-94 and 1994-95 for its secondary and senior secondary courses was:

Year	Secondary	Senior Secondary
1992-93	31,375	20,932
1993-94	35,098	25,777
1994-95	36,766	29,054

It is proposed to extend the open learning facilities in a phased manner at the secondary level in all parts of the country. In order to facilitate setting up of state open schools, the NOS provides consultancy services to the state goverments and serves as an agency for effective dissemination of information related to distance education and open learning.

The National Council of Educational Research and Training (NCERT) was established in September 1961 in New Delhi as an autonomous body. Qualitative improvement and excellence in school education and teacher education are some of its major objectives. They maintain effective liason with state education authorities for providing academic inputs to school education system.

The NCERT develops curricula, syllabi and prepares textbooks for classes I-XII which form the basis for prescription of schemes of studies by Central Boaard of Secondary Education (CBSE) for the schools affiliated to the Board. It also develops instructional material for childhood education and training packages for teacher educators and supervisory personnel. It provides technical assistance for national population education programmes designed to introduce population education in the formal education system. NCERT also provides its expertise to states/UTs. It also designs courses and material, generates software systems and sets up resource centres for computer literacy and studies in school project. NCERT organises Jawaharlal Nehru National Science Exhibition every year in which a large number of school students from all over the country participate. The Council produces science kits for the use of school students. It prepares comprehensive guidelines for curriculum evaluation and school industry linkages as well as for pre-service education of teachers on vocationalisation of education. Training courses for the officials involved in the Integrated Education Programme for Disabled Children are also conducted.

The NCERT is providing very useful assistance to the Department of Education in implementing the District Primary Education Projects (DPEPs) in several states towards fulfilment of the recommendations made in Education For All (EFA) Summit of nine high population countries held in New Delhiin December1993.Oneof the major projects entrusted to the NCERT is the Sixth All India Educational Survey which the Council is implementing in collaboration with the National Informatics Centre (NIC).

The objective of inculcating the message of small family norms and other population related issues in the minds of school and college students and the clientele of adult and non-formal education is being achieved through National Population Education Project.This project is now being implemented through school and non-formal education, higher education and adult education.

Since its inception in 1980, NPEP has done much towards achieving its main objective of institutionalising population education through the school education system. During the second cycle (1986-1990) the main focus was on consolidation of the project's multidimensional activities and further expansion of its network. During the third cycle, special attention was paid to girls and SCs/STs through various curricular activities with an emphasis on community participation. The process of interweaving population education elements into the syllabi, textbooks and of instructional and training materials will continue.

One of the main factors responsible for slow pace of growth of enrolment of adolescent girls of rural, tribal and other remote areas is the traditional social inhibitions against their movement outside the family precincts. Moreover the high/higher secondary schools in schools in such places are sparsely located. In order to actualise the recommendation in POA 1992 for formulating a special enabling plan to ensure increased enrolment of girls in secondary education and the NPE directive for encouraging NGO participation in education, the scheme for strengthening of boarding and hostel facilities for girl students of secondary/higher secondary schools was launched in 1993-94 with the objective of providing the following types of assistance to the existing hostels run by the NGOs: (i) Non-recurring assistance as non-time grant for provision of essential furniture, utensils and meeting basic recreational needs at the rate of Rs. 1,500 per boarder: and (ii) recurring assistance for food, emoluments of cook and bearer at the rate of Rs. 5,000 per annum per boarder.

Culture

Culture of India which is composite in nature is essentially an expression of inner urges and cumulative beliefs of people gathered through centuries of experience. It is the perennial flow of this culturtal stream which determines the nation's strength, character and capacity to survive as an integrated living reality despite heavy odds and its continuous march forward on the path of progress. Keeping this in view, preservation of cultural heritage, inculcation of art consciousness among people and promotion of high standards of creative and performing arts and dissemination of culture have been made part of the objectives of State policy.

The Central and state governments strive for promotion and dissemination of art and culture through national and regional academies of art, dance, drama, music and letters. Zonal cultural centres have been set up for projecting, preserving and sustaining cultural kinship that transcends territorial limits. In addition, Indira Gandhi National Centre for Arts has been set up at New Delhi as a resource centre and data base. All these institutions and Departments of Art and Culture are helped in their objective by media and voluntary agencies. Apart from this, some eminent persons in the field of fine arts are nominated by the President to the Rajya Sabha.

To promote and propagate understanding of Indian art, both within and outside the country, the Government established Lalit Kala Akademi (National Akademi of Fine

Arts) at new Delhi in 1954. To decentralise its activities, the Akademi has set up regional centres called Rashtriya Lalit Kala Kendra at Lucknow, Calcutta, Madras and Bhubneswar as well as a small office at Bombay. The Akademi has also set up Community Artists Studio Complex with workshop facilities in painting, sculpture, printmaking and ceramics in Garhi village in New Delhi. The workshops and all regional centres are headed by experts to give technical guidance in these disciplines.

Since its inception, the Akademi organises national exhibition of contemporary Indian art with 10 national awards, each of Rs. 25,000. Three to four special exhibitions every year are organised with some concept involving known and eminent artists of India. Every three years, the Akademi also organises Triennale-India, a most significant exhibition of contemporary art in this part of the world. The last, Seventh Triennale was held in 1991 while the next one was inaugurated on 16 February 1994. The Akademi also organises a Rashtriya Kala Mela (National Art Fair) where artists from all over India present their work. The Eighth Rashtriya Kala Mela was held in Bangalore in 1995, while sixth was held in Bombay in January 1993 and the seventh Mela was held in New Delhi in February 1994.

The Akademi honours eminent artists and art historians every year by electing them as fellows of the Akademi. So far 45 persons have been conferred with this fellowship. To propagate Indian art outside, the Akademi regularly participates in International Biennales and Triennales abroad and also organises exhibitions of works of art from other countries. To foster contacts with artists ouside, it sponsors exchange of artists with other countries under the various Cultural Exchange Programmes and Agreements of the Government of India.

The Lalit Kala Akademi accords recognition to art institutions/associations and extends financial assistance to these bodies as well as state Akademis every year. It also gives scholarship to deserving young artists of its regional centres. Under its publication programme, the Akademi brings out monographs on the works of Indian contemporary artists in Hindi and English and books on contemporary, traditional, folk and tribal arts authored by eminent writers and art critics. The Akademi also brings out bi-annual art journals, Lalit Kala Contemporary (English), Lalit Kala Ancient (English) and Samkaleen Kala (Hindi). Apart from these, it brings out large size multicolour reproductions of contemporary paintings and graphics from time to time. The Akademi has started a regular programme on research and documentation. Scholars are given financial assistance to undertake projects in contemporary folk, tribal and traditional arts. It has set up an Artists-Aid Fund to give financial assistance to ailing artists and other artists who may be in penury. The first National Exhibition of Photography was held in 1995. The Akademi has decided to give five awards of Rs. 10,000 each and five Hon'ble Mentions for the Exhibition.

Centre for Cultural Resources and Training (CCRT) was set up in May 1979 as an autonomous organisation by the Government of India. The CCRT took over the scheme 'Propagation of Culture' among college and school students which was being implemented by Delhi University, since 1970. The Centre is under the administrative control of Department of Culture, Ministry of Human Resource Development.

The broad objectives of the CCRT have been to revitalise the education system by creating an understanding and awareness among students about the plurality of regional cultures of India and integrating this knowledge with the education. The main thrust is on linking education with culture and making students aware of the importance of culture in all development programmes. The training being imparted stresses on the role of culture in science and technology, housing, agriculture, sports, etc. An important component of training is creating an awareness amongst students and teachers of their role in solving environmental pollution problems and conservation and preservation of the natural and cultural heritage. To fulfil these objectives, the Centre organises a variety of training programmes for teachers, educators, administrators and students throughout the country. It has also been organising academic programmes on Indian art and culture for foreign teachers and students. Workshops are conducted in various art activities lilke drama, music, narrative art forms, etc., to provide practical training and knowledge in the arts and crafts. In these workshops, teachers are encouraged to develop programmes inwhich the art form can be profitably utilised to educational curriculum.

The CCRT organises various educational activities for school students, teachers and children belonging to governmental and non-government organisations under its extension and community feedback programmes, which includes, educational tours to monuments, museums, art galleries, craft centres, zoological parks and gardens, camps on conservation of natural and cultural heritage, camps on learning crafts using low cost localilty available resources, lectures and demonstrations by artists and experts on various art forms, demonstrations by artists and crafts persons in schools.

The CCRT collects materials on the arts and crafts of the country in the form of audio recordings, slides, photographs, films and written texts in order to disseminate the information on culture and provide participants and other research institutions with material on the arts of India. The Centre also aims to disseminate information and foster an understanding of Indian culturre amongst teachers, administrators, educators and students. Publications for institutions and members of the community are prepared on topics related to aspects of Indian culture and ecology and the natural environment.

The CCRT implements the Cultural Talent Search Scholarship Scheme, which was taken over from the Department of Culture in 1982. The scheme provides scholarships to outstanding children in the age-group of 10 to 14 years studying, either in recognised schools okr belonging to families practising traditional, performing or other arts to develop their talent in various cultural fields particularly in rare art forms. The scholarship continues till the age of 20 years or first year of university degree. The Centre has also instituted CCRT Teacher's Award which is given every year to selected teachers in recognition of the outstanding work done by them in the field of education and culture.

Zonal cultural centres have been conceptualised with the aim of projecting cultural kinships transcending territorial bounds. The idea is to arouse and deepen awarreness of the local cultures and how these merge into zonal identities and eventually into the rich diversity of India's composite culture. Besides, these are also intended to document, preserve and to sustain the vanishing art forms and oral traditons. The involvement of artists and creative people has been in built in the set-up through a system of autonomous governance.

The seven zonal cultural centres established under the new scheme are: (i) North-Zone Cultural Centre, Patiala; (ii) East Zone Cultural Centre, Santiniketan; (iii) South Zone Cultural Centre, Thanjavur; (iv) west Zone Cultural Centre, Udaipur; (v) North-Central Zone Cultural Centre, Allahabad; (vi) North East Zone Cultural Centre, Dimapur and (vii) South-Central Zone Cultural Centre, Nagpur. The participation of states in more than one zonal cultural centre according to their cultural linkage is a special feature of the composition of the zonal centres.

The Ramakrishna Mission Institute of Culture, Calcutta is engaged in the promotion of thought, knowledge and education. Apart from being engaged in cultural activities at national and international level, the Institute also maitains several schools of instructions.

Indira Gandhi National Centre for the Arts (IGNCA) was established to commemorate the memory of the late Prime Minister, Mrs Indira Gandhi. This Centre launched on 19 November 1985 as a fully funded autonomous trust, is visualized as a centre encompassing the study and experience of all the arts-each for its own integrity, yet within a dimension of mutual interdependence, inter-relatedness with nature, social structure and cosmology. Through diverse programmes of research, publication, training, creative activities and performance, the IGNCA seeks to place the arts within the context of the natural and human environment. the fundamental approach of the Centre in all its work is multi-disciplinary and inter-disciplinary.

The Indira Gandhi National Centre for the Arts, comprises five main divisions viz. (i) Kala Nidhi; (ii) kala Kosa; (iii) janapada Sampada; (iv) Kala Darshana and (v) Sutradhara. During 1994-95, the reference library of Kala NIdhi Division added 2,204 selected works of eminent authors to its collection, 478 rolls of microfilms of rare Indian manuscripts from abroad and 1,532 microfiches from SMPK, Berlin University of Vienna were also added to its collections. The Kala Kosa Division under its programme of Kalathttvakosa, a lexicon of fundamental concepts of Indian arts, is engaged in the preparation of its volume engaged in the preparation of its volume III and IV. The institution organised a 17 day workshop on 'Manuscriptology and Palaeography' in collaboration with Shri Lal Bahadur Shastri

Rashtriya Sanskrit Vidyapeetha as part of training programme for younger generation of researchers from within IGNCA and outside. During the year, the janapada Sampada Division under its Loka Parmapara programmes, recieved interim reports on various projects including Santhal Perception of Sound", "Seed and Eaarth in Oral Tradition of Vraja", etc. Under its publication programme, a number of manuscripts were assigned to the co-publishers. The first and second issues of IGNCA Newsletter, Vihangama, have been brought out during the year and the third issue is under publication. The Kala Darshana Division organised a number of exhibitions abroad in collaboration with Mr. Jacques Pimpaneau of Musee Kwok On, France, photographic exhibition of photographs by David Ulrich titled Hawalii Landscape of Transformation; and Raja Deen Dayal Exhibition at Bombay and Bhopal. The IGNCA also co—sponsored a session on "Cave art of India and China" at Dunhuang (China), and deputed three delegates to participate in the International Seminar held there as a part of the Dunhaung Academy Golden Jubilee celebrations.

One of the important activities undertaken by the Government of India has been the commemoration of the centenaries ofdistinguished Indians who have left an indelible impression on the history and life of our country. National committees are set up for centenaries which are considered to be of such importance. Year long programmes are drawn up by the committees for implementation during the centenary year. These programmes normally include organisation of national seminars, installation of statutes, other functions, stamp release, publications and exhibitions. The Department of Culture also provides financial assistance to registered voluntary organisations for celebrating the centenaries of outstanding personalities which are not taken up for celebration by the Government of India. Another mode of organising centenaries is where one or more state governments are requested to set up the centenary committee and the Government of India on its part organises a few programmes like release of commemorative postage stamps, seminars/lectures, publication, etc.

Gandhi Smriti and Darshan Samiti (GSDS) was set up by the Department of Culture in 1948 primarily to maintain and look after the national memorial where gandhiji was assisinated and now called 'Gandhi Smriti', and a permanent photo exhibition at Rajghat called' Gandhi Darshan', which was created at the time of Gandhiji's birth centenary in the year 1969. The institution has brought out a number of books on Gandhi, communal harmony and national integration. It also publishes a quarterly newsletter to create awareness about the GSDS and also organises annual Gandhij Memorial Lecture by an eminent scholar both in India and abroad.

The year 1994-95 happens to be the 125th birth anniversary year of Gandhiji and, therefore a series of programmes commenced with an inaugural function at Vigyan Bhawan on 2 October 1994 chaired by the President. The Samiti has since organised a programme of painting by the children, a photo exhibition put up at Paris on the eve of the 1st UNESCO Gandhi Memorial Lecture delivered by the Prime Minister; a massive programme of creating awareness for the youth in all the districts of Kerala; another programme involving several thousand youths and others for creating awareness about the literature on Gandhi. Programmes have also been organised for women, especially for those elected for Panchayats. Orientation programmes comprising discussions, film shows, visit to an exhibition and cultural programmes in several rural settings were the other highlights. The GSDS also participated and collaborated in the regional Conference organised by UNESCO on tolerance in April 1995 at New Delhi.

Maulana Abul Kalam Azad Institute of Asian Studies, under the administrative control of the Department of Culture is the centre for research and training of the life and works of Maulana Abul Kalam Azad and with the study on social, cultural, political and economic movement in Asia from the middle of the 19th century. The Institute also maintains library of books, newspapers, still photographs and materials on the secular traditions of modern India and events of the 19th century which is suitable for the public to collect papers and library sources for study and research from India and abroad. It also maintains personal museum at the former residence of Maulana Abul Kalam Azad. The Museum highlights the life and works of Maulana Abdul Kalam Azad as a distinguished national leader and thinker.

All festivals have a common purpose of creating a greater awareness amongst the people of the receiving country of India's rich cultural heritage and contemporary development in vrious spheres of modern India. This helps to generate an appropriate climate of goodwill and understanding for mutual exchanges in different spheres including technology, commerce and tourism on a more permanent footing. The main thrust of the Festival of India has been to project its multifaceted cultural life, while also highlighting scientific and technical progress and advancement through a series of exhibitions, programmes of performing arts as well as through seminars, readings, workshops, youth meetings, sports festivals etc.

The Festival of India in China was inaugurated on 9 May 1994 at Ply Plaza at Beijing by the Human Resource Development Minister and his Chinese counterpart. The inaugural ceremony consisted mainly of performing art event with the underlying theme 'Harmony'. Eight Indian films were screened at different venues in China during the Festival of India. The National Institute of Fashion technology mounted fashion shows during the festival.

The Performing Arts programme for the Festival of India in China was the single largest component among the festival events. About 75 performers visited China during the period of festival. Indian handicrafts combine varied styles and colours, fine workmanship, profound traditions and have a distinctive national flavour, Karigari provided a glimpse of these patterns of handicraft traditions that have survived in India for many thousand years. It was inaugurated on 10 May 1994. In this exhibition, an effort was made to give the viewers an impression of Indian science as a whole, in all its rich diversity through Indian experience in science and technology in its long history of 4500 years.

Around 1500 titles, mostly recent and some old titles of perennial value, brought out by almost 150 publishers were displayed at the exhibitions in China. The books selected for the exhibitions in China covered a wide range of subjects such as arts, history, biography, literature, philosophy, religion, social sciences, technology and books of general reference.

The Government encourages development of all Indian languages including classical, modern and tribal. Its policy lays emphasis on training of teachers in relation to adoption of the three-language formula and production of university-level textbooks with ta view to facilitating media switch over from English to regional languages. In order to assist non-Hindi speaking states/union territories to effectively implement the three-language formula, support for provision on facilities for provision on facilities for teaching of Hindi in these states/union territories is provided by sanctioning financial assistance for appointment of Hindi teachers in schools and for establishment of Hindi teachers training colleges in these states/union territories, under a Centrally-sponsored scheme. The grant-in-aid is provided mainly to assist the consolidation and further development of Hindi teacher training colleges in non-Hindi speaking states/union territories and to a limited extent, to assist the setting up of a new institution in such areas which are in need of such assistance. Assistance is also given to voluntary organisations for enabling them to hold Hindi teaching classes, conducting research on methodology of its teaching and providing Hindi books to various organisations. Various schemes are in operation to promote and develop tribal, calssical, modern Indian languages and prepare and publish books, dictionaries, research and instructional material besides training of teachers in Hindi. Through the kendriya Hindi Sansthan, Agra the Government .of India promotes development of improved mentodology for teaching Hindi to the non-Hindi speaking students. A full-fledged academic course for teaching Hindi to foreigners is being conducted by the Sansthan under the scheme 'Propagation of Hindi Abroad'. Central Hindi Directorate runs programmes relating to pruchase and publication of books and their free distribution to non-Hindi speaking states and to the Indian missions. The Directorate also brings out Hindi journals like UNESCO DOOT, Bhasha and Sahityamala. It is also implementing a scheme of teaching Hindi through correspondence courses in the media of English, Tamil, Malayalam and Bengali.

The Commission for Scientific and Technical Terminology, New Delhi, prepares and publishes definitional dictionaries and terminology in various disciplines and Pan-Indian terminology. Hindi-English glossaries in Basic sciences, humanities, social sciences, university level textbooks in agriculture and engineering and other subjects are also published. Fifty scholarships are awarded every year to foreign students for studying Hindi in Kendriya Hindi Sansthan, Agra.

Financial assistance is given to voluntary organisations and individuals to bring out publications like encyclopedias, dictionaries, books of knowledge, original writing on linguistic, literary, indological, social anthropological and cultural themes, critical editions of old manuscripts etc., for the development of modern Indian languages. Grants are also given for holding literary conferences, seminars and exhibitions besides purchasing copies of printed publications. States are given special help for the production of university level books in the regional languages. the Bureau for Promotion of Urdu was set up in 1969. Apart from working as a secretariat to Taraqqie-Urdu. Board which has been converted into an autonomous body known as National Council for Promotion of Urdu Language to advise the government on development of Urdu, it also develops educational literature in Urdu. It gives financial assistance to calligraphy centres. A National Council for promotion of Sindhi language has been set up as an autonomous body.

Government also provides facilities for study of language other than mother tongue. For this the Central Institute of Indian Languages (CIIL), Mysore conducts research in the areas of language analysis, language pedagogy, language technology and language use. Study of tribal languages is one of important functions. It runs six regional language centres at Bhubaneswar, Mysore, Patiala, Pune, Solan and Lucknow to help meet the demand for trained teachers to implement the three-language formula and one extension centre at guwahati to do research for development of tribal languages of north-eastern region.

The Central Institute of English and Foreign Languages (CIEFL) Hyderabad, set up as an autonomous body n 1958 is engaged in bringing out qualitative improvement in teaching of English. Subsequently, teaching of major foreign languages viz., Russian, German, French and Arabic and their literatures was also included in its activities. In 1973, it was declared to be an institution of higher learning deemed-to-be a university. It has two regional centres at Shillong and Lucknow.

Financial assistance is also provided to states for setting up CIEFL's district centres for English with a view to improving the standard of English language, teaching and learning. So far 28 district centres have been set up. These centres aim at imparting training to teachers of English in their areas through orientation course. Under another scheme, financial assistance is given to regional and state institutes of English for strengthening their programmes of training with respect to improving standard of English language teaching.

There are many schemes for propagation, popularisation and development of Sanskrit and other classical languages like Arabic and Persian. These include schemes for financial assistance to state governments and voluntary sanskrit organisations and their development into Adarsh Sanskrit Pathshalas, for incentives to retired scholars as Shastra Chaudamani pandits, for publication of original writtings of contemporary authors, editing and publication of rare manuscripts and catalogues of manuscripts, reprinting of important out-of-print Sanskrit texts, promotion of oral vedic tradition, vocational training to products of Sanskrit Pathshalas, national awards to eminent Sanskrit, Arbic and Persian scholars and preparation/publication of Sanskrit dictionaries.

Registered organisations engaged in the development and propagation of Sanskrit are given recurring grants for salary of teachers, scholarships to students, construction and repair of buildings, library books, research projects etc., upto 75 per cent of the approved expenditure. About 550 voluntary institutions conducting courses on traditional Sanskrit education and about 200 institutions working in the field of propagation and promotion of Arabic, Persian are benefitteed under this scheme every year. Institutions having potential for greater development are identified and brought under the scheme of Adarsh Sanskrit

Mahavidyalayas and Shodh Sansthans. So far, 14 post-graduate Sanskrit Mahavidyalayas and two research institutions have been brought under the purview of this scheme. To encourage more students to learn Sanskrit, the amount of scholarship under the voluntary organisation scheme has been increased from Rs. 100 per month to Rs. 300 per month with effect form 1 April, 1995.

Department of Education also conducts an all-India Vedic Convention through Maharishi Sandipani Rashtriya Ved Vidya Pratishthan and an all-India Sanskrit elocution every year where scholars in different Shastras and a team of eight contestants from all states are invited with a view to identifying the rare Veda Shakhas and their repositiories, devising ways and means for preserving the ortal traditions and encouraging extempore speech on classical subjects. As a special measure to preserve oral tradition of Vedic studies, a scheme was introduced in 1978 under which each Swadhyayin is required to train two students each below 12 years, in a particular Veda Shakha. The scholar gets an honorarium of Rs. 1250 and the student Rs. 175 per month. At present, 18 such units are functioning. During 1994-95, five more units were selected. Annual Elocution contest was held at Sadashiv Kendriya Sanskrit Vidyapeetha, Puri from 26 to 28 February 1995 in which about 90 students from 13 states participated.

Maharishi Sandipani Rashtriya Veda Vidya Pratishthan had been set up in 1987 with the objective of preserving and developing all aspects of Vedic studies. During 1994-95 the Pratishthan organised one all India and six Regional Vedic Sammelans, seminars and workshops on different topics, gave financial assistance to Vedic institutions, aged Vedic Pandits and Nityagnihotris, stipend to Veda students, fellowships, conduct of vedic classes for general public, tape recording of Vedic recitation etc.

To encourage scholars in Sanskrit, Arabic and Persian a scheme for awarding "Certificate of Honours" with a suitable monetary grant to eminent Sanskrit, Arbic, and Persian scholars was introduced in 1958. Eminent scholars of Pali and Prakrit languages are also considered for the award. A monetary grant of Rs. 10,000 per annum for life is granted to each scholar and a Sanad and a Robe of honour (Shawl) is also presented when the distinction is conferred by the President at the investiture ceremony. The award money has been enhanced from 10,000 to Rs. 20,000 per annum from 1995-96.

Rashtriya Sanskrit Sanstha, an autonomous organisation under the Ministry of Human Resource Development with its headquarters at Delhi, exercises academic and administrative control over seven Kendriya Sanskrit Vidyapeethas at Jammu, Allahabad, Guruvayoor, Puri, Jaipur, Lucknow and Sringeri where Sanskrit education in traditional shastras and research in various fields is conducted. Vidyapeethas of Delhi and Trupati were declared deemed-to-be universities in 1987. The Vidyapeethas located as Sringeri and named after late Shri Rajiv Gandhi was inaugurated by the President of India on 5 March 1992. Rashtriya Sanskrit Sansthan also plans to open more Kendriya Sanskrit Vidyapeethas at Madhya Pradesh (Bhopal), Himachal Pradesh and Maharashtra (Bombay) during 1995-96. The Sansthan also conducts examination for prathma to Vidyavaridhi (Ph.D.) and Vachaspati (D.Litt) and in addition to its own institutions over 50 other institutions all over the country are affiliated to it.

Under the Centrally - sponsored scheme of development of Sanskrit, cent per cent grant is given to the state governments/uhnion territories for: (a) financial assistance upto Rs. 4,000 per annum to eminent Sanskrit scholars in indigent circumstances, (b) for appointment of teachers for teaching selected modern subjects in the traditional Sanskrit pathshalas; (c) for providing facilities for teaching Sanskrit in high and higher secondary schools; (d) for scholarships to students studying Sanskrit in order to attract good students in IX to XII classes and (e) for their own schemes for promotion of Sanskrit.

Under a scheme, registered voluntary organisations working for the promotion of Arabic and Persian are given financial assistance towards salary of teachers, scholarships, furniture, library, books etc., and other activities which are conducive to development of Arabic and Persian. Financial assistances is available to the extent of 75 per cent of the approved expenditure. About 150 voluntary Arabic and Persian institutions were sanctioned financial assistance during 1994-95.

A new scheme, modernisation of 'Madrasa Education; has been introduced in 1993-94. The objective of the scheme is to encourage traditional institutions like Madrasas and Maktabs by giving financial assistance to introduce science, mathematics, social studies, Hindi and english in their curriculum. However, the process of modernisation of traditional madrasas and maktabs is entirely voluntary. The scheme provides opportunities to students of these institutions to acquire education comparable to the national eduction system. Assistances is given to these traditional institutions for the activities which contribute to this objective. In the first phase, modernisation will only cover about 250 educational institutions providing primary education.

The primary objective of the Indian Council for Cultural Relations (ICCR) is to establish and strengthen cultural relations and mutual understanding between India and other countries. One of the major activities of the Council is administering scholarship schemes for international students. There are at present 1,792 international students from around 70 countries pusruing a variety of courses on scholarships. Two new scholarship were instituted in the memory of the late Appa Saheb Pant, the first Commissioner of India in Kenya, and the Okita Memorial Scholarship at the request of the family of the former Japanese Foreign Minister, the late Dr. S. Okita.

The ICCR celebrated the birth anniversary of its founder, Maulana Abul Kalam Azad on 11 November as 'International Students Day'. Special get-togethers and cultural programmes were arranged on this occasion for international students and Indian students.

Festival of India in China held in May 1994 has been one of the major highlights of ICCR in 1994. Some of the other major events include 'India Today 1994' in Australia, which was inaugurated by the Vice-President of India; the India Trade Fair at St Petersburg; 'India in Dubai'; the 125th Death Anniversary Celebrations of Miraz Ghalib in Mauritius; and the 'India Night' at Alter Opera, Frankfurt. During April-december 1994, the ICCR sponsored visits of 17 cultural troupes abroad. The ICCR also organised performances by a number of incoming delegations and several Indian cultural programmes in honour of visiting delegations and several Indian cultural programmes in honour of visiting delegations/VVIP functions.

On the occasion of 125th Birth Anniversary of Mahatma Gandhi, the ICCR organised a major exhibition titled 'Ashoka-Gandhi-Nehru-The Healing Touch' at the Tokyo Fuji Art Museum in October 1994. Other exhibitions organised by ICCR during 1994 are the exhibition of Indian Children's Paintings (Republic of Korea) and the Children's Paintings (Cairo). The ICCR also presented busts of Gandhiji to the USA (for installation at International Peace Garden, Salt Lake City,

San Francisco) and Cuba (for installation at Central Park, Havana) and that of Gurudev Rabindranath Tagore to Japan (for installation at Soka University Campus).

The Council sponsored and assisted 45 Indian scholars, intellectuals, academics and artists to participate in seminars, symposia, study tours, etc., abroad in 21 countries and received 78 visitors from 11 countries. The ICCR organised the International Symposium of India Studies (ISIS) during November-December 1994 at Kovalam, Kerala in which 31 scholars from vrious parts of the world participated.

In keeping with India's foreign policy that has a cultural dimension for promoting greater people-to-people contact, the Council has set up cultural centres in Geogetown, Jakarta, Moscow, Port Louis, Paramaribo, Cairo, Berlin, London, Tashkent and Almaty. These centres, except in Berlin and London, impart lessions in Indian music, dance, yoga and languages and organise lectures,l symposia, exhibitions, essay competitions, performances of dance and music, staging of plays, screening kof films and publication of news bulletins. ICCR presently has 18 professors teaching Indian languages, Indology and allied subjects in Belgium, Bulgaria, China. Finland, France, Hungary, Indonesia, Republic of Korea, Mauritius, Poland, Thailand, Turkey, Trinidad and Tobago.

In August 1994, Ted Tanen from American Secretariat of the Indo-US Sub-Commission on Education and Culture visited India and had meetings with the Indian Co-Chairman of the Sub-Commission, Shri Salman Khurshid and several other leading persons, in various cultural and academic fields. The Press Information Bureau in collaboration with the ICCR sponsored the visit of four women delegates from the media to participate in the 'Women & Media' programme in the USA in October 1994. The ICCR hosted the visit of four Indian film directors from USA to India to participate in the film festival'From India to America; New Directions in Indian American Films and Video' in New Delhi and Bombay in December 1994 organised by the Smita Patil Foundation in collaboration with the Indo-US Commission and Whitney Museum of American Art, USA.

The 28th Maulana Abul Kalam Azad Memorial Lecture was delivered on 9 September 1994 by Secretary General of the United Nations on 'Current World Challenges as Reflected in the United Nations Today' and the 29th Lecture was delivered on 12 January 1995 by Tan Sri Ghazali Shafie, former Malaysian Minister for Foreign Affaisrs, Home and Education. Renowned Canadian environmentalist Mr. Naurice FS Kong was nominated for the Jawaharlal Nehru Award for International Understanding, 1992.

The Council brings out six quarterly journals in different languages: English (India Horizons and Africa), Hindi (Gangananchal), French (Recontre Avec L'Inde), Spanish (Papeles de la India) and Arabic (Thaqafatul Hind). A special issue of Indian Horizons on India-China Relations was brought out on the occasion of Festival of India in China and is considered to be one of the finest and most comprehensive books available on the age-old contacts between the two countries. The ICCR co-published India and Egyypt: Influences and Interactons and 'The Divine Peacock: Understanding Contemporary India'.

The ICCR also participated in the 11th New Helhi World Book Fair, the Exhibition of Indian Books in China, the Australian Book Fair in Sydney, the 46th Frankfurt Book Fair, the Exhibition of Indian Books in

Male, the Special Book Exhibition in New Delhi and the Book Exhibition of ICCR publications at New Delhi. The ICCR gifted 1,050 books to institutions, distinguished persons, academicians and opinion makers in 35 countries and 200 musical instruments, audio/ video tapes and art objects to institutions in 18 countries.

Health

The Government has reaffirmed the crucial role of public investment in social sectors like health. It has also been recognised that alongwith the States, the Centre also bears the responsibility to ensure that primary health care is provided to every citizen.

Providing access to good primary health care has been included in the minimum needs programme.

Specific plans will be drawn up during the Ninty Plan to ensure that new primary health care entre is established for a population of 5,000 people and is efficiently managed. The primary health care centre provide basic health and family welfare services to the rural population.

The Chief Ministers' Conference held in July 1996 has recommended that all out efforts will be made to attain 100 per cent coverage ofprimary health service facilities in rural and urban areas by 2000 A.D. The Panchayati Raj System will be activised in association with voluntary organisations in extending family planning and primary health care services.

The Central assistance for building the infrastructure for delivery of primary health care will be stepped up and the norms for this purpose will be relaxed further in areas inhabited by SC/ST/primitive/tribal groups and hill and desert areas. Indigenous systems of medicine like Ayurveda, Unani and Siddha and Homeopathy will be given adequate coverage indelivery of primary health care service.

The Government will work to achieve tangible results in promoting the small family norms so that the gains from development reach everybody.

Family Welfare programme has been given an over—riding national priority. Totally reoriented towards clients' needs and quality care, the programme now plans to provide services through an integrated Reproductive and Child Health Package. The essential components of RCH services have been classified under four braod heads viz. Prevention and Management of Unwanted Pregnancy, Maternal care including ante—natal, delivery and post—partum services, Child survival services fro new born and infants and, Management of Reproductive tract infections/Sexually transmitted diseases.

From April 1996, the Family Welfare Programme has become target free in its quest for improved performance. While changing from provider driven approach to a demand driven approach, decentralised, participatory planning has been introduced to create a sense of belongin among the people at grassroots level. Planning is now being encouraged through involvement of more private rural medical practitioners, anganwadi workers and non—government organisations.

To enhance community participation in the Programme, a scheme has been introduced on watershed development for small farmers, integrating Family Welfare issues with provision for community mobilisation and participation. A comunity award scheme has also been introduced for the best performing village in the district.

The campaign mode approach adopted in he Pulse Polio Immunisation (PPI) programme has led to record social mobilisation and immunisation of 8.7 crore children on December 9, 1995 and 9.3 crore children on January 20, 1996. PPI is being repeated this winter on December 7 & 18 January.

Through the same campaign mode of approach, a special health check—up programme was arranged for all primary school children all over the country during this summer. This programme is also likely to be repeated next year.

A register of births and deaths will be maintained by every village panchayat.

A National Illness Assistance Fund is being set up for the poor who ae below poverty line. This will assist them for specialised treatment for life threatening illness and treatment for injuries in hospitals where the treatment cost exceeds Rs. 1.50 lakh. Budget provision for 1996—97 of Rs. 5 crore for the Centre and Rs. 2.50 crore for the States has been made. States have also been asked to set up similar funds for this purpose. Fund will be supported by donations which will be given 100 per cent income tax exemption.

The State Health System project, which was earlier in operation in Andhra Pradesh will now be extended to Punjab Karnataka and West Bengal. The objective is to put in place a first referral health system which would provide vital support and lend credibility to primary helath care services. This will help in the development of a cohesive, efficient and sustainable health system.

Step are being taken to eliminate donation of blood by professional donors; all blood banks will be licensed within two years. These steps will ensure that blood transfused is free from infections.

Nearly half of the budget provision 1996—97 for medical and public health has been provided for National Programmes for Control of Communicable and Other Diseases.

There are over 6.5 lakh of practitioners the Indian Systems of Medicine in the country. They largely work in remote rural as well as urban slum areas and thus, could play an important role in improving the quality and outreach of health care. During the Eighth Plan the DEptt. of ISM & H has been formed to provide a new thrust and focus to the ongoing programmes. The focus will be to ensure quality and relevance of the undergraduate training, a period of internship with possible multi-professional inter-action and periodic qcourses to update the knowledge and skills of the practitioners.

Lack of close supervision and monitoring at the peripheral level and the inadequate community awareness and participation have come in the way efficient and effective implementation of the Health programmes. With the seventy third and seventy fourth Constitutional amendments, the Nagar Palikas and Panchayati Raj Instutitions will play increasing role in ensuring planning, implemntation and monitoring of health services at the local level. They will also ensure effective coordination of programmes at the local level between related sectors such as sanitation, safe drinking water and women and child development, so that optimal benefit and the vulnerable segments receive the attention that they need.

At the time of Independence communicable disease had been the major cause of morbidity and mortality in the country. Though health is a state subject, several centrally sponsored programmes for control of communicable diseases were initiated over the last four decades. National Malaria Eradication Programme was the oldest of all these. It was launched in 1953 and had achieved spectacular success in rapidly reducing the morbidity and mortality due to malaria from estimated 75 million cases and 0.8 million deaths at the time of Independence to 0.1 million cases and no death in 1965. Unfortunately since then there has been a resurgence of malaria in several parts of the country. Increasing prevalence of Falciparum malaria, resistance of mosquitoes to insecticides and malarial parasite to commonly used antimalarial drugs have been the source of concern. The Modified Plan of Operation is being implemented; special attention is being paid to the vulnerable North-Eastern States by providing 100 per cent Plan assistance for this programme. Other vector borne diseases also have been receiving due attention. Re-emergence of diseases like Kala Azar has been a cause of concern.

Deteriorating urban and rural sanitation, poor water and solid waste management and ever increasing overcrowding result in communicable disease which continue to be the major cause of morbidity and mortality in the country. Emergence of new infections like HIV add to the existing disease burden due to communicable diseases. The emergence of drug resistance in many bacteria and resistance to insecticides among vectors have added to the existing problems of disease control.

Other major National Programmes that have received attention of the Eighth Plan aim to combat tuberculosis, leprosy and HIV infection. The performance in many of these national programmes has been suboptimal due to lack of critical manpower at the primary health care level. Efforts are underway to identify the gaps in infrastructure and manpower, and fill them as expenditiously as possible so that the programmes become fully operational. In addition efforts are being made to improve the operational efficiency, the quqality of services, make services more responsive to client needs, ensure that health care providers have the necessary skills and support including referral facilities and supplies they need. Simultaneously through health education efforts will have to be made to improve the client and the community awareness of the existing services and how to utilise them optimally, so that available services are effectively utilised and community participation in the programme optimised.

At the time when many of the disease control programmes were initiated sufficient health infrastructure and manpower were not available for managment of major health problems; so a vertical programme infrastructure was created to operationalise these programmes in the absence of primary health care infrastructure. By the end of the Eighth Plan the primary health care infrastructure is well estiablished and so efforts are being made to ensure that existing vertical programmes are horizontally integrated at district level so that the primary health care institution truly becomes the nodal agency for channelising comprehensive Health Services to the population.

In order to assist the primary health centre/CHCs officers to carry out horizontal integration, it is envisaged that the middle level public health programme managers who are currently heading the vertical programme at district level will be given the additional task of ensuring coordination and implementation of integrated Health Programme at Primary Health Care institutions in defined blocks.

Provision of appropriate drugs of good quality at affordable cost is essential for success of disease control programmes. Equally important is to restrict, and if possible, eliminate, the use of irrational drug formulation and fixed dose drug combination. Recognising this, provisions for strengthning the food and drug control organizations in the States and Centre were made in the Eighth Plan. However, implementation of the scheme has been patchy and tardy. This will be taken up on priority basis during the next few years.

Any health programme is as good as the personnel who constitute the health system. Both in the State and in the Central Sector over 75 per cent of the budget goes to meet the salary of the employees. Unlike health service planning, the health manpower planning in India did not receive adequate attention. There is gross inadequacy of the number of para—professionals and over production of doctors and specialists in the country. There are regional disparities both in quantity and quality of the health care professionals. These have come in the way of effective implementation of the health programmes. It is imperative that health manpower appropriate in quality and adequate in quantity is available for catering to the health care needs of the populaltion. In addition to the existing institutional mechanisms, the open university system and the vocational courses will assist the States in production of adequate number of the para-professionals of appropriate categories and ensure that the quality of preservice training is optimal.

It is essential to establish an institutional mechanism for health manpower planning at district, State and Central level so that the task of health manpower planning, based on the data on availability and needs at the district, State and the national level, and the function of health manpower production proceed in tandem. This will ensure that appropriate mix of the health personnel of requisite quality are produced to meet the existing and changing health care needs of the population in the public, private and voluntary sectors.

In the rapidly changing health care scenario it is essential that all professionals and para-professionasl undergo periodic retraining so that their knowledge and skills are updated. Continuing multi-professionals education enables the professionals and para-professionals to function effectively as a team for effective and efficiently delivery of health care. In addition to the existing inservice training courses in various institutions, the Open universities will play an increasingly important role in this direction.

The Indian Council of Medical Research has been the nodal agency forbio-medical research in the country. Bio-medical and health systems research is carried out by research institutions, universities, medical colleges and non-governmental organisations and are currently funded by several agencies including ICMR, DST, DBT, CSIR and concerned Ministries. Basic, clinical, applied and operational research studies relevent to major health and population problems in the country have been the focus of research programmes. It is noteworthy that most of the National Health Programmes in the country are based on applied and operational research studies carried out by ICMR.

Efforts are underway to achieve koptimal coordination of the research activities by networking and if needed by multi-agency funding of important projects. Development, testing and quality control of drugs in the modern system of medicine and ISM & H, development of immunodiagnostic tests for common communicable diseases which could be used at the primary health care institutions, development and testing of alternative strategies for control of communicable and non-communicable diseases and operational research for efficient implementation of the RCH (reproductive and child health) package through PHC planning are some of the major research areas which have been initiated in the recent years.

Given the existing conditions of poor environmental sanitation and the weakness of the public health system it may not be possible to completely prevent out breaks of communicable diseases in the near future. Nevertheless, early detection and prompt response could result in rapid containment and control of the outbreak, reduction in morbidity and mortality. The building up of the disease surveillance and response mechanisms have received considerable attention during the Eighth Plan period. It is felt disease surveillance and response must be based at district level ensure prompt response. This system needs to be given the necessary back up laboratory support and epidemiological expertise so that containment measures are based on suond data and are logical. This back up system should be evolved through strengthening and optimal utilisation of the facilities and expertise available in the National Institutions/medical colleges.

Increasing incidence of hospital acquired infections and accidental infection in health care providers and waste disposers renders it imperative that efforts are made to improve infection control and waste management through utilisaton of appropriate affordable technology at all levels of health care. Planning Commission and the Ministry of Health and Family Welfare Programme have initiated steps to take up specific pilot projects.

Increasing longevity, demographic transition resulting in rapidly rising numbers of aged population, urbanisation, increasing pollution, a change over from traditional diets, sedentary life style and increase in the stress of day to day living have led to the increase in life style related disorders and noncommunicable diseases. Noncommunicable diseases such as cardio-and cerebro-vascular diseases resulting in heart attacks and strokes, diabetes and common malignancies are emerging as major public health problems in the country. Pilot projects for district based integrated noncummunicable disease control programmes carried out through the existing primary and secondary level facilities, using diabetes as a model, have been initiated in the Eighth Plan. The experience gained will be used to expand such programmes.

Rapidly growing population, urbanisation, changing agricultural, industrial and water resource management, increasing use of pesticides and fossil fuels have all resulted in perceptible deterioration in the quality of environment and attendant adverse health consequences. Pilot projects exploring the dimensions of the problem and aimed at seeking realistic solutions were initiated during the Eighth Plan period. Efforts are also under way to document extent of the problem of environmental pollution and its impact on health status of the population. Prevention and management of health consequences of environmental deterioration will receive increasing attention.

Over the last two decades occupational health has received considerable attention. Continuous monitoring of safety of work environment and workers' health status, both in the organised and unorganised sector with emphasis on gender specific and child labour related issues, documenting the magnitude and types of the occupational health problems, initiating appropriate preventive and remedial measures will be developed into a structured health programme are being taken up wherever possible.

Several major development activities in any field such as Agriculture, Industries, Urban and Rural Development have resulted in environment changes; some of these could have health implications. In order to minimise these it has been suggested that all large development projects should have Health Impact assesment and then necessary provision for health care of people involved in development activities and prevention and management of health consequences of developmental activities on the population living in the vicinity of the project should be incorporated and costed as part of the project. These suggestions are being considered by appropriate implementing agencies.

The past fifty years have witnessed the development of a vast health care infrastructure and manpower aimed at providing health care to the population. National Programmes have been evolved and implemented to control major public health problems. The investment in Public health has shown considerable increase over the plan periods. However there has not been any increase in the proportion of the Plan outlay allocated to health sector. There is an increase in the disease burden due to communicable and non-communicable disease caused by the growing population, newer diseases and changing life styles. There are evolving technologies for health care and increasing expectations of the population for health care. All these have resulted in the ever widening gap between what is possible and what is affordable. It is imperative that in the coming decades this gap is bridged and at the same time equity and excellence are ensured in health care services.

The post-Independence era has witnessed the development of a vast health care infrastructure in the country to control major public health problems. However, ever growing population, changing lifestyles and emergence of new disease have increased the health care burden resulting in a widening gap between what is possible and what is affordable. India is one of the pioneers in the health service planning with a focus on primary health care. The Bhore Committee report which laid the foundation of the health care system in Independent India preceded the Alma Ata declaration by three decades. At the time of Independence, the country's health care infrastructure was mainly urban and clinic based. These hospitals and clinics provided curative care to patients who came to them. Outreach of services in the rural areas was very limited; there were very few preventive and rehabilitative services available.

From the First Five year Plan efforts were made to build up primary, secondary and tertiary care centres and to link them through appropriate referral system. National Programmes for combating major public health problems were evolved and implemented. These efforts have resulted in a discernible impact on mortiality with Crude Death rate (CDR) deslinning from 27 in 1951 to 9 in 1995 Sample Registraton system (SRS 1995 provisional). However the morbidity due to communicable and nutrition related diseases has not shown a parallel decline. In addition, there is now an increasing morbidity due to non—communicable diseases and newly emerging infections such as those with HIV.

Over the last Eight Plan periods the Rural Primary Health Care infrastructure has been built up throughout the country. Adequate number of subcentres and PHCs have been created so that at the national level the norms for these have been met by the end of the Seventh Plan. Efforts are underway to build adequate number of Community Health Centres (CHCs) so that there is effective emergency services available in rural areas. However the staffing of these infrastructure is often inadequate and lack of key personnel have come in the way of effective delivery of health and family welfare service and implementation of the major national programmes. Yet another problem has been in building up of effective referral services between these three tiers of health services.

There is a need to assess the requirement of personnel based not only on population, but also on the basis of workload, distance to be covered, and problem in utilization of health services by the population. Flexible approach to recruitment of staff if necessary on contract basis has to be taken up to ensure that programmes do not suffer due to lack of key personnel.

In 1991 it was estimated that nearly 30 per cent of India's population lived in urban areas. Urban migration over the last two decades had resulted in rapid growth of urban slum population. Though initially the health care services were mainly urban based, the existing services have become inadequate to serve the needs of the growing population. Realising this unmet felt need for health care, several organisations including Municipalities, State Governments, non-governmental organisations and externally aided projects undertook efforts to create necessary infrastructure and provide the manpower there. Unlike the rural health services, there has not been any clear cut and well organised efforts to provide primary secondary and tertiary care services in geographically defined areas in urban health care. As a result, there are substantial under-utilisation of some facilities and over crowded tertiary care centres. Efforts have been initiated to build up appropriate linkages between centres providing primary health care services and those providing secondary and tertiary care in the same areas, so that there is optimal utilisation of the available health care facilities.

- Although housing is basically a State level activity, the Central Government is responsible for the formulation of broad policy framework of this sector and overseeing the effective implementation of the social housing scheme, particularly for the weaker sections of the Society.

- The Central Government strives to create a conducive environment for generating housing activity so as to meet its growing demand. The Delhi Rent Bill, 1994 has been passed by both the Houses of Parliament and it recieved the assent of the President on 23.8.1995. Soon after the Delhi Rent Act, 1995 was passed by the Parliament, representations were received from a section of traders-tenants demanding changes in some of the provisions of the Act. On the other hand, some forums representing house owners are pressing for an early notification of the Act and enforcement thereon. All these issues are under the consideration of the Government.

- The Indira Awas Yojana (IAY), meant for the poorest of the poor belonging to scheduled castes and scheduled tribes and free bonded labour in the rural areas, had been further extended to cover non-SC/ST poor families, subject to certain conditions. Houses, under IAY scheme are built in clusters so that common facilities can be provided easily. Under IAY, 2,81,754 houses were built during 1996-97 (upto October, 96) as against 8,63,889 in 1995-96.

- The Urban Basic Services for the Poor (UBSP) scheme was launched with a total outlay of Rs. 100 crore for the Eighth Plan period. The aim of the scheme is to improve the quality of life of the urban poor specially the most vulnerable sections of the population such as women, children, youth, Scheduled Castes/Scheduled Tribes and minorities. As on 30th November, 1996, more than 8000 Neighbourhood Development Committees comprising primarily of urban poor women have been set up in 318 towns for the provision of basic services. 3877 mini plans have already been prepared and 574 community organisers are in the field working as catalysts for enriching community participation.

- In its efforts to enchance the flow of funds particularly in rural areas and its easy accessibility to the needy rural populaltion, the National Housing Bank (NHB) till the end of April 1996, has subscribed to the "Special Rural Housing Debentures" (SRHDs) of State Level Cooperative Land Development Banks (SLDBs) to the tune of Rs.180.91 crore to the cooperative sector institutions, the share of SLDBs works out to 51.1 per cent. Recognising the importance of providing housing to women, particularly those belonging to the vulnerable sections, NHB has announced a "Direct Financing Scheme for Housing for Women". Under the scheme, NHB will directly finance the projects of public agencies and local bodies for the benefit of women belonging tot he Economically Weaker Sections (EWS) and Lower Income Group (LIG) categories.

- Water supply and sanitation are important basic needs for the improvement of quality of life and enchancement of productive efficiency of the citizens. Although State Governments are responsible for supply of drinking water in villages, Central assistance is being provided under the Accelerated Rural Water Supply Programme

(ARWSP) with 100 per cent grants—in—aid subject to a matching provision (except for DDP areas where matching provision is regular) being made by State Governments under Minimun Needs Programme (MNP). The National Drinking Water Mission (NDWM) renamed as the Rajiv Gandhi National Drinking Water Mission (RGNDWM) is looking into the need for providing sustainable safe drinking water to entire rural population over the next few years.

- The coverage of rural population with drinking water supply and sanitation facilities in rural and urban areas increased rapidly. An outlay of Rs.1170.86 crore has been provided in 1996-97 budget for the Rural Water Supply and Sanitation Schemes.

- The scheme of rural sanitation is aimed at supplementing the efforts made under different Central and State sector programmes for improving sanitry facilities in the rural areas. It includes, inter alia, construction of sanitary latrines for individual households below the poverty line, village-complexes for women, drains and other sanitation facilities. A total number of 1,66,353 and 37,422 sanitary latrines were constructed for Scheduled Castes and Scheduled Tribes respectively during 1995-96.

Housing

Housing is a State subject but the Union Government is responsible for the formulation of policy with regard to programmes and approaches for effective implementation of the social housing schemes, particularly those pertaining to weaker sections of the society. The National Housing Policy is enunciated in the Five Year Plan and the state goverments implement the schemes in accordance with the plan priorities and local requirements.

In tune with the policy of the Government, a National Housing Policy (NHP), taking into account the developments on national and international scene on Shelter Sector after 1988 and also in the light of comments received from state governments and different sections of the community has been evolved. Special emphasis has been given in the policy paper on the specific needs of rural housing. The policy document outlining the strategy under the Eighth Plan has since been endorsed by Parliament in 1994. The long term goal of the NHP is to eradicate houselessness, to improve the housing conditions of the inadequately housed and to provide a minimum level of basic services and amenities to all. It recognises that the magnitude of housing task calls for involvement of various agencies including government at different levels, cooperatives, the community and the private sector. The policy envisages a major shift in Government's role to act more as a facilitator than as provider. The needs of vulnerable sections of society will continue to be atended to by the Government. It envisages to facilitate housing activity of the lower and middle income groups and to encourage within the framework of housing policy and local planning, the voluntary agencies in efforts to upgrade shelter, extend basic services, augment incomes and promote environmental conservation. The policy has been incorporated in the Housing Chapter on the Eighth Plan.

During the Eighth Plan, emphasis will be on social housing schemes including Minimum Needs Programme projects in rural areas, strengthened role of HUDCO, shelter for the homeless, technology transfer, housing information system and housing for Central Government employees. All the state governments have been requested to formulate detailed action plans for implementation of the policy.

The world Conservation Strategy has recommended greater public participation in planning and decision-making concerning the use of living resources and proposed environmental education programmes and campaigns to build support for conservation. The Panchayati Raj is institutionalization of public participation in planning and decisison-making in rural India. The following issues can be listed for capacity building in Panchayati Raj for environment protection and improvement.

Through Panchayati raj institutions are not directly linked with the Indian federal system, they are closely related with State governments. Most State government departments, particularly departments of agriculture, education, public health, forests and finance have close functional relationship with PRIs. The activities of State governments may be broadly analysed as general administration, technical assistance in the fields ofpersonnel, financial assistance, correction of errors, excesses and negligences. State governments provide administrative guidance and advice to PRIs n problems and issues. The 73rd Constitutional Amendment Act 1992 has strengthened the organizational aspects of PRIs. The success or failure of the object of environment protection through PRIs would largely depend on administrative ability, leadership and motivation of personnel. It becomes even more significant because of the fact that administrative capability is an important means of converting programme inputs into outputs with economy and efficiency. The administrative and transforming quality of the leadership would significantly determine the administrative capability of the Panchayati Raj. The administrative capability involves the ability to mobilize, allocate and combine the actions that are needed to achieve the objectives of environment protection.

India is one of the few countries of the Third World which has enshrined in its Constitution a commitment to environment protection and improvement. The environment law ia a new division of law. Even though it appears to be of recent origin and yet it not a sudden creation. Many provisions dealing with the environment are scattered in pieces and found in different enactments. The Environment (Protection) Act 1986 was enacted with the objectives of protection, regulation of the discharge of environment pollutants; handling of hazardous substances; speedy response in the event of accidents threatening environment safety and health. The World Conservation Strategy has suggested reviewing and strengthening of legislation concerning living resources to ensure that it provides sufficiently for conservation, paying particular attention to enforcement as also to remove loop holes. The lack of proper co-ordination and co-operation among the administrative institutions is an important loophole. A greater degree of co-ordination and co-operation between Central, State and local governments is needed for the implementation of environmental programmes. The other important weakness of the legislative enactments is its lack of recognition of the crucial role that the PRIs can play. The involvement of PRIs as the eyes and ears of the government in terms of grass roots monitoring of environmental quality, needs to be duly recognized. In due course, as experience is gained, particularly with regard to the respective roles of PRIs, enactment of new legislation for environment protection could be considered.

Though PRIs are not sound in their organization for technical tasks and do not have technical and professional experts, decentralization below the State level ensures technical expertise of a high order required for environment protection and improvement in rural India. The Ashok Mehta Committee on Panchayati Raj has asserted that technical assistance and organization of a high order is necessary to sustain the momentum. The State governments have the requisite competence in this regard and the decentralization process at the district level is now under way. When the process of administrative decentralization is already taking place, analysis of the changes, and the ensuring emphasis on development point to the need for democratic management or rural development below the State level so that the entire programme can be effectively implemented, co-ordinated and supervised. The inescapable conclusion is that the first point of decentralization should be at the district level. District heads of sufficient competence are already stationed here. Their capabilities ae also being upgraded. The district is also traditionally a unit of administration to which all are acclimatized. Further, it is the key planning unit for evolving the overall strategy, resource allocation including credit and the delineation of the different types of projects. The establishement of a strong Panchayat tier at the district level appears to respond both to the organizational needs within district and the demands of emerging links with the State.

Despite the emphasis on the active role to be played by PRls, they were not, much effective in the past. A number of efforts were undertaken to bring forward the Constitution Amendment Bill 1992, to provide constitutional status to Panchayati Raj bodies and to strengthen them by making suitable provisions for this durability, continuity, adequate representation to all the sections of society and financial allocations. The Act has empowered the State legislatures to authorize the Panchayats to levy, collect, and appropriate suitable local taxes and also provide for making grants-in-aid to the Panchayats from the Consolidated Fund of the State. In addition, a Finance Commission has to be constituted once in every five years to review the financial position of the Panchayats and make suitable recommendations to the State on the distribution of the funds between the State and the local bodies. The Central Finance

Commission shall also suggest measures necessary to augment the Consolidated Fund os a State to suppliment the resources of the PRIs in the State. Thus, a large amount of assured funds will flow to the PRIs involvement in environment protection and improvement.

In rural India, all the life support systems are now under serious stress and strain. Both human and animal population pressures have reached a level where the flora, fauna, soil and water and also atmospheric conditions are getting more and more depleted and pollutted. Consequently, in a predominantly agricultural country, the renewable base of land resources has been eroded and environmental degradation has taken place in the name of development. The Panchayati Raj institutions have existed for long in India, but these institutions have not been effective in environment protection and improvement. Against this backdrop, the 73rd Constitution Amendment Act assumes greater importance. Now it will no more be possible for any State government to fiddle with these institutions, as has been the case in the past. The continuation of these institutions will automatically result into strengthening of both horizontal and vertical linkage with the administration at different levels. This, in turn, will provide these institutions an opportunity to play their legitimater role in environment protection and improvement. Besides this, PRIs can play an educative role in environmental matters for younger generation as well as adults, with due consideration to the underpriviledged. This is essential in order to broaden the basis for an enlightened opinion and responsible conduct by individuals, enterprises and communities in protecting and improving the environment in its full human dimension.

Integrating environemntal considerations into development planning is not an easy task. Unless concern is backed by an ability to take ameliorative action, little can be achieved. India has been very conscious of this and has, over the past few decades, taken important steps to increase its capacity to handle environmental issues.

The initiatives have come equally from the Government, NGO's and individuals. Many collaborative and joint programmes exist today between the Government and the NGO's.

Environment and development problems are complex and there cannot be generalized and simplified solutions. Answers have to be found which are ecologically, economically and socio-culturally consistent in the particular milie. Given the size and diversity of a country like India, this task becomes extremely difficult.

Expertise is requied in framing appropriate policies and legislation, in planning, in creating mechanisms for implementation, in * education and public awareness. India also needs to be above to bring its perspective to global forums and participate in evolving international treaties, protocols and conventions. Most importantly, with the increasing emphasis on decentralized decision—making and the stress on micro-planning, this capacity-building is taking on a greater urgency. Capability is required to enable decisions to be made in a decentralized manner—decisions which are not imported solutions, but are appropriate to the particular situation.

Addressing the plenary session of the UN Conference on Human Environment in Stockholm in 1972, Prime Minister Indira Gandhi and said, "Even though our industrial development is in its infancy and at its most difficult stage, we are taking various steps to deal with the incipient environmental imbalances, more so because of our concern for the human species, whic is also imperilled." It was at her initiative that a National Council Environmental Planning and Coordination (NECPC) was set up in 1972 to identify and investigate the problems of preserving or improving the human environment in the country, and to propose solution to environmental problems.

Another Empowered Committee, the Tiwari Committee, was set up in 1980 to review and recommend legislative measures and administrative machinery for ensuring environmental protection. On the recommendation of this Committee, the Department of Environment was set up in 1980 as the focal agency in the administrative structure of the Central Government for planning, promotion and coordination of environmental programmes. This department became part of the new Ministry of Environment and Forest in 1985.

The Ministry is the apex body under the Government of India for planning, promotion and coordination of environmental and forestry programmes. Its activities include conservation and survey of flora and fauna, prevention and control of pollution, afforestation and regeneration of degraded areas, impact assessment, forest conservation and research, and education and information. The National Wastelands Development Board and the Ganga Project Directorate are major components of the Ministry.

Most of the states have also set up their own Departments of Environment, Pollution Control Boards and other associated bodies. Various other ministries and departments, including those of Urban Development, Oceanography, Non-Conventional Energy Sources etc., at the state and central levels, are also concerned with different aspects of the environment. Greater coordination among these various agencies—government and non-government-would strengthen environmental efforts. State Governments are in the process of involving themselves seriously in environmental planning.

The Directory of Environmental NGOs, brought out by the World Wide Fund for Nature - India (WWF-I) in 1989, lists about 850 NGOs working in this field, but there are porbably at least four times this number. Their involvement is clearly seen. As the Secretary General of WWF-I says, "India's impressively large body of NGOs is becoming active on the environmental front because fo the increasingly clear nexus between meaningful, equitable, sustainable economic growth and the conservation of the environment...For instance, the National Environmental Awareness Campaign promoted by the Ministry has successfully encouraged many NGOs whose primary concerns are rural development, appropriate technology, civil rights, women's development, tribal welfare etc. The interaction between NGOs and State Governments is largely confined to functional matters (clearance, information, advice etc.) whereas for financial and technical support various central departments and agencies have to be relied upon. However now there is a concerted effort by the Government to use their expertise for their own programmes."

NGOs range from clubs which encourage and assist in adventure travel, exploration, and dissemination of knowledge about an ecosystem to agencies which deal with various issues like creating gainful employment, wastelands development, afforestation, rehabilitation of tribals, and with preparation of educational materials and aids. They may be as small as groups of two or three persons, or as large as organizations with an eight-thousand-strong membership.

One of the most important signs of environmental awareness in India is the rise of people's movements which are challenging existing socio-political structures and development models, and are showing alternative paths. These have led not only to action at the grassroot level, but are also helping to shape developmental policies.